The Roots of Rough Justice

The Roots of Rough Justice

Origins of American Lynching

MICHAEL J. PFEIFER

University of Illinois Press

URBANA, CHICAGO, AND SPRINGFIELD

First Illinois paperback, 2014
© 2011 by the Board of Trustees
of the University of Illinois
All rights reserved
Manufactured in the United States of America
1 2 3 4 5 P C 5 4 3 2 1
∞ This book is printed on acid-free paper.

The Library of Congress cataloged the cloth edition as follows:
Pfeifer, Michael J. (Michael James), 1968–
The roots of rough justice: origins of American lynching /
Michael J. Pfeifer.
p.   cm.
Includes bibliographical references and index.
ISBN-13: 978-0-252-03613-2 (cloth : alk. paper)
ISBN-10: 0-252-03613-1 (cloth : alk. paper)
1. Lynching—United States—History.
2. Culture conflict—United States—History.
3. Social control—United States—History.
4. Capital punishment—Social aspects—United States—History.
5. Discrimination in capital punishment—United States—History.
I. Title.
HV6457.P43   2011
364.1'34—dc22   2010046041

PAPERBACK ISBN 978-0-252-08008-1

In memoriam, Father John P. Boyle

Contents

Acknowledgments

The publication of this book marks more than twenty years that I have been working on the topic of lynching, starting with an undergraduate senior thesis written in 1990–91 at Washington University in St. Louis. Many debts, intellectual and otherwise, have been incurred in those years. Among the greatest of those debts is to this book's dedicatee, Father John P. Boyle. Fr. Boyle, who died in 2006, never tired of listening to soliloquies about lynching and offered crucial support as I wrote my dissertation in Iowa City during the 1990s. Even more importantly, Fr. Boyle, a distinguished theologian, offered a vital model of the moral engagement of the intellectual with the world that I can only hope to emulate and to which this book aspires.

I am also grateful to friends Coleen Maddy, Ginger and Matti Vehaskari, and Michael Smith, who provided lodging as I conducted portions of the research. Babacar M'Baye, Christopher Waldrep, William Carrigan, Fitz Brundage, James Robertson, Bill Thomas, Carl Hallberg, Carolyn Conley, Allison Kavey, Barry Latzer, Eli Faber, Jerry Markowitz, Andrew Buchman, David Marr, and Sam Schrager read portions of the manuscript or offered ideas or support. Conversations with the late filmmaker Gode Davis influenced aspects of the initial stages of research and writing; Davis's passionate quest for the history of American lynching contributed significantly to the public discourse on the history of racial violence in the United States. Many librarians and archivists assisted with the research, including ones at the State Historical Society of Iowa, the Wisconsin Historical Society, Tulane University, Texas A & M University at Corpus Christi, the Library of Michigan, the Minnesota Historical Society, the Washington State Library, the New Mexico State Archives and Library, the Wyoming State Archives, the Mississippi Department of Archives and History, the Freedmen and Southern Society Project at the University of Maryland, the University of Virginia, the National Archives, the Tennessee State Library and Archives, the Huntington Library, the National Archives of the United Kingdom, and the National Archives of Scotland. Also essential were the ministrations of interlibrary loan librarians at The Evergreen State College, the University of Western Ontario, and the John Jay College of Criminal Justice. Financial support for portions of the research came from the Provost's Office at Evergreen, the State Historical Society of Iowa, and the Professional Staff Congress at the City University of New York, and crucial release time was proffered by the History Department at John Jay College. Earlier iterations of some of this material appeared in the *Journal of American History* 97, no. 3 (December 2010), *Louisiana History* 50, no. 2 (Spring 2009), and the *Annals of Iowa* 64, no. 2 (Spring 2005); the editors of those journals graciously granted permission to reprint portions of those articles. Erin Greb efficiently and skillfully designed the book's maps. Laurie Matheson at the University of Illinois Press offered invaluable support for and patience with this project, and several anonymous readers improved the manuscript with their close reading and comments. Thanks as well to Jennifer Clark for her coordination of the publication process and to Karen Hallman for her skillful copyediting. Any flaws herein are mine alone.

The Roots of Rough Justice

Introduction

On June 13, 2005, the U.S. Senate approved a resolution apologizing for its historical failure to enact antilynching legislation. The Senate's action in 2005 culminated more than two decades of work by descendants of lynching victims and scholars that has sought to recover and illuminate the history of a practice of collective violence that claimed the lives of thousands of persons in the United States in the nineteenth and early twentieth centuries, including several thousand African Americans and hundreds of Hispanics and whites. As a result of these efforts, we now know much more about lynching in the postbellum United States, including where, when, why, and how it occurred. But where did lynching come from, and why and how did it develop into a pervasive practice in the United States?

This book examines the antecedents of American lynching in an early modern Anglo-American legal heritage and in the transformation of ideas and practices of social ordering, law, and collective violence in the American colonies, the early American Republic, and, especially, in the decades before the American Civil War. The heart of the book is an extensive analysis of the lynching violence that emerged in the middle decades of the nineteenth century on the southern, midwestern, and far western frontiers of the United States. In novel places such as Mississippi, Iowa, and California in the 1830s, '40s, and '50s, I argue, white Americans seized upon lethal group violence unsanctioned by law—particularly hangings—to enforce mandates of racial and class hierarchy and to pull into definition tenuous and ill-defined understandings of social order and community. Collectively murdering African American slaves and free blacks, Native Americans, Mexicans, and working-class, nonlanded whites, white Americans rejected growing legal reforms that offered the promise of legal fairness to the unpopular and powerless by protecting the rights of those accused of crimes. Antebellum vigilantes mimicked public punishments, the pillory and the gallows, even as reformers sought to abolish those punitive customs on grounds of humanitarianism and public efficacy. Invoking elastic notions of popular sovereignty and republicanism—ideas holding that government was rooted in virtuous citizens and could be reclaimed by them if their life, liberty, and property were threatened—whites on the pre–Civil War frontiers imposed racial and class codes and fashioned practices of repressive violence that would dominate the societies and cultures of the American South, West, and Midwest into the twentieth century.

The field of U.S. lynching studies, which has burgeoned in the last twenty years in case studies,[1] state studies,[2] regional studies,[3] in national studies of mob violence,[4] in studies of gender and lynching,[5] and in studies of lynching and cultural production,[6] has taught us a great deal about lynching in the decades after Reconstruction. Southern historians have led the way, producing rich analyses of postbellum lynching violence below the Mason-Dixon line. The literature on western and midwestern mob killings has been far more limited until recently, but finally historians have acknowledged in their work that the practice of lynching has a national history, that the victims of racially motivated lynching were as diverse as the targets of American racial prejudice,[7] and that western lynching cannot be dismissed as insignificant compared to southern lynching or simply explained through the invocation of the lawless frontier. We now know a great deal about the so-called lynching era of the late nineteenth and early twentieth centuries, a characterization that holds for the South, where most lynching occurred in the postbellum era, but not for the West, where lynching was most prevalent in the mid–nineteenth century.

Overall, historians have told us rather little about lynching as a practice before the 1880s.[8] A pioneering 1990 study of racial violence in Kentucky argued, with considerable evidence, that lynching proliferated in Reconstruction in the Upper South,[9] yet no studies since have systematically explored in quantitative or qualitative terms the transformation of lynching violence in Reconstruction in 1860s and '70s in the Lower South, although scholars in recent years have published suggestive work on Reconstruction lynching violence in central Texas, Louisiana, Mississippi, and the Carolinas.[10] A recent study of Colorado has evocatively sketched the dimensions of lynching violence in the early West of the 1850s and 1860s,[11] but historians have done relatively little to analyze this significant time and place in the annals of American lynching violence. The lynching of slaves in the antebellum

South has been similarly understudied. On the basis of limited evidence, some scholars have argued that lynchings of slaves were rare because slaves were white men's property and planters had an interest in protecting their property holding.[12] Others have suggested that mob killings of slaves occurred regularly.[13] But systematic analysis of the phenomenon has been lacking.

There are additional gaps in American lynching historiography. Several recent studies of lynching have demonstrated an admirable chronological and geographical scope in enlarging and complicating our understanding of the history of the rhetoric surrounding the term *lynching,* but have only periph-erally addressed the very real practices of collective violence that the word actually connoted in particular times and places.[14] Perhaps most egregiously, scholarship on the history of lynching in the United States to this date has been largely an exercise in, and an argument for, American exceptionalism, most particularly, the exceptionalism of the American South. U.S. lynching historians have done little to analyze the antecedents for American extrale-gal collective homicide in early modern Irish and British cultures and have neglected comparison of American lynching with the analogous practices of illegal collective murder that have occurred across global cultures and eras.[15] Though focus on the "lynching frenzy" of the Jim Crow South is fully warranted in light of the several thousand African Americans that died at the hands of southern whites in that era, analysis of earlier contexts for racially motivated mob violence may help to discourage the parochial and ahistorical temptation to view Jim Crow–era southern lynching as sui generis. Informed by the strengths and weaknesses of this rich body of recent lynching scholar-ship, my argument in this book is that the origins of American lynching in the nineteenth century can only be fully understood in national, and indeed transnational,[16] terms.

This book has evolved out of my own contribution to lynching scholarship, a 2004 monograph entitled *Rough Justice. Rough Justice* interpreted lynch-ing as an important aspect of a cultural conflict over criminal justice waged across the regions of the postbellum United States. Yet as I was writing that book, it became clear to me that the dynamics it depicted did not begin in the years after the Civil War. Though the postbellum context is essential to understanding the lynching frenzy of the late-nineteenth-century South, the "nadir" of southern race relations in fact marked the apex of phenomena with much earlier roots in American history. To best understand what happened in the United States in the late nineteenth and early twentieth centuries, I realized it would be necessary to discern the development of ideas and practices regarding criminal justice and violence over the course of "the long nineteenth century," that is, stretching back to the years before the American Revolution in the late eighteenth century. *Rough Justice* had sought to transcend the sectional parochialism that has too often walled off particular American regions from comparative analysis. However, as I began writing this book, it became clear that analysis of the origins of American lynching must also transcend continental and political boundaries to encompass the British Atlantic, that is, Britain and its colonies on both sides of the Atlantic in the seventeenth and eighteenth centuries,[17] and beyond. Although the term *lynching* probably originated in the United States[18] and, as is shown in the succeeding chapters, a practice of collective murder known as lynching took profound root in the nineteenth-century United States, group murder that resembles lynching has in fact occurred across historical and contemporary world cultures and eras.

However, to acknowledge that informal group murder inspired by motivations of criminal justice, race, or ethnicity, or lynching as the practice would come to be known in the United States in the early to mid–nineteenth century,[19] has analogues dating to the ancient world[20] and across global cultures[21] should not be the same as suggesting that the practice ultimately lies outside of history, is unrecoverable or unknowable by historians, is knowable only as language or rhetoric, or that in the interest of stressing cultural universals we might ignore or elide the particular historical contexts in which collective murder has actually taken root as a widespread practice, such as in the regions south and west of the Allegheny Mountains in the United States in the nineteenth century. Such assertions are ahistorical. Although lynching has, perhaps since the onset of human societies, expressed a universal impulse toward summary collective punishment of social enemies defined as criminal, the practice over the last several hundred years can best be understood as a specific cultural response to the ambiguities of legal change, especially concerns over the efficacy of formal criminal justice, in particular times and places.

American lynching arose in the early to mid–nineteenth century as a response to alterations in law and social values (the shift from a penology of retribution and deterrence to one centered on reform of the criminal, the rise of the adversarial system and aggressive defense lawyering, the shift from private to public criminal prosecution, and the professionalization of criminal justice) that occurred throughout the Anglo-American world. Crucially, the emergence of the extralegal group murder of lynching was shaped with reference to particular American conditions, most notably the violent libertarian tradition bequeathed by the Revolution and the mobile, fractious social settings of the early to mid–nineteenth century cotton, mining, and agrarian frontiers. Diverging from much of industrializing Britain and the northeastern United States, the developing American South, Midwest, and West lacked established social elites and strong middle classes that pressed for legal regularity and advocated for legal reforms that recognized the dignity and rights of criminal defendants. Instead, in the regions of the United States south and west of the Alleghenies, skepticism of legal change combined with racial and class republicanism to assert that the communal violence of lynching and vigilantism offered the surest path to the performance of criminal justice that would sustain racial and class prerogatives over slave, free black, Hispanic, and white miscreants whose resistance and criminality threatened the social order.

Crucially, unlike England and western Europe, the United States' transition to a capitalist economy was not accompanied by the emergence of a strong, centralized national state that claimed and enforced an exclusive monopoly over violence and the administration of criminal justice to secure the rule of law. Rather, American criminal justice developed along a distinctive path that emphasized local authority and opinion, self-help and ad hoc law enforcement practices, and the toleration of extralegal violence. Lynching was an important aspect of this distinctive American trajectory in the long nineteenth century, registering many Americans' rejection of due process and the exclusive claims of state authority in criminal law.[22] The formation of American criminal justice was a highly contested process, as lawyers, judges, and middle class reformers fought for due process and the rule of law against rural elites and working class people who sought to retain "rough justice," that is, criminal justice grounded in local prerogatives of honor, class, race, ethnicity, gender, and crime control. Because of factors of demography, economics, and historical development that included industrialization, urbanization, slavery and westward migration, the due process forces were at their strongest in the Northeast but weakest in the South, with the West and Midwest lying in between. Beyond the United States, British-controlled Catholic Ireland was another cultural and legal periphery in the Anglo-American world. In the early to mid–nineteenth century, the Irish developed practices of extralegal violence in ambivalence and opposition to British laws.[23] As will be seen in chapter 4, these practices would be transposed to the northern United States by Irish Catholic immigrants in the form of racial lynching in the 1860s, effectively bridging Irish and American practices of collective violence.

The book is organized chronologically and topically. The analysis begins in the first chapter with a brief survey of collective violence across the early modern Anglo-American world. Then the second chapter traces, in the social and legal context of the southern, midwestern, and western frontiers, the lethal transition from the nondeadly collective violence (typically floggings) perpetrated by regulator movements in the late eighteenth and early nineteenth centuries, to the prolific extralegal hangings of gamblers, alleged slave insurrectionists, horse thieves, and murderers in Mississippi, Iowa, and Wyoming Territory from the mid-1830s through the late 1860s. The third chapter charts the emergence of racially motivated lynching in the antebellum United States. This chapter documents how southern planters created legal institutions that protected the master class's interest in slave property, but also how antebellum southern whites resorted to the lynching of slaves through burning or hanging at times when the master's property interest was effectively nullified by a slave's murder of a member of the master class, or when portions of the white community rejected the criminal justice system's ability to enforce racial control. The focus then shifts to other racial frontiers, examining lynching violence against Native Americans and Hispanics on the midwestern and far western frontiers of Wisconsin, Minnesota, California, New Mexico, and Washington Territory in the 1840s and '50s.

Chapter 4 treats the Far West, the Upper South, and the Midwest in the mid-to-late 1850s as a laboratory for a variety of lynching violence that would become widespread in the postbellum era. In the late antebellum era, westerners, upper southerners, and midwesterners performed carefully targeted collective violence that protested the adjudication of particular cases in the criminal justice system amid a deepening commitment of the northern legal culture to due process law. The book's fifth chapter traces the pivotal transformation of racial lynching across the United States in the era of the Civil War and Reconstruction. The chapter begins with an analysis of lynchings of African Americans in the early to mid-1860s in Wisconsin, New York State, and Michigan, highlighting the role northern whites played in forging a national practice of racial lynching during the Civil War and Reconstruction. The chapter ends by examining the emancipation of the slaves and the transition in legal and social arrangements in Louisiana in the Reconstruction era, identifying within emerging patterns of collective violence and shifts in legal institutions the advent of the ritualized racial violence that would plague the South in the late nineteenth and early twentieth centuries. The epilogue expands to a global, transnational focus, briefly suggesting the implications of the book's analysis for understanding contemporary lynching violence in locales as different as Latin America, sub-Saharan Africa, and the Caribbean.

1. Collective Violence
   in the British Atlantic

The legal and cultural antecedents of American lynching were carried across the Atlantic by migrants from the British Isles to colonial North America. Collective violence was a familiar aspect of the early modern Anglo-American legal landscape. Group violence in the British Atlantic was usually nonlethal in intention and consequence but it occasionally shaded, particularly in the seventeenth century in the context of political turmoil in England and unsettled social and political conditions in the American colonies, into rebellions and riots that took multiple lives. In the years before and after the Declaration of Independence in 1776, Americans transformed older British notions and practices of crowd action and imbued them with new meanings amid the egalitarian and reformist implications of the Revolution and the early American Republic.

Though early modern crowd violence sometimes took on antiauthoritarian implications, seventeenth- and eighteenth-century crowd actions were rooted in a hierarchical conception of society as a corporate body linking gentry and plebeians in an English commitment to and participation in a "rule of law" that reputedly distinguished Englishmen from most Europeans. Such an understanding of an encompassing, participatory rule of law linked members of English and colonial American communities in institutions of criminal justice that included attendance at public punishments such as the pillory and the scaffold. Public spectacle executions meted out a "bloody code" intended to convey the consequences of serious crimes and the majesty of legal authority in a monarchical, hierarchical society. Around the British Atlantic, grass roots criminal justice was also manifested in the "hue and cry" communal apprehension of criminals and, increasingly in the eighteenth century, the posse comitatus, which gave the sheriff the authority to call upon all physically able men to assist in capturing felons. Elites accepted, sometimes grudgingly, that under such a corporatist constitutional arrangement, commoners might occasionally turn to collective action to seek restoration of what they perceived as their customary rights. Crowd actions often took the form of rituals of misrule, performances that inverted social rank or gender in holiday processions or in charivari that temporarily overturned social arrangements in order to reaffirm conventional political or gender arrangements such as gentry domination of the polity or benevolent patriarchal control of the household (in correction of the aberrant behavior of cuckolds, wife-beaters, overly headstrong wives, or newlyweds of disparate ages).[1]

There is little evidence that informal group murder, that is, what would later become known as lynching, occurred with any frequency in the early modern British Isles or Colonial America, and certainly not sufficient evidence to argue that the practice ever became an aspect of a ubiquitous Anglo-American tradition of crowd violence, which seldom culminated in the deaths of the targets of crowd action. However, summary collective executions did occasionally occur in the early modern British Atlantic, typically in the heat of deep popular passions over situations characterized by perceptions of legal, social, or political injustice. In June 1628, a crowd of London apprentices murdered John Lambe "with stones and cudgels and other weapons." Lambe, who was probably in his early eighties, worked as a "magical healer and counselor" and had escaped capital convictions for witchcraft and rape through a reprieve and a royal pardon. Significantly, Lambe was also an associate of the Duke of Buckingham, George Villiers, a favorite of Charles I who had become the focus of opposition in Parliament and would soon be assassinated. The crowd murder of Lambe can be read as an act of collective justice that sought to punish a convicted witch and rapist in light of the failure of the legal authorities to do so, but also as a "subversive" act of popular politics in an escalating conflict between Charles I and Parliament over the destiny of the English nation. Furious over the act of political disorder, the king ordered the City of London to punish the rioters and those that had failed to prevent their actions. The city jailed a number of law officers for failing in their duty, but no individuals were arrested for their participation in the crowd. The king responded by suing the city, and the court levied a £1,000 fine.[2]

A collective murder similarly inspired by legal and political anxieties occurred in Edinburgh in September 1736. Captain John Porteous had ordered militia to fire on a crowd that rioted at the gibbet after the hanging of a smuggler, Andrew Wilson. Six died among the Scottish rioters infuriated by the Crown's harsh enforcement of the excise laws. A jury, possibly influenced by a large crowd that gathered outside the courtroom, convicted Captain Porteous of murder, and he was sentenced to death. Angered at news of a reprieve of Porteous's execution, and fearing that he might ultimately escape hanging through an appeal of his conviction and the intervention of the prime minister, Robert Walpole, an armed mob of several thousand pulled Porteous from the city's jail, the Tolbooth, and hanged him from an improvised gallows. Dismayed by the failure of local authorities to intervene to prevent the collective homicide, Parliament responded to the crowd execution by dismissing the provost of Edinburgh and fining the city £2,000.[3]

Another crowd execution occurred on the northwestern periphery of the British Atlantic, in Marblehead, Massachusetts, in July 1677. After Indians commandeered a number of settler fishing boats, a colonist community distraught over devastating losses to Natives in King Philip's War reacted with furor. When some of the fishermen that were feared lost instead arrived at Marblehead with two Natives they had overpowered, intending to ransom them for goods that had been captured by Indians, local settler women refused to consent to a transfer of the Natives to local authorities. Asserting that legal processes could not avail the community's psychic wounds in the way that murderous retribution would, the Marblehead women seized the two Natives and killed them.[4] One of the fishermen, Robert Roules, testified in a deposition.

> Being on shore, the whole town flocked about them, begining at first to insult them, and soon after, the women surrounded them, drove us by force from them, (we escaping at no little peril,) and laid violent hands upon the captives, some stoning us in the meantime, because we would protect them, others seizing them by the hair, got full possession of them, nor was there any way left by which we could rescue them. Then with stones, billets of wood, and what else they might, they made an end of these Indians. We were kept at such distance that we could not see them till they were dead, and then we found them with their heads off and gone, and their flesh in a manner pulled from their bones. And such was the tumultation these women made, that for my life I could not tell who these women were, or the names of any of them. They cried out and said, if the Indians had been carried to Boston, that would have been the end of it, and they would have been set at liberty; but said they, if there had been forty of the best Indians in the country here, they would have killed them all, though they should be hanged for it. They suffered neither constable nor mandrake, nor any other person to come near them, until they had finished their bloody purpose.[5]

Although these incidents resembled later lynchings in significant ways, there is little to suggest that early modern Anglo-American group killings constituted a well-accepted or widespread practice in any meaningful sense.[6] In the seventeenth- and eighteenth-century English and Scottish crowd executions, the Crown responded vigorously to send a message that crowd violence that crossed a threshold into murderous public disorder would not be tolerated. In the Marblehead killings, observers stressed the anomalous quality of the violence. Yet, looking beyond the gender composition of the crowd, the collective killing of Natives by settler women was in another sense entirely consistent with an emerging pattern in settler-Native relations in Colonial British America, one that would persist for another two centuries. Given the significant cultural differences and Anglo-American assumption of superiority, conflict between settlers and Natives could easily escalate into individual and collective lethal retribution, and the complications of laws and legal authority would prove more of an inspiration than an obstacle to the perpetrators of settler-Indian violence. Indeed, the London, Edinburgh, and Marblehead cases each revealed, through exceptional moments of crowd violence, tensions between legal authority and popular views of the law in the early modern British Atlantic, stresses that would expand markedly in the United States in the decades after independence.

Participants in the American Revolution drew upon and reworked older Anglo-American ideas and practices of crowd violence. Consistent with patterns of crowd action earlier in the eighteenth century, most revolutionary popular violence was nonlethal, directed against property, and based upon the customary Anglo-American notion that the people might use violence to protest unjust government. However, from 1765 through the early 1780s, a period during which revolutionary sentiment developed, independence was declared, and a vicious civil war between Patriots and Tories erupted in the backcountry, novel forms of crowd violence directed against persons emerged. Tarring-and-feathering, a melding of older practices of public humiliation of aberrant individuals through "ridings," judicial public punishments, and the punitive folkways of sailors, became a ubiquitous punishment for customs informers and others that offended Patriot sensibilities. In the Blue Ridge Mountains of Virginia, summary punishment of Tories, typically through the infliction of thirty-nine lashes, would be commemorated by some sources in subsequent decades as giving birth to a practice of summary, collective, and nonlethal violence called "lynch-law." Yet lynch-law dovetailed with the American rhetoric and practice of "regulation," predating the Revolution by several decades, in which neighborhood groups informally punished deviants and social enemies and sought to impose their vision of order in backcountry regions, most notably in the Carolinas in the late 1760s and early 1770s. Consistent with traditions of Anglo-American crowd violence, lynch-law and regulation, which would be carried south and west as the backcountry expanded in the decades that followed, usually entailed violence that sought to humiliate and wound, not kill, victims.[7]

Laying the groundwork for the emergence of a lethal practice of American lynching, the egalitarian transformation of American politics and society from the Revolution through the Jacksonian era illuminated a division between reformers who sought to render criminal justice more rational and humane versus popular opinion that continued to insist on harsh retribution for serious crimes. As a sanguinary but highly discretionary administration of criminal justice tied to well-accepted hierarchical, corporatist relationships gave way to a criminal justice system that emphasized rationality, regularity, and the reform of the criminal, an increasingly democratic polity asserted not merely its customary rights within a hierarchical framework, but now its very right to define the nature of criminal justice and its administration, just as their forefathers had waged a revolution against British tyranny and had written a constitution and as they themselves vigorously contested local political offices and avidly participated in state and national politics. Accentuating the cultural division over the transformation of criminal justice, the years of the Revolution and the early Republic had bequeathed a contradictory constitutional legacy. Some argued that the founding documents of the American nation had settled the key questions regarding the relationship between the people, governmental institutions, and laws, and that under a republican form of government, the duty of citizens was now to obey laws and to seek any necessary changes through the political process. But other Americans argued, invoking the tradition of the Anglo-American crowd and the substantial precedents of popular violence in the Revolution, that communities might legitimately disregard laws and usurp the functions of criminal justice when government could not or would not act to protect the interests of citizens.[8] This cultural conflict over the contours of law and criminal justice would give birth to American lynching in the social flux of the developing regions south and west of the Alleghenies in the early-to-mid–nineteenth century.

2. Vigilantes, Criminal Justice, and Antebellum Cultural Conflict

On January 27, 1838, in his Address to the Young Men's Lyceum of Springfield, Illinois, the young lawyer Abraham Lincoln deplored the vigilante execution of gamblers and alleged slave insurrectionists in Mississippi in 1835 and the mob execution of an African American in St. Louis in 1836, asserting that the passions of mob law endangered American self-government.[1] Lincoln rejected the arguments of apologists for vigilantism who insisted that the inadequacy of laws and ineffectiveness of legal institutions in thwarting dangerous criminality justified vigilante violence. Although his specific examples of mob violence came from the Mississippi River Valley, Lincoln argued that lawless mobs that substituted their judgments for those of legally constituted courts had become a national problem, "from New England to Louisiana. . . . they spring up among the pleasure hunting masters of southern slaves, and the order loving citizens of the land of steady habits."[2] Lincoln believed that rampant mob violence unleashed social havoc by eroding the "walls erected for the defence of the persons and property of individuals."[3] In Lincoln's view, only "a reverence for the constitution and laws" that eschewed political passions and extremism and safeguarded individual rights could ensure the perpetuation of republican political institutions inherited from the American Revolution.[4]

As Lincoln understood, antebellum vigilantes and their opponents participated in an emerging discourse over the nature of law, criminal justice, the state, and individual rights. Drawing on an expansive and elastic notion of popular constitutionalism,[5] an understanding of the right of the people to make and supervise laws that stemmed from the Anglo-American legal tradition and the American Revolution, vigilantes asserted the prerogative of communities to usurp legal functions and to deploy violence to protect their neighborhoods from lawlessness. By contrast, those who criticized their actions argued, as had Lincoln, that only the observation of laws and the use of the political process to correct problems in criminal justice could safeguard social order and protect individuals from the dangers of "mob law."[6] As they disputed the boundaries of law and the proper response to criminality, vigilantes and those who criticized them pondered the legacy of the American Revolution and the challenges of republican government in the antebellum United States.

Antebellum advocates of vigilantism in the Midwest, South, and West drew on Anglo-American and American revolutionary traditions of community violence that suggested that citizens might reclaim the functions of government when legal institutions could not provide sufficient protections to persons or their property.[7] Trans-Appalachian vigilantes' highly instrumentalist practice pulled into definition lines of social status and community, the now-respectable against the now-unrespectable versus alleged murderers and transgressors of property, such as slave insurrectionists, horse thieves, counterfeiters, and claims-jumpers.[8] In their temporary, republican usurpation of the prerogatives of legal authority, vigilantes invoked popular sovereignty to reject a style and philosophy of criminal justice that had crystallized in the Northeast from the late eighteenth through the mid–nineteenth centuries. Legal changes emanating from the Northeast included a newly ascendant respect for the rights of the defendant (enshrined in the Fifth Amendment to the U.S. Constitution, holding that no citizen would be deprived of due process protections), a burgeoning interest in the potential for the reform of the criminal, and a fear of the effects of harsh punishments on the masses that enthusiastically viewed them.

The reform of criminal justice in line with humanitarian considerations and a growing emphasis on legal rights and fairness accompanied capitalist transformation and middle class and working class formation in the Northeast from the American Revolution through the first half the of nineteenth century.[9] The adversary system, in which lawyers dominated trials and vigorously contested criminal procedure, was also a recent development in the history of criminal justice, taking root in Anglo-American law only in the eighteenth century.[10] As with movements to limit capital punishment, the adversary system took fullest root in the Northeast. In the Northeast, middle class persons committed to due process principles and the reform of criminal justice institutions and accepted the necessity of aggressive lawyering in the interest of legal fairness, although cohesive urban working class communities continued to acquit or convict defendants in line with traditional understandings of community justice.[11] In the South, whites persisted in observing customary communal notions of criminal justice for whites in and out of court, evinced comparatively little interest in reform of capital punishment, and sought to keep African American slaves out of court and instead subject to the punitive whims of the slaveholding class and the larger white community. However, these popular views clashed with an increasing emphasis in southern criminal law in the antebellum years on bringing slaves under the same courts and legal procedures as whites to demonstrate the ostensible consistency of slavery with developing American notions of legal fairness.[12] Complaints about an overabundance of lawyers and their intolerable manipulation of legal process abounded on the backwoods southern frontier, sometimes inspiring regulator movements.[13] Southerners in the early republic and the antebellum era had not committed fully to due process law nor to the adversary system that supported it. The story was more complex, however, on the midwestern frontier, where Yankees and settlers from the Old Northwest and Upper South wielded competing notions of criminal justice. Frontier midwesterners with roots in New England and the Mid Atlantic tended to stress legal regularity and due process, whereas residents of the Lower Midwest who came from border regions and the South emphasized harsh and rapid punishment that coincided with communal prerogatives. The West would see an analogous mixture and clash of northeastern, southern, and backcountry legal cultures as Americans migrated to regions beyond the Mississippi in the 1830s through the 1860s.[14]

Setting the stage for antebellum vigilantism, in the mid-to-late-eighteenth-century North British migrants to regions south and west of the Alleghenies had participated in regulator movements that transposed English, Scottish, and Ulster traditions of organized violence within the novel conditions of the American backcountry. Complex backcountry regulator movements both united and factionalized yeoman farmers against social antagonists such as coastal elites, corrupt local officials, bandits, hunters, debtors, merchants, and lawyers. Backcountry regulation entailed brutal, but not usually lethal violence; regulators often tarred and feathered, flogged, and banished their enemies, but only infrequently hanged the recipients of their punishment.[15] Backcountry migrants carried patterns of regulator violence westward to large portions of the Old Southwest and the Old Northwest in the late eighteenth and early nineteenth centuries. In the antebellum decades in the developing South, Midwest, and West, vigilante violence retained characteristics of backcountry regulation,[16] but also took on new forms and meanings. Vigilante movements became a characteristic response to concerns about frontier criminality, as well as a means of constituting social hierarchy and community in regions undergoing rapid in-migration. Empowered but also alarmed by the erosion of the deferential social and political hierarchies that had characterized the early decades of the republic, Jacksonian era vigilantes asserted that the growing emphasis on due process in criminal law posed a particular danger in frontier regions where the reliability of legal and political institutions was jeopardized by a still nascent and unstable social order. In response to this purported threat, antebellum vigilantes now often sought to murder, not merely physically chastise, their enemies. Mimicking the ritual of the public executions that reformers now criticized as unseemly and inhumane, vigilantes hanged their enemies in a practice that was increasingly labeled lynching.[17]

Defending their actions, vigilantes articulated a preference for criminal justice that privileged local opinion over a neutral commitment to due process law and the rights of the defendant, a stance that rejected an emerging commitment in reformist circles and in the legal culture to the notion of a fair-handed, omnipotent state as arbitrator of community differences and guarantor of individual rights. This latter "due process" perspective, articulated in embryonic form by Abraham Lincoln in his 1838 speech to the Young Men's Lyceum, asserted that the people, through their elected representatives, made laws and could alter them when circumstances required, but that the only reliable path toward social and economic progress was the faithful observation of legal process. Old Northwest and Old Southwest vigilantes asserted by contrast their own "rough justice" vision of constitutionalism, one in which communities might temporarily disregard the law and usurp the power of courts through vigilante violence that enforced preferences for harsh communal punishment if the observation of legal process seemed to circumvent local views. Like virtually all antebellum Americans, vigilantes articulated a cultural perspective based upon republicanism, an ideological commitment to a responsive government elected by virtuous, qualified (white) citizens. However, for vigilantes and their defenders, republicanism was a highly elastic ideology and language more consonant with the defense of kin and neighborhood than with an abstract allegiance to an evenhanded, benevolent state and formal legal system that Lincoln and other proponents of due process law constitutionalism advocated.[18]

The Cotton Frontier

Vigilante movements, often self-designated as members of "Captain Slick's Company" or "Slickers," were a ubiquitous aspect of the social landscape of the cotton frontier.[19] Influenced by early modern Anglo-American traditions of regulator violence and the practices of ad hoc, extralegal communal supervision and collective punishment associated with the American Revolution and the early American Republic,[20] cotton frontier Slickers also imbibed the racial republicanism of the expanding slaveholding South and deployed a particular vision of law confronting growing notions of legal regularity and due process in the antebellum United States. Slicker violence, like much regulator violence in the antebellum Midwest and West, revealed and constituted factions within communities that were recently established or experiencing substantial in-migration, by seeking to define, through a praxis of collective violence, questions of social order, community leadership and respectability, criminality and disrespectability. Often these contests for social leadership were fiercely contested in multiple venues, through nocturnal informal violence as well as by day in civil and criminal court proceedings, and they took on particular intensity in a region where the compulsion for white racial solidarity underlined the defense of slavery and the protection of slaveholding.

Several examples from Alabama illustrate how Slicker movements took place amid a social and legal competition for community leadership and power in a slaveholding republic. Slickers seized Woody Martin in the area of Huntsville on the night of October 12, 1830, took him out to the woods, and flogged him "til scarcely a spark of vitality remained."[21] Woody Martin's son, James, responded a few days later by shooting William Burton amid an argument, a Huntsville newspaper reported, as to "the merits and demerits of Capt. Slick's band of lawless miscreants."[22] A "Riot" followed at the market house, in which friends of Burton and the Slickers protested James Martin's actions.[23] In the legal process that followed, James Martin was convicted of assault and battery and the participants in the riot were fined.[24] But the social competition that pitted the Martins versus Burton and the Slickers had a longer legal pedigree. In 1822, a jury had acquitted Woody Martin of selling liquor without a license at a "house of entertainment" in Huntsville; in 1829, a jury had fined James Martin $100 and had him flogged at the pillory, branded with a "T" and imprisoned for horse theft.[25] In another example, a Slick Company self-designated as the "best citizens" formed in Chambers and Randolph Counties in eastern Alabama in the mid-1830s in response to an allegation that a gang of thieves was stealing slaves and horses, secreting them in man-made caves, and selling the stolen property into Mississippi. Slickers arrested a man named McClendon in Randolph County, whereupon a portion of the Slick Company in disguise took McClendon from a guard, tied him to a tree, and flogged him until he confessed that a missing slave had been removed to Mississippi. The Slickers then ordered McClendon to leave the area.[26] Slickers also were at work in Jackson County in northeastern

Alabama in July 1831, when they tied Alanson Huff to a tree and whipped him. Huff brought suit against four participants in the Slicker company that had punished him, but he feared further retribution, asserting that the Slickers counted five or six hundred supporters. The court granted Huff's request for a change of venue to Madison County in light of the influence the Slickers exerted in Jackson County, but Huff decided not to pursue the case, settling for the defendants' payment of legal fees.[27]

Cotton frontier Slickers and their apologists embodied a stance on and an approach to law. They sometimes used the legal process to bring formal charges against the men they flogged literally outside the courthouse door; in turn, Slickers were the targets of legal actions, occasionally financially ruinous ones, brought by their victims.[28] Even as they used courts or were brought to court, Slickers and their defenders lambasted the effectiveness of local criminal justice institutions. In 1833, a Huntsville editor asserted that the recourse to "Slick's law" was absolutely essential in Jackson County, as the "laws were powerless" there in light of the organized activities of a criminal class of "rogues and counterfeiters" that could manipulate the legal process through serving as jurors who would acquit their criminal allies, or by committing perjury through false testimony as witnesses in cases involving their criminal accomplices.[29] A participant armed with multiple weapons in the 1830 riot in Huntsville that followed James Martin's attack on the Slickers and shooting of William Burton "swore if the law would not defend him he would defend himself."[30] But even as they stepped outside of law to punish their social enemies, Slickers mimicked the punishment legally administered in Alabama at the whipping post, imitated militia organization by designating a "captain" to command activities (although coordination sometimes collapsed in the heat of personal animosities and vengeance), and designated themselves as "the best men," republican citizens instrumentally devising informal institutions that might protect community order and property in slaves and horses against the challenge posed by economic competitors and a purportedly burgeoning cotton frontier criminal class.

Reworking Slicker traditions, vigilantes in Mississippi helped to refashion collective violence in a lethal direction in the summer of 1835. On July 6, a group styling itself as "the most respectable citizens" of Vicksburg hanged five gamblers on a scaffold in front of a large crowd. A conflict between town residents and gamblers had erupted two days before, on the Fourth of July, when a gambler named Cabler insulted members of the Vicksburg Volunteers at a barbecue and then threatened them as they paraded in the public square. In customary republican Slicker fashion, "a crowd of respectable citizens" took Cabler out to the woods, flogged and tarred and feathered him, and ordered him out of the area. A Vicksburg newspaper editor explained that the inability of the law to reach miscreants who threatened the community but who had not yet consummated their designs led to the recourse to Slick law. "It was determined to take him into the woods and *lynch* him—which is a mode of punishment provided for such as become obnoxious in a manner which the law cannot reach."[31] Vicksburg residents met that evening to adopt resolutions expelling gamblers from the town and shutting down "faro-dealing" houses. On the morning of July 6, militia accompanied by "a file of several hundred citizens" descended on a gambling house. After they opened the back door, a shot from within struck and killed a leader of the mob of townspeople, Dr. Hugh S. Bodley. The enraged crowd seized five gamblers from the dwelling and quickly executed them. The gamblers' corpses hanged until the next morning, when they were cut down and buried.[32]

Defenders of the Vicksburg vigilantes asserted that their actions reflected an analysis of the defects of the cotton frontier criminal justice system. A Vicksburg editor defended the mob execution as a response by thoughtful citizens to a gaping hole in cotton frontier law, the difficulty of securing a homicide conviction. "The laws, however severe in their provision, have never been sufficient to correct a vice which must be established by positive proof, and cannot, like others, be shown from circumstantial testimony. It is practiced, too, by individuals whose whole study is to violate the law in such a manner."[33] Intervening in an emerging antebellum cultural conflict over the appropriate nature of criminal justice and punishment, the editor excoriated those, such as northern reformers, who might criticize the Vicksburg summary execution as inhumane, unjust, and as a grievous violation of due process law. "Whatever therefore sickly sensibility or mawkish philanthropy may say against the course pursued by us, we hope that our citizens will not relax the code of punishment which they have enacted against this infamous and baleful class of society."[34]

Mississippians also interpreted the Vicksburg vigilante execution in reference to the precedents offered by Slicker violence and they noted continuity but also an important change in direction. An editor in Manchester, Mississippi, commenting on the Vicksburg events, emphasized that the summary execution of the gamblers was a hanging, *not* a lynching, a term that until that time had connoted an extralegal flogging. Recasting Slicker rationales for stepping outside the law, the editor of the *Manchester Herald* argued that the Vicksburg vigilante violence occurred against the context of a functioning cotton frontier legal system that could not offer adequate protection against a dangerous criminal class.

This is a harsh and summary mode of inflicting punishment for crimes however black—but the exigency of the times requires it. There is some radical defect in our laws or in their administration.—The Judges say it is the defect of our popular constitution: it may be; but we know that crime frequently goes un-punished, and our citizens must resort to themselves for protection—and, as Squire Lynch has proved ineffectual, Squire Jack Ketch has been substituted . . . We are opposed to mob-law; but it would be a mockery of justice to go through the formality of a trial with such villains.[35]

Despite the Manchester editor's careful distinction between lynching and hanging ("Jack Ketch" was a colloquial Anglo-American term referring to the hangman), historian Christopher Waldrep has persuasively shown that the burgeoning popular press reported the Vicksburg vigilante execution as a "lynching." As a result of their reporting of the event, the term *lynching* broadened to connote any sort of collective extralegal punishment, lethal or nonlethal. Within months, newspapers were reporting a frenzy of lynchings throughout the country.[36] Yet, as the Manchester editor emphasized, the shift was not merely a semantic and rhetorical one but, crucially, also one of praxis, from vigilante flogging, to vigilante execution by hanging, backed by familiar arguments alleging the ineffectuality of cotton frontier legal institutions, but now seeking to justify not merely thirty-nine lashes but communally imposed death. Southern, midwestern, and western vigilantes absorbed this lesson, deploying in the 1840s and '50s an expanded punitive repertoire alternating flogging and hanging, often after polling the assembled crowd in a republi-can ballot, and justifying their actions by asserting that functioning courts could not touch an expanding criminal class manipulating the vagaries of due process law.

Mississippi vigilantes invoked similar arguments in the weeks that followed the Vicksburg mob execution to justify the suppression of a purported region-wide conspiracy of blacks and whites to overthrow the slave system. Inspired by a pamphlet authored by Virgil A. Stewart that supposedly chronicled the confessions of John Murrell, a white thief and counterfeiter who was the al-leged mastermind of the plot, panic-stricken slaveholding whites in Madison County formed a "Committee of Safety" and tortured blacks into implicating a number of local whites and revealing supposed details of the insurrection. Summarily hanging the slaves and free blacks who had "confessed" involve-ment, the Madison County committee put the alleged white participants on trial, convicting and hanging five of them and flogging and banishing others. The accused whites were marginal men in the slaveholding region's social order; several of them had been born in the North and they made a precarious living in the slaveholding region as "Thompsonian" doctors who offered steam cures and homeopathic medical treatments.[37]

Drawing on eighteenth- and early-nineteenth-century precedents for the harsh and lethal suppression of slave insurrections,[38] Madison County vigilantes utilized collective violence that also reflected the legal and social context of the late cotton frontier. Invested with extraordinary extralegal powers by a mass meeting of "respectable citizens" in the Madison County seat of Livingston on July 3, 1835, the Madison County Committee consisted of thirteen "freeholders" who asserted the authority to summarily arrest and try whites and blacks "with the power to hang or whip being always governed by the laws of the land so far only as they shall be applicable to the case in question, otherwise to act as in their discretion shall seem best, for the benefit of the country, and for the protection [of] its citizens."[39] As in Vicksburg, self-consciously republican procedures and a rhetorical broadside against the antebellum criminal justice system bridged comparatively benign traditions of Slicker violence with a shift toward vigilante execution by hanging. Falsely promising those they accused "something like a *trial,* if not *formal,* at least *substantial,*" the Madison Committee argued that their lethal vigilantism was necessary because the potential of "the law's delay or evasion" would not sufficiently deter the allegedly profound threat posed by the conspirators.[40] To the question of why the committee did not turn over those it had apprehended to the civil authorities and the legal process, the committee's secretary argued that the whites accused of participation in the insurrection plot would have inevitably manipulated legal procedure, found ways to have crucial testimony excluded, pressured or threatened witnesses, committed perjury on the stand, or broken out of jail with the aid of their "confederates in guilt."[41] The mass meeting, which authorized the committee's actions, instead asserted "the law of self-preservation, which is *paramount to all law.*"[42] But, in its resolutions investing the committee, the mass meeting also sought to avoid the threat that a litigious antebellum culture posed to vigilantes by pledging "ourselves to sustain said committee against all personal and pecuniary liability which may result from the discharge of the duties hereby assigned them."[43]

Lethal vigilantism thus arose on the late cotton frontier as an evolution of Slicker regulator traditions and as a refashioning of the deadly reprisals with which slave insurrections had been typically suppressed in eighteenth- and early-nineteenth-century America. Vigilantism took root amid fluid social conditions as an explicit and conscious rejection of the evolving antebellum criminal justice system. Vigilante hangings, which were increasingly labeled lynchings, emerged amid a dynamic and unfinished cotton frontier social order, as a means of sifting and sorting out definitions of social class among whites in a cultural landscape of substantial in-migration and mobility. These patterns were in play in the 1850s just beyond the southwestern periphery of the vast cotton kingdom, in the complex ethnic and social landscape of South Texas. The region surrounding San Antonio saw extensive collective violence in the late 1850s. Vigilantes hanged seven horse thieves along the San Antonio River in the spring of 1857;[44] a member of a vigilance committee fatally shot "desperado" Bill Hart and two of his companions in San Antonio in May 1857;[45] a year later, vigilantes hanged four Mexican horse thieves from a tree in the vicinity of San José Mission.[46] A Bexar County grand jury staffed by Anglos and Tejanos, reporting in September 1858, lamented the plague of "summary vengeance" in the community, asserting that it was rooted in a history of lax enforcement of laws in the region and the Texas governor's excessive use of executive clemency to release dangerous criminals.[47] As the extralegal violence in Texas indicated, the implications of the increasingly lethal emphasis of vigilantes on the late cotton frontier would be profound. Lynching, typically by hanging, became a familiar occurrence throughout the regions beyond the Alleghenies from the late 1830s through the '50s, often as an explicit rejection of the effectiveness of the deliberative and ostensibly neutral criminal justice administered by courts and officeholders.

The Midwest

From April through December 1857, a large-scale vigilante movement swept across the late midwestern frontier of eastern Iowa. Eventually encompassing five counties, the movement collectively hanged and shot fifteen white men, accusing them of murder, horse theft, and counterfeiting.[48] The movement and the opposition it elicited pulled into sharp definition evolving antebellum midwestern notions of law and authority, class, culture, and community. The vigilantes in Iowa in 1857 acted not in the absence of legal institutions, which were already well-established in the region,[49] but because a changing legal system offered tenuous and unsatisfying solutions to problems of authority and social control in a region where lines of social hierarchy, culture, and community leadership were ambiguous and ill-defined.

The 1857 eastern Iowa vigilante movement reflected the legal and social context of the late midwestern frontier. Organized criminals who stole stock and circulated counterfeit currency exploited a widely dispersed prairie population, nascent connections to markets that still relied largely on equine and maritime transportation (only minor portions of eastern Iowa were connected to railroad lines and the East by 1857[50]), and the lack of centralized banking and standardized currency exchange. Significant population increase and in-migration from different regions of the antebellum United States meant that social identities and networks were recently established and insecure, even as highly localistic neighborhoods provided the basis for cultural and political identification.[51] According to the U.S. Census, population growth between 1850 and 1860 was dramatic in the three predominately rural counties that formed the epicenter of the 1857 vigilante movement, with population more than doubling in Jackson County, more than tripling in Cedar County, and more than quadrupling in Jones County. The two more urbanized counties on the periphery of the vigilantes' activities, Scott and Clinton, saw equally dramatic gains by 1860 with population multiplied between four and six times what it had been a decade earlier.[52] Amid this social flux, participation in vigilantism became a means of asserting an identity as a respectable property-holder collectively defending livestock and the reliability of market exchange against culturally marginal persons who threatened those commodities and ostensibly the very basis of prosperity on the agrarian frontier. Membership in a vigilante committee thus served to both define and enact community, pulling into definition respectable agrarian proprietors against a supposedly parasitical rural criminal class that threatened honest livelihood in a recently planted and rapidly changing society.

However, vigilantism also pulled other individual and collective identities in antebellum eastern Iowa into definition, particularly around the issue of the sanctity of law. Vigilantes defined themselves as those who would step outside of law to ensure that the ultimate purpose of all law, self-preservation, was served. Their actions constituted a critique of legal institutions that, because of a growing emphasis on legal fairness and procedure and the novelty and tenuousness of social relationships, seemed to them incapable of expressing the will of the dominant residents of the neighborhood or of effectively keeping social order. Simultaneously, vigilantes defined those whom they flogged or hanged as members of a disrespectable criminal class, unworthy of citizenship or of the mutuality expected of good neighbors. These events constituted a third social group as well, those editors, entrepreneurs, Quakers, and members of the legal culture (for example, judges and lawyers) who placed their faith in due process law and a respect for the rights of those accused of crime. Echoing Abraham Lincoln's response to vigilantism, due process advocates in antebellum Iowa argued that, even in light of the real problem of frontier criminality, the actions of the vigilantes were intolerable because they endangered the very foundation of republican government, the willingness of citizens to defer to the governmental and legal institutions that they had created and could alter through the political process. Due process proponents, asserting their superior knowledge and judgment on the basis of their social class and emphasizing individual conscience and humane conduct, argued that the actions of mobs represented the ignorant majority tyrannically extinguishing the rights of the accused and the unpopular. For due process supporters on the late eastern Iowa frontier, only the safeguarding of the majesty of law could ensure that the rights of all would be protected and that a stable social order could be erected.

The eastern Iowa vigilantes asserted that they had no choice but to turn to the natural law of self-preservation and that their ultimate goal was to achieve the reinforcement of the administration of law. The Jackson County Vigilance Committee, led by H. K. Landis, postmaster of Iron Hill, who claimed that the committee was "composed of from three to four hundred citizens," adopted resolutions demanding that the state's criminal law be enforced in that county "to the very letter." The Iron Hills Vigilants resolved to rigorously investigate counterfeiting, horse theft, and murders committed in the county and asserted that they would be "governed" by the state penal code in this endeavor "so far as it is convenient." The Jackson County mobbers sought the resignation of county officials whom they accused of avoiding the prosecution of serious criminal cases "by going a duck hunting." The vigilantes promised to closely scrutinize the behavior of officials and the conduct of criminal prosecutions.[53]

Eastern Iowa editors interpreted the regulators' argument by means of a systematic critique of the legal system. The *Maquoketa Excelsior* expressed some doubts about "mob law," but argued "there are times when Vigilance Committees are very beneficial in clearing the county of desperadoes." The Maquoketa editor suggested that excessive concern for proper procedure and fairness in due process law had precipitated a crisis situation in Jackson County. "When Judges so construe the law as to give new trials to felons who have been many times convicted of the most outrageous of crimes—when convictions cannot be had, and all sorts of villains go scot free without fear of the law—it is then past endurance."[54] In its reporting of the lynching of Michael Carroll and William Barger, the *Excelsior* stressed that the court's decision to grant Barger a new trial and Carroll a change of venue had inspired the vigilante violence against those men.[55]

Other newspapers in eastern Iowa picked up this theme of legal conflict in responding to the vigilante movement. The editor of the *Dubuque Express and Herald* argued that the problem lay in an aspect of the growing emphasis on due process, particularly the unwillingness of juries to convict on anything short of "the clearest evidence." "In consequence of this acquittal, the malefactor goes abroad into the community, fearless of the law, and regardless of any new evidence which may come to light. . . . either our criminal code, or the mode of executing it, must ere long, undergo a change. To the utter inefficiency of one or the other, or both, can be traced the causes of the disgraceful lynching scenes which have done dishonor to our country."[56] Four months later, the *Dubuque Express and Herald* resumed this critique of the administration of criminal justice in Iowa. The Dubuque editor excoriated the weakness of jurors and the machinations of lawyers in the Hawkeye State, contrasting the unpredictability of American law unfavorably with the reputed efficiency and fairness of legal institutions in England. The *Express and Herald* blamed the "record [of] so many mob executions as have taken place within the last twelve months" on the unreliability of legal institutions in Iowa.[57]

Vigilantes and editors who defended their actions emphasized the incompetence and inconstancy of jurors, lawyers, prosecutors, and county officials because the actions of those parties to the administration of criminal justice were relatively unpredictable in an era and locale where personal reputations and ideological and factional loyalties were recently formed and potentially malleable.[58] Respective positions regarding due process law, the sanctity of property-holding and the suppression of its infringement, and the reputations of neighbors were up for grabs and led to a variety of results in legal process. In contrast to the formal legal system, vigilantism offered the satisfaction of the swift, harsh, and collective punishment of those who had allegedly committed crime.

Eastern Iowans who opposed the vigilantes shared their understanding that the events must be understood in the context of a stance on law. A "large number of the citizens" that assembled at the Friends meeting house in Springdale in Cedar County on July 18 adopted a preamble and resolutions that condemned the "lawless violence" of the "'Vigilance Committee.'" The Anti-Mob Law Association that gathered at the hall of local Quakers sought the legal punishment of "horse thieves and all other criminals." But the antimob law meeting argued that vigilantism imperiled the rights of all citizens in a republic by abandoning the neutrality and rationality of law in favor of "summary vengeance." Echoing criticisms of mob actions that refrained throughout the antebellum era, they resolved "that when a portion of the people, acting under excitement, may with impunity trample the laws of the country under foot to effect their purpose, the rights of the good citizens of a free and enlightened government are no longer secure, but may be wrested from them by any puff of passion." The Anti-Mob Law Association, whose resolutions were noted by its secretary, Thomas Winn, who would serve as a delegate to the Republican state convention a month later in Iowa City, demanded that the press condemn the "mobocratic proceedings" and asserted a class division in opinion on vigilantism. They argued that "the enlightened community" should withdraw their support for the portion of the press "which is not high-toned enough" to condemn the violence. The antivigilantes concluded with the wish that "all good citizens" protest and employ their "influence" against the violence and seek to lawfully punish it for "the peace, prosperity and welfare" of the community.[59]

The citizens that formed the Anti-Mob Law Association were not alone in condemning the vigilantes' abandonment of due process law. Other eastern Iowans participated in a debate that sought to define the nature of republican government and criminal justice on the late midwestern frontier. The editor of the *Daily Iowa State Democrat* made an impassioned defense of republican legal institutions as he condemned the "butchery" of the "Jackson County Mob" and the "respectable journals" that defended them. In deploring the mobbers' resort to extralegal murder, the Davenport newspaper compared their actions with the attacks hostile Native Americans made against white settlers. Invoking the common notion among antebellum white Iowans that Native Americans were culturally inferior to white Americans, the *Democrat* asserted that vigilantism was in fact barbarism that eschewed the institutions of civilized society in favor of private vengeance and social disorder.

> The Chief danger to the peace and order of a people self governed, is their efforts to take the execution of the law into their own hands, from the authority legally constituted by them to perform the duties of preserving public order, punishing crime and redressing wrong. . . . A combination of desperadoes, impatient of the necessary delays of the law in the administration of justice, and each having some private spite and malice to gratify, are more fearful than a band of brutal Indians let loose upon Society with reeking knife and dripping tomahawk. In its frenzy it confounds innocence with guilt, takes suspicions for proof and executes vengeance instead of justice upon the victims of its hate.[60]

Another newspaper, the *Maquoketa Excelsior,* condemned the actions of the regulators who hanged William Barger, pulled down his corpse three hours later, and drove it in a buggy to Cobb's Hotel, where they placed "a slip of paper" in the corpse's hands that "called for dinner and horse feed." The *Excelsior* argued that this act unveiled the uncouth style and unrefined values of the vigilantes: "Such are some of the natural out-croppings of this lower strata, in the midst of a community that boasts decency, some degree of refinement, and a modicum of Christianity."[61] The disapproval and remorse with which some eastern Iowans responded to the actions of the vigilantes could also take a more private form. A man identified as the "son of Deacon Finch, of Massilon, Cedar County" had participated in the vigilante committee that voted to hang "Kelso and his comrade." Finch left before the hanging, but upon arriving home his mother asked him if the vigilantes had apprehended the men. He replied that "they had" and that he had voted to hang the men. His mother admonished him that "he ought not to take that which he could not give." Finch went out to "his plowing" and after "awhile. . . . he hitched his horse" and used one of the reins to hang himself from a tree.[62]

Although some officials publicly identified or participated with the vigilantes, such as Iron Hills Postmaster H. K. Landis, and Cedar County judges Samuel A. Bissell, a forty-five-year-old migrant from upstate New York, and Wells Spicer, a young Know-Nothing from Illinois who was also editor of the *Tipton Cedar County Advertiser*,[63] other members of the political class denounced the Regulators' lawless violence. On September 18, Judge William Tuthill, a forty-nine-year-old early settler and banker who had been born and educated in New York City, delivered a charge to Jones County grand jurors that underlined the advantages of adhering to due process law.[64] Admonishing the grand jurors to fully investigate the vigilante activities that had occurred in the county, Tuthill stressed that law safeguarded "order and harmony in our government, prosperity in our social relations, and peace and security to the community at large." Tuthill asserted that if citizens were to determine merely on the basis of their opinions what was crime and how to punish it, "anarchy" and the "overthrow of the government would ensue." Reading the full text of the Fifth Amendment to the U.S. Constitution to the grand jurors, Tuthill emphasized the sanctity of due process protections. He castigated the vigilantes' recourse to hanging, arguing that their actions in fact were "wilfully and wickedly trampling upon and setting at naught that glorious Constitution, framed by our patriotic forefathers, that we have been taught to regard as the very foundation and bulwork [*sic*] of liberty and prosperity as a people, and perpetuity as a nation." Tuthill argued that the very continuation of American democracy depended upon the respect of citizens for law.[65] However, grand jurors failed to indict regulators for their illegal actions in 1857. One grand juror blamed the vigilantism on an organized band of horse thieves active in the state and the difficulty of bringing them to justice in light of "our sparse population." The grand jurors petitioned the state legislature for a statute that would enable county judges to increase the awards for the conviction of horse thieves to the value of the stolen stock and the penalty of conviction to no less than ten years' imprisonment. Stressing what they sought in criminal justice, the grand jurors hoped that their suggestions might "secure certain, sure, expeditious, and effective justice." The abstract values inherent in due process law mattered less to them than the rapid suppression of horse thievery.[66]

The discourse surrounding the vigilantism in eastern Iowa in 1857 also drew into focus political allegiances and ideologies. The resolutions adopted by the Jackson County Vigilance Committee excoriated not only the administration of criminal justice in the county but also the general conduct and policies of the clique of ex-Whigs and Republicans who held Jackson County offices. Deploring what they termed the "robbery" and "smuggling" of county bonds and the "Drainage Fund," the regulators argued, in tones redolent of the working class and yeoman republicanism of Jacksonian Democracy, that the officeholders were in cahoots with the criminals who plagued eastern Iowa "to carry their sway over the people of the county, and to roll in their silks and purple and wealth at the expense of the hard earnings of the farmer and the hard working mechanic."[67] Replying to criticism from Republican newspapers in Bellevue and Maquoketa that it had unjustly maligned Jackson County officials and had backed vigilantism, a Democratic newspaper in Dubuque, the *Express and Herald,* urged Jackson County citizens to purge their county's offices of the "bad men" who had held them for "a series of years" distinguished by excessive taxation, misappropriation of public funds, "tricks, mismanagement, negligence and corruptions." The *Express and Herald* argued that it had "not approved mobocracy" and indeed had "in a better spirit" sought to dissuade "further acts of public punishment, no matter how justly merited" than had the "foul sheets" of the *Maquoketa Excelsior* and the *Bellevue Republican.* Support or apology for the vigilantes and their critique of the overly deliberative and procedural style of law supposedly practiced in the courts of the region thus coincided with Democratic rhetoric and ideology that stressed the virtues of laissez-faire economics and minimal government, versus the public institutions and funding and moral reforms sought by Whigs and then Republicans.[68]

Along with the cultural, ideological, and political conflicts the regulator violence in 1857 embodied and elicited, the Iowa vigilantes' actions reflected a transition in patterns of collective violence in the United States. As with cotton frontier vigilantes, the eastern Iowa regulators' praxis of violence included both customary and novel elements linking older Anglo-American traditions of communal violence with newer procedures, most significantly the lethal hanging and shooting of many of their victims. The regulators flogged several of their victims; communal flogging, typically with thirty-nine lashes on the bare back, was among the most typical of popular punishments in the eighteenth and early nineteenth centuries. The eastern Iowa vigilantes self-consciously adopted republican procedures that suggested the neighborhood basis of summary justice. Sometimes the regulators conducted a ballot among the crowd to determine whether a victim should be flogged or hanged: For instance, thirty vigilantes voted to whip Bennet Warren and three hundred voted to hang him in Clinton County.[69] The 1857 regulators bound themselves to each other through bylaws pledging to suppress criminality and swore oaths of loyalty, secrecy, and collective self-defense.[70] The eastern Iowa regulators staged comprehensive mock trial procedures, evoking the legitimacy of legal forms while eschewing the meaningful protections of due process law. The regulators elected a captain, who directed their activities, and sometimes conducted full-fledged informal trials of the men they accused, to the extent of appointing a judge, jury, and attorneys and examining witnesses.[71]

The eastern Iowa regulators' hanging of suspected horse thieves, murderers, and counterfeiters connected easily with Anglo-American traditions of community morals regulation. Such a practice was manifested in Cedar County on July 1857 amid the wave of violence against alleged murderers and property criminals. A Scottish-born farmer named John Chappell recounted in his diary on July 6 that a society had organized at Rogersville for protection against horse thieves. Five days later, Chappell wrote that the "Regulators," led by "Capt. Wm. Dallas" seized and brought before "Judge Lynch" a man named David Winterringer, whom they tried "before Squire Rigby, Elder Ferguson and Samuel Yule and others for the hinous offence of asking and at-temptimg [sic] to take a kiss of Miss Smith, schoolmadam at the Brick school house, Red Oak." At first the regulators "could not make out an evil case of it." But then after "serious advice from Elder John Ferguson," the "company" extracted a confession, although "the prisoner" continued to laugh about the matter. But when "Capt. Dallas" displayed a rope, Winterringer cried "tears of penitence" and soon "agreed to leave the county of Cedar forever under the pain of having his head bored by a bullet."[72] The Red Oak regulators were well-established farmers who had been among the first white settlers of Cedar County; Chappell, Dallas, Ferguson, Yule, and Rigby had arrived in 1837 and 1838. Embodying the strong cultural connections between North Britain and the American backcountry, at least four of the Red Oak regulators had been born in Scotland and had migrated to America in the late 1820s and in the early to mid-1830s. Three of the future vigilantes had sojourned in New York and Indiana and one in Ohio before arriving in frontier Iowa; one of them, William Dallas, would be arrested six months later for his role in the vigilante murder of Hiram Roberts, whose death concluded the 1857 eastern Iowa vigilante movement.[73] Informal neighborhood scrutiny and punishment of offenses that violated prevailing gender and sexual standards was a common feature of rural American, British, and European society in the early modern era.[74] But this custom transmogrified into nearly lethal regulator violence in the context of a flurry of deadly vigilantism on the late midwestern frontier. In the years that followed, lethal vigilantism would take on an extended life in the Lower Midwest as the experience of the Civil War and Reconstruction exacerbated backcountry whites' ambivalence regarding state authority. Endemic, localized vigilante killings punished allegations of property crime and homicide across portions of southern and western Iowa and southern Indiana into the 1880s.[75]

The West

Shortly after the Civil War, as the Union Pacific Railroad staked out a route across the southwestern edge of the Dakota Territory in 1867 and 1868, speculators and settlers that included diverse entrepreneurs, laborers, and professionals flooded in, creating instant towns at prospective rail centers. The tracks reached Cheyenne by November 1867, and this infant metropolis in a few weeks numbered approximately 6,000. Laramie City also sprouted instantaneously several months later, as did points west as 1868 progressed. The editor of the *Cheyenne Leader,* Nathan Baker, noted the transient nature of much of the population and deplored extensive prostitution, consumption of alcohol, gambling, and general "lawlessness," embodied in ubiquitous criminal activity and a boisterous style of recreation. Baker derided what he perceived as the opportunistic anarchism of these "end-of-the track" towns, which was a function of the rambunctious capitalism they temporarily attracted.[76]

The burgeoning railroad towns possessed a semblance of government and law enforcement. Encouraged by Union Pacific, citizens in Cheyenne elected a provisional city government in August 1867 (which was replaced by a legal, elected government in January 1868), as did residents of Laramie in May 1868. Informal citizen organizations supplemented limited municipal police forces in crime control, and police courts functioned. Marshals and judges oversaw the administration of Dakota territorial law. However, apologists for vigilantes claimed that legal institutions of the Dakota Territory remained weak and that vigilante committees active in 1868 responded to rampant criminality and violence, driving out the "scum" and imposing social order.[77]

The record of lynching violence in the railroad towns in 1868 is a mixed one, and it belies simple explanations. A highly organized vigilante committee in Cheyenne expelled three supposed thieves in early January, and then traveled thirty miles west to Dale City and hanged three men who had drunkenly shot into a dance hall and saloon. Following another shooting incident at a saloon in Cheyenne, the committee ordered approximately a dozen men to leave the town, and in the succeeding weeks expelled a number of persons, including some acquitted of crimes by local authorities. In March, a masked mob hanged Charles Martin, who had been acquitted of murdering his partner in the ownership of a saloon, and Charles Morgan, accused of horse theft. The final lynching in Cheyenne occurred when a mob hanged a German brewer named Landgraber when he refused to pay a debt owed to a saloonkeeper.[78]

Laramie's brief spasm of lethal vigilantism began in August 1868, when approximately twenty men collectively murdered an alleged robber nicknamed "The Kid," who was accused of drugging his victims. In October, five hundred vigilantes led by Major T. B. Sears, a Civil War veteran, mounted raids on drinking, dancing, and gambling establishments, hanging four. Five masked men hanged supposed-thief H. C. Thomas in Laramie in November 1868. Mobbers then hanged five "desperadoes" in Bear River City, a prospective rail town recently established west of Laramie, and correspondents speculated that members of the Laramie vigilante committee participated. Another committee, led by the Union Pacific's chief tie driver, hanged three more alleged robbers in Bear River City on November 11, provoking a riot in which at least fourteen died and which was finally suppressed by the arrival of soldiers from Fort Bridger.[79]

Although evidence concerning the 1868 vigilante killings is sparse, it is obvious that political factionalism, economic competition, and a struggle over social status and the definition of respectability in newly formed and relatively unstable communities motivated much of the collective killing. For example, the committee that hanged four in Laramie in October 1868 selected victims who held municipal offices; the Bear River City lynchings and riot resulted from a battle for control that pitted a newspaper editor and his "respectable" camp versus the "roughs" who had originally dominated the town. Although these highly organized mobs tended to be led by moneyed men who cited their sterling reputations in contrast to those of the "lawless" element, sometimes the roughs targeted by a committee shifted allegiances and joined the vigilantes. Only a few of the collective hangings elicited uniform support. Many were vocally opposed or at least questioned by the local newspaper, the marshal stationed in town, and numerous townspeople. Moreover, the vigilante committees acted not in the absence of law enforcement, as law officers and courts operated in the towns, but instead often in usurpation of the judgments of legally constituted courts. Vigilante executions ceased in Cheyenne and Laramie when public opinion held that the vigilantes had gone too far and had begun killing innocent men. Significantly, vigilante committees fell dormant after the first few months of white settlement and did not revive after the implementation of legal institutions under the newly formed Wyoming Territory in 1869.[80]

The spasm of vigilante executions in early Wyoming in the late 1860s constituted a relatively late manifestation of a pattern of collective violence that erupted across the expanding West in the mid–nineteenth century, most prominently in San Francisco in the 1850s and in Montana in the 1860s.[81] Western vigilante movements typically aggrandized political and economic power through the extermination of social antagonists branded as participants in insidious criminality or corruption that infringed the livelihood of honest, respectable republican proprietors. Yet western vigilante committees merely elaborated, on a somewhat larger scale, ideologies and practices of collective violence that had been forged in earlier frontier contexts east of the Rockies.

In sum, antebellum vigilantes had refashioned traditions of backcountry regulation in an emerging pattern of collective violence that emphasized the informal execution of victims, most often through hanging. This vigilante violence, which was increasingly labeled *lynching*, took meaning and context from dynamic conditions of in-migration and contests over social and legal legitimacy on the southern, midwestern, and western frontiers. In novel and unstable social settings, vigilantes seeking to eradicate those they perceived as their social enemies spurned local criminal justice institutions that were being reshaped by an emerging emphasis on due process. As they asserted the sovereignty of neighborhoods to deploy violence against those that purportedly threatened lives, property, and social values,[82] vigilantes encountered opposition from due process advocates who argued that problems of endemic criminality and inefficient legal institutions could only be safely and fairly redressed by rewriting laws and better enforcing them. This vigorous antebellum debate over the boundaries of constitutionalism shaped discourses and practices of lynching violence that would inhabit decades of American social and cultural life.

3. Racial and Class Frontiers

*Lynching and Social Identity
in Antebellum America*

During the antebellum era, practices of collective murder took root on the cotton and resource extraction frontiers as white planters, farmers, and miners stepped outside of formal law to execute slaves, free blacks, Indians, and Mexicans who challenged white authority with acts of resistance or criminality. White Americans in the developing South, Midwest, and West justified summary executions through racial and class republicanism, that is, through their notion of their superiority as virtuous, productive American citizens with a responsibility to ensure the safety of whites and the viability of recently planted and complex socioeconomic orders that included purported racial inferiors and dangerous criminal classes. In the years before the Civil War, practices of racial lynching became a means for white southerners, midwesterners, and westerners to assert that their regions would constitute a "white man's country" regardless of the protections due process law might theoretically extend to black, Indian, and Hispanic defendants.

The South

In July 1859, whites in Navarro County in east central Texas hanged a slave accused of murdering and robbing a white man, Mr. English, who was traveling through the area en route to his home in Fort Worth. The white community reportedly offered to compensate the slave's master, Mr. Blanton, with the same sum that he would have received from the state if his slave had been legally executed. The 1859 mob hanging in Navarro County reveals how white communities in the antebellum South sometimes deflected slaveholders' claim of their right to human property by resorting to the collective killing of slaves.[1]

Scholars have only tangentially examined the lynching of slaves. Influential monographs on slavery and antebellum southern violence study the matter only slightly and take contradictory views of the issue. In *Roll, Jordan, Roll,* Eugene Genovese argued that the lynching of slaves was relatively rare. Estimating that a mere 10 percent of the three hundred or so persons lynched in the South between 1840 and 1860 were black, Genovese asserted that slaveholders preferred legal executions to mob executions because slaveholders were compensated by states if their slaves were legally executed. Genovese conceded that planter class and lower class whites sometimes turned to collective violence amid the racial panic of insurrection scares.[2] In contrast to Genovese, Kenneth Stampp in *The Peculiar Institution* argued that mob killings of slaves occurred frequently, typically by burning or hanging.[3] However, neither of these historians conducted a thorough analysis of mob violence against slaves in local sources. Local studies of slavery in fact suggest that collective killings of slaves were not rare events. Thomas G. Dyer found that between 1847 and 1859, at least eleven slaves were murdered by mobs of whites in Missouri, most in the area along the Missouri River known as "Little Dixie" where that border state's slaveholding concentrated; mobs burned three of the slaves to death.[4] Scholars of slavery in Arkansas, Alabama, Texas, Georgia, and Missouri have asserted that the lynching of slaves occurred fairly frequently, although these events often went unreported in newspapers.[5] One scholar has argued that when it comes to slaves the term *lynching* may not be especially meaningful because slaves were so often subject to homicidal violence that may or may not have taken collective or extralegal form.[6] Other scholars have recently unearthed evidence that southern whites collectively murdered slaves when their interests diverged from those of slaveholders, who sought in vain to protect their property from the punitive demands of the larger white community after allegations of murder or rape.[7]

Accounts of mob executions in newspaper sources and in state, local, and regional histories (which often quoted newspaper sources verbatim), help to shed light on the social and legal dynamics of the lynching of slaves. Analysis of the collective killing of slaves complicates understandings of antebellum slavery, the law, black-white relations, social and cultural differentiation among whites, and the lineage of racial violence in the South. Whereas slaves' status as property left them vulnerable to the punitive whims of individual slaveholders, slaves' position as the investment of masters provided some protection from the legal consequences of serious crimes and the racial antipathies of nonslaveholding whites. Southern mob executions of African Americans, informed by a praxis of the formal and informal capital punishment (sometimes by burning alive) of slaves stemming from the colonial era, were increasingly labeled *lynching* after the mid-1830s and excoriated by the northern abolitionist press as an aspect of an atavistic system of racial slavery. The antebellum lynching of African Americans flowed from the imperfections of the slave system and disparate southern whites' commitment to an explosive popular constitutionalism, the notion of the fundamental right of citizens to make and supervise law.[8]

The lynching of slaves, which may have occurred more frequently than some scholars have acknowledged, transpired when the master's claim to the protection of their investment in human property was effectively nullified, either through a slave's murder of a master or his family or by the white community's insistence that the collective execution of a slave outside of law served a good greater than the preservation of the value of the master's investment. Lynching punctuated a vigorous conversation among whites with divergent relations to slavery over the role of the criminal law in securing control of African Americans. Nearly half of documented southern white mobs burned alive their African American victims, asserting that immolation offered a more terrifying message to black miscreants than the most common legal punishment in the antebellum South, hanging. In an era marked by the territorial expansion of slavery, the staunch defense of the Peculiar Institution from internal and external threats, and the erosion of the status of "free negroes" as an intermediate legal and social caste, mobs of whites also collectively murdered free blacks. Evidence suggests that the lynching of African Americans may have been most common on the western periphery of slavery, in Missouri and Texas, where slaveholding was recently planted, the slave population was rapidly growing, slaveholders possessed comparatively less social and political power, and nearby cultural challenges to bondholding made slaveholding whites especially defensive about the perpetuation of the Peculiar Institution.[9] The lynching of blacks, though seemingly contradictory in a society that placed a high premium on the value of a master's slave property, emerged from traditions of crime and punishment in slavery, the response of white southerners to legal reforms and, most importantly, the inability of slaveholders to ever achieve the full mastery of African Americans and southern society that they sought. Hardly anomalous in the antebellum South, the practice of the lynching of blacks would be seized upon and reinvented by white southerners after emancipation, absent the consideration of the master's property interest that had previously shaped and constrained the actions of southern mobs.

Through an examination of primary and secondary sources, I have compiled an inventory that includes fifty-six mob executions of blacks in the South in the years 1824–1862 (see appendix). This is necessarily an incomplete database, shaped by my selective research in southern and northern newspapers, the choices that southern editors made regarding the coverage of events in their localities, northern editors' decisions concerning coverage of slavery and events in the South, and the emphases of state historians of slavery. Nonetheless, the partial tally suggests that lynching violence against blacks in the South may have been more pervasive than historians such as Genovese have asserted, and that the phenomenon of the mob execution of African Americans in the South substantially predated the Civil War and Reconstruction. The sources document at least forty-four mob killings of slaves and at least three mob murders of free blacks (the slave or free status of black mob victims was not specified in some cases). Viewed conservatively, the evidence indicates that a practice of the mob execution of blacks had emerged in the South by the 1830s, if not before,[10] and that the practice had become a familiar one in the South by the 1850s (more than two-thirds of the documented lynchings of blacks occurred in the years between 1850 and 1862).[11] The inventory does not include the hundreds of slaves summarily executed during insurrection panics in the antebellum era. Although retaliatory white violence in the wake of real and purported slave rebellions bore substantial similarities to the mob executions of individual slaves accused of particular criminal offenses such as murder and rape, anti-insurrection violence resulted from the perception of large-scale crises in racial control and thus tended to be considerably more indiscriminate and far-reaching.[12]

The issue of the property value of a slave, and the potential uncompensated loss to the master of that sum if a slave were to be lynched, loomed large in the calculation of whether a slave would be mobbed or left to the punishment provided by the legal system. The issue was significant enough in Texas that in 1857 state legislators considered a bill that would have provided compensation to the owners of slaves "executed by the people without the authority of law."[13] Texas, following the practice in other southern states, compensated the slaveholder in the event that a slave was legally executed. An 1852 Texas statute stipulated that the jury of conviction assessed the value of the slave condemned to death, with the amount not to exceed $1,000, with half of the assessment to be paid to the executed slave's master. However, the proposal to also compensate masters for the loss of their chattel property to lynchers was rejected by the state senate as a possible encouragement to mobs. A senate committee instead advocated that masters who lost their human property to lynchers might turn to the courts for redress.[14] This was exactly the remedy several slave owners sought in 1857 when they sued the city of Louisville, Kentucky, for the value of two slaves, George and Bill, who had been taken from the city jail by a mob and hanged, and for the value of a third

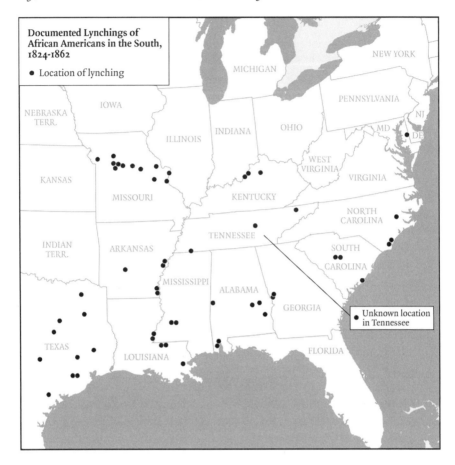

Documented Lynchings of
African Americans in the South,
1824-1862

● Location of lynching

Unknown location
in Tennessee

slave, Jack, who had cut his throat to avoid death at the hands of the mob. The three slaves had been accused of murdering the Joyce family.[15] Despite the importance of the issue of compensation, it did not necessarily deter the lynchers of slaves and those who defended their actions by asserting that dramatic, communal punishment outside the law would bolster the social control of slaves.

The lynching of slaves occurred within a legal context that privileged slaveholder authority and property-holding.[16] Antebellum southern states possessed slave codes inherited from colonial statutes that offered legal sanction to masters and overseers who killed slaves in the process of correcting them and that offered compensation to the owners of slaves who were legally executed.[17] In Louisiana, Virginia, and South Carolina, separate systems of slave courts administered a harsh and swift mode of criminal justice for slaves accused of crimes. In Louisiana, special slave tribunals denied slaves basic due process procedural safeguards and ensured that slaveholders would be adequately compensated for any loss of their property through a legal execution. Tribunals, staffed by slaveholders, often sentenced slaves convicted of killing slaves to floggings and to wearing iron collars or shackles for periods of years. Such punishments meant a slave could continue to labor for a master as they served their sentence.[18] Capital crimes for which slaves could be sentenced to death in the late antebellum era in Louisiana, with a method of execution to be chosen by the special slave tribunal, included a broad array of offenses that emphasized the lethal punishment of virtually any act of overt African American slave resistance or criminality. These included "wilful murder," assault with a dangerous weapon with the intention to kill, poisoning, strangling, drowning, the rape of a white girl or woman, plotting insurrection, arson, "striking the master, mistress, their children, or white overseer," burglary, and theft.[19] A judge or magistrate sitting on the special tribunal was required to appraise the value of the convicted slave and pay half of the value to the slave's owner and the other half to the victim of the slave's crime in the event of a death sentence.[20]

In most other slave states, however, the tendency in the antebellum era was toward bringing slaves into the same courts and under the same formal legal procedures as whites.[21] Courts could be solicitous of slaves' rights, particularly if influential masters sought to protect slaves or employed skilled legal counsel. A growing tendency toward the protection of slaves' legal rights aligned with an antebellum defense of slavery that asserted the slave system's essential benevolence and its consistency with American laws, legal culture, and an increasing emphasis on procedural fairness in American criminal law.[22] In lieu of execution, in a practice that originated in the early nineteenth century as an attempt to avoid the spectacle of public hangings, slaves convicted of capital crimes were often instead sold to contractors and transported out of the country; around nine hundred slaves were transported from Virginia from 1801 through 1858.[23] In practice, then, the law served the interests of slaveholders and ensured that the administration of criminal law would not unduly threaten their control or disposition of their property-holding, but the planter's prerogative was sometimes in tension with the views of the larger white community and an expanding emphasis on legal fairness for slaves.

Regardless of antebellum legal trends, most slaves who resisted white authority never made it into court. Masters and overseers typically exacted physical and sometimes lethal punishment without the formal process or deliberation of a court or tribunal, although the consideration of the master's property investment offered a check against indiscriminate lethal violence. Moreover, the testimony of blacks against whites was not admissible in court, which in some cases effectively protected whites from legal repercussions for their assaults and homicides of blacks. Recalling legal systems as experienced by slaves in Louisiana to a white interviewer decades after emancipation, Octavia George highlighted the mercurial nature of white authority: "There were no jails; the white man was the slaves' jail. If whipping didn't settle the crime the Negro committed—the next thing would be to hang him or to burn him at the stake."[24] Similarly, in 1836, an escaped slave, Moses Roper, questioned the very concept of the neutrality of the law as he described a legal execution by burning in South Carolina. Roper posited that with regard to "the protection which the law is supposed to extend to the slave's life," in his view "that whatever the law may be, no such protection is in reality enjoyed by the slave."[25]

Beyond slaveholders and overseers, southern law and practice institutionalized an important role for the white community in policing slave behavior, linking whites of diverse socioeconomic statuses in a common defense of the slave system and white supremacy. The slave patrol originated in the early eighteenth century in South Carolina and Virginia in response to fears of slave rebellion and it became a means of controlling the movement of slaves and preventing their unauthorized assembly. Slaveholding and non-slaveholding whites joined forces in the patrol, which was authorized to go on to private property to inspect slave cabins and to demand to see the passes of slaves who traveled on the roads. Often making nocturnal rounds in bands of four or five, sometimes costumed in dark clothing or in hoods that suggested ghosts, patrollers flogged slaves who lacked permission for travel, bound them, and turned them over to the sheriff or their master. The master's interest in preserving his property may have mitigated the degree of violence the patrollers could inflict.[26] Many years after emancipation, former slaves recalled the violence of the "patterollers" and how masters sometimes clashed with the patrol and sought to protect slaves from its punitive activities. The patrol offered the larger white community a significant function in the supervision and punishment of slave behavior and the control of racial boundaries, albeit one that frequently conflicted with the authority over slaves that masters claimed for themselves.[27]

The southern legal system sought to mediate between the competing goals of the control of black deviancy, the sanctity of slaveholders' property-holding, and the observation of the formal legal procedures that existed for the prosecution of slaves accused of committing particular crimes. Allegations that slaves had committed crimes such as murder and rape could disrupt the delicate balance between crime and racial control, the preservation of the value of the master's property, and the observation of legal process. Forty of the fifty-six documented antebellum mob executions of African Americans (71.4 percent) involved allegations of murder. Significantly, fifteen of forty-four slaves that were lynched (34 percent) were collectively executed for murdering, or attempting to murder, their master, mistress, or other members of the master's family. Slaveholders perceived the killing of a master or his relatives as a grave threat to the preservation of slaveholding authority, a literal destruction of the master's patriarchal authority over his slaves and family. Killing the master or his family negated, at least in an emotional sense (although not necessarily in a practical sense, in terms of the legal claims of the master's surviving legatees), the property interest that normally would have led slaveholders to attempt to intercede in the legal system for the mitigation of the severity of punishment and the preservation of the life of the slave offender. Murder of the master or his relatives typically flowed from slaves' anger at the far-reaching and often cruel effects of authority exercised by members of the master class, sometimes in the context of the personal toll upon slaves of the cotton frontier's westward expansion of slavery.[28] These dynamics were at play in April 1859, when Alfred, a slave in Tyler County in southeast Texas, axed to death his master, Mr. Roper, and burned his corpse. Alfred believed the master's death would mean the family's return to Alabama, from where they had recently immigrated at the behest of Mr. Roper against the wishes of the rest of his family. A "large number of the citizens of the counties of Liberty, Polk, and Tyler" immolated Alfred near the site where he had murdered Mr. Roper. An "eye witness" newspaper correspondent explained that "Judge Lynch opened and adjourned the Court."[29] The trauma of forced migration westward provided a similar context for the collective killing of a slave in 1836. William allegedly axed to death the members of a party migrating to Texas, including his master, another white man, and five slaves. Tennessee law officers apprehended William in his previous home near Memphis and conveyed him to the locale of the crime, Hot Springs County, Arkansas, where whites seized the slave from the sheriff and burned him to death.[30]

Another case of the murder of a master occurred in Montgomery County in central Alabama in 1854. A planter, Dr. McDonald, punished a slave for disobedience. The slave allegedly responded by lying in wait for McDonald in a stable and clubbing the slaveholder to death when he came to get his horse. After the slave surrendered to authorities, hundreds of whites came into town demanding rapid punishment, with most of the crowd advocating burning. After the mob seized the slave, they tied him to a stake, piled on pine-knots and applied turpentine and a torch. After burning the slave to death, the crowd reportedly raised a collection of $850, the equivalent of the value of the deceased slave, and gave it to the dead master's family, thus honoring the principle of compensation for taking the life of slave property.[31] Although the *Huntsville Democrat* quibbled with the mob's choice of method, it defended the collective killing as an orderly act done in the public interest of racial and crime control: "We think it would have been better simply to have hung the scoundrel with the promptness with which he was burned. But in matters involving the control of that class of population, we hold that the law of self-protection, which abrogates all other law, must necessarily find its exponent in the action of the majority of those immediately interested."[32] A mob execution similarly ensued in Lincoln County in Missouri's slaveholding Little Dixie region in January 1859, after a slave stabbed to death his master, Simeon Thornhill. At the "annual Negro sales" at the county seat of Troy, James Calaway, the deceased slaveholder's brother-in-law, mounted a box and exhorted the crowd to "take the black murderer out of jail and burn him at the stake in the presence of all the negroes that were there, to set an example before them, and show them what will be the result of all such conduct if there should ever be such again."[33] The mob of whites, estimated at 800–1,000, used crowbars, axes, and sledgehammers to extricate the prisoner from the jail and tied him to a stake that they planted in the jail yard. The lynchers borrowed the didactic formula of the gallows speech from the antebellum rite of legal execution. Before the mob set alight the wood it piled around its victim, it compelled him to address the 200–300 blacks gathered to watch the execution in a final statement asserting that he had had a good master, had been treated better than he deserved and had been given too many liberties, and that they must take warning and heed the lesson of his execution.[34]

Unprotected by prevailing white understandings of gender and deviancy, slave women were also executed by mobs for harming members of the master class. In his travelogue of his journey through East Texas in early 1854, Frederick Law Olmsted chronicled a case near Fannin in which a mob hanged a slave woman who had murdered her mistress and her two children with an axe.[35] In May 1850, in Clay County, Missouri, a mob similarly hanged a slave woman after she struck her mistress with an axe, and another Missouri mob, in Callaway County in 1860, hanged a young slave female accused of murdering a young white woman in her master's family toward whom she had "known ill feeling."[36] Whereas a slave's murder of a slaveholder and his family could lead to calls for punishment outside of legal channels, so could other slave offenses. Mobs also executed African Americans accused of organized criminality and the murder of whites off of the plantation. For instance, in 1841, a crowd of Mississippi whites in a river town south of Natchez burned to death a "runaway slave" accused of participation in a criminal gang's spree of murder and robbery after the pyre was lit by a white woman the gang had kidnapped and raped.[37]

Allegations of rape also catalyzed southern mobs that pursued African Americans. Eleven percent of documented mob executions of blacks in the antebellum South resulted solely from an allegation of rape, whereas 27 percent of documented black victims were accused of rape in addition to other serious crimes such as murder. Recent scholarship has complicated our understanding of the white community's response to sexual relationships between black men and white women in the early- to mid-nineteenth-century South, finding that harsh repercussions for interracial sex depended upon factors of class and circumstance. White communities sometimes cleaved along class lines, as planters manipulated the legal system to protect slaves accused or convicted of raping lower class white women. Such tensions may have been a factor in an 1861 Georgia case in which a master sued the lynchers of his slave, George, who was to stand trial for raping a white woman but was instead seized and burned to death by neighborhood whites who could not abide "the law's delay."[38] In another instance of lynching for rape, a mob seized a slave from jail and hanged him after he was arrested for attempting to rape a white woman in Hopkins County in northeast Texas in 1859.[39] Mobs similarly murdered slaves accused of rape in North Carolina[40] and in Missouri in 1850 and 1859.[41] The relatively small number of slaves executed by mobs solely on an accusation of rape may have reflected the fluidity of antebellum southern white responses to interracial sex, as well as the ability of slaveholders to wield their social authority and legal influence to shield slaves from communal violence.

The antebellum southern mob's choice of a method of execution occurred within the context of traditions of racialized punishment and alterations in the administration of the death penalty. More than 43 percent of documented lynchings of blacks involved execution by burning (twenty-four victims), whereas mobs murdered 47 percent of documented black victims through hanging (twenty-six victims). Execution by burning had been a staple of capital punishment in Colonial America, inherited from English jurisprudence (where it had been used as a punishment for heresy and witchcraft in the late medieval era), but, by the seventeenth and eighteenth centuries, it was reserved for those convicted of petit treason, the reversal of the patriarchal order of the household through the revolt of wife against husband or slave against master. In the American colonies, the highly dramatic punishment of burning at the stake was reserved for slaves convicted of participating in insurrection plots or of murdering their masters or, less frequently, for wives convicted of murdering their husbands. However, colonial authorities seldom inflicted death by burning, often preferring to hang slaves that had murdered masters and wives that had killed husbands.[42] Execution by burning was elimi-

nated in northern states with the extensive statutory reforms that sought to
rationalize the capital code in the era of the American Revolution. Influenced
by Enlightenment notions that emphasized sympathy with the humanity of
the offender, the reformability of the criminal, and the deterrent effect of mild
but predictable (as opposed to the traditional system of severe but random)
punishments, legislators discarded traditional punishments such as the gibbet
(hanging in irons), dismemberment, and burning.[43] Despite the reform of the
capital code in much of the United States, execution by burning lived on in
the antebellum South. In states such as South Carolina, special tribunals tried
slaves and selected the method of their punishment, occasionally choosing
to burn convicted slaves alive.[44] Even as legal tribunals in some slave states
still imposed burning at the stake, hanging became the predominant method
of legal capital punishment in the antebellum South. Some southern white
mobs and their apologists asserted by contrast that the sanguinary tradition
of burning African Americans at the stake provided an especially powerful
assertion of racial supremacy.

   Antebellum southern mobs, and those who pondered their actions, debated
the propriety of burning versus hanging in a conversation in which white citizens sought to define the jurisprudence of racial mastery in a white republic.
An editor in Mobile, Alabama, defended a mob's immolation of two African
Americans convicted of murdering two white children in May 1835, by asserting that the only legal punishment available, hanging, was not adequate to the
"barbarity" of the crime. "As the court pronounced the only sentence known to
the law—the smothered flame broke forth . . . Their lives were justly forfeited
to the laws of the country, but the peculiar circumstances demanded that the
ordinary punishment should be departed from—they were seized, taken to
the place where they had perpetrated the act, and burned to death."[45] In some
cases, the matter of whether to burn or hang an African American offender
was determined in republican fashion, through a public meeting and then a
vote. In July 1851, a slave was arrested for the murder of Mr. and Mrs. Baker
near Austin, Texas. Whites in the vicinity held a meeting in which a minority advocated burning at the stake, but the majority "were not so barbarous"
and voted down the idea. The meeting appointed a committee that, denied
access to the defendant by the sheriff, broke into the jail, seized the slave, tried
and found him guilty, sentenced him to death, and hanged him.[46] Similarly,
a mob of whites hanged two slaves "according to a statute of Judge Lynch" in
southern Mississippi in 1843. A Gallatin editor argued that the mob would
have been justified had it fulfilled its original intention to burn the slaves alive
in retribution for their rape, assault, and robbery of a white woman and her
child, which constituted grave offenses against "the domestic circles of life":
"If the perpetrators of this excessively revolting crime had been burnt alive,

as was first decreed, their fate would have been too good for such diabolical and inhuman wretches."[47]

A public debate among whites over the efficacy of burning versus hanging an African American offender erupted in a courtroom in Columbia, Missouri, in August 1853. A slave on trial for the attempted rape of a white woman confessed his guilt. Spectators watching the trial determined to immediately burn or hang the accused, but the prosecutor, Odon Guitar, admonished the crowd that if they insisted on executing the prisoner outside of legal process they should "go about it coolly and . . . decently and in order, not as demons." The crowd then formed a committee, chaired by a prominent slaveholder, Eli E. Bass. Bass took a voice vote of the crowd, the majority of which voted for hanging over burning. The vigilantes seized the prisoner and hanged him.[48] Yet the republican mob, faithful to racialized traditions of the execution rite, reserved burning at the stake exclusively for black miscreants. A posse of whites in Chicot County, Arkansas, in 1857, captured a biracial gang of rapists and murderers. The posse burned the blacks alive, but shot the white ringleader.[49] Even as southern lynchers debated among themselves the propriety of burning African American victims, some antebellum northern commentators saw the propensity of southern mobs to burn their victims alive as an atavistic vestige and a profound marker of sectional difference. The *New York Times* rejected a Tennessee editor's spirited defense of a mob that had burned its black victim alive, asserting that "Civilized communities, as a general thing, have long since discarded the notion that they were to inflict punishment for the sake of torture,—or that the *deserts* of the culprit were to be the measure of the personal torment they should bestow upon him."[50]

Just as antebellum southern mobs sometimes argued that the conventional capital punishment, hanging, did not transmit a sufficiently harrowing message to African American offenders, mobbers and their apologists similarly asserted that the avowedly neutral legal process could not respond with the speed and harshness necessary to deter black deviancy. As slaveholders in many cases controlled the courts, and masters sought to employ legal counsel to protect their chattel property (and indeed were required to do so in some states), such cases reflected tensions between slaveholders and nonslaveholders over the proper response to slave crime as well as a more general reaction against an expanding tendency toward legal fairness for blacks (and whites) in southern courts. Mobs responded with anger at instances of observation of legal procedure that delayed the punishment of black offenders. In Sumter County in western Alabama in 1855, a slave allegedly murdered a white girl. When the circuit court granted a change of venue to another county, a mob extricated the slave from the jail and burned him to death before a crowd of two thousand.[51] The next year in Barbour County in southeastern Alabama, the state supreme court voided the death sentence of a slave, Bob, by granting him a new trial. Over the reported objections of some residents, a mob took the slave from the jail and hanged him anyway.[52] In September 1855, after a judge granted a continuance, a mob in East Tennessee hanged a "runaway negro" accused of murdering a white woman.[53] Beyond frustration at the slowness and unpredictability of legal process, southern mobbers sometimes insisted that a court's sentence was too lenient. A mob in Montgomery in southeast Texas in 1857 reportedly hanged a slave accused of the attempted murder of his mistress because they "were impatient of the law's delay, and indisposed to let him off with less than capital punishment."[54] A portion of the white community in Columbus, Georgia, in August 1851, held a mass meeting to protest the governor's pardon of a slave, Jarrett, who had been convicted of raping a white girl and sentenced to death. The mass meeting transformed into a mob that stormed the jail, pulled out Jarrett, and hanged him.[55] Frustration over the lacunae of a racially disparate criminal justice system could also lead mobs to claim white victims. A mob hanged a slave woman and a white man, McClintock, in Clay County in western Missouri in 1850 due to the fact that her inability to testify as a witness against him (slaves could not give testimony against whites in Missouri courts) meant that he would have escaped legal repercussion for his purported role in her axe attack on her mistress.[56]

A mob similarly cited the purported leniency of the criminal justice system in October 1854 on Maryland's Eastern Shore. In Denton, a free black, Dave Thomas, was tried for the murder of William H. Butler. The court convicted Thomas of manslaughter and sentenced him to sixteen years and seven months in the penitentiary. Neighbors and friends of the murdered man, angered at what they perceived as a light sentence, took Thomas out of the jail and hanged him to fulfill "the sentence of Judge Lynch to its deadliest extent."[57] The lynching of Dave Thomas underlined the precarious status of free blacks in the antebellum South. Lacking whatever protection a slaveholder's interest in his property may have afforded slaves, at times viewed as a threat to the survival of the slave system, and increasingly stripped of the legal rights that had distinguished them from slaves, free blacks also fell victim to the wrath of antebellum southern white mobs.[58] In 1858, a Louisiana mob murdered a free black who had allegedly raped a white child.[59] Northern African Americans traveling in the slave states were also at risk. In April 1836, a St. Louis mob burned to death Francis L. McIntosh, a "mulatto" boatman from Pittsburgh who had killed a deputy sheriff.[60]

Mob executions of African Americans resulting from frustration over the deliberative and unpredictable nature of legal process highlighted the lack of unanimity among southern whites.[61] Amid circumstances of racial crisis, and in light of legal institutions that privileged slaveholder's interests, whites with varying relationships to slavery did not necessarily agree on what the proper response was to allegations of slave criminality. This may have been especially true in western portions of the upper, border-state South, where slaves and slaveholders were less numerous, large portions of the white population were less invested in the peculiar institution, and laws and legal institutions less perfectly meshed with the prerogatives of slavery and racial control.[62] For instance, in central Missouri in July 1859, whites hanged and burned four slaves whom they accused of murdering, assaulting, and raping whites. After the conviction of one of the slaves, John, for murder in the first degree, the judge enraged the crowd in the courtroom by telling John's attorneys that he would listen to motions to put aside the verdict or for a new trial before sentencing him. Shortly afterward, the crowd angered by the formalities of legal procedure transformed into a mob that pulled John from the jail where he been placed as the court temporarily recessed and chained him to a tree and burned him to death.[63] The central Missouri lynchers were enraged by the possibility that slaveholders might intercede to thwart criminal justice. One of the slaves, named Holman, had been arrested for assault. His owner had sent him from jail to a locale outside of the county with the hope of selling him; authorities captured the slave and jailed him again. A mob seized Holman and hanged him shortly after they had collectively immolated John.[64] White defenders of the lynchers of the four slaves argued that the legal punishment for slaves convicted of rape in Missouri, castration, was not severe enough, and that slaveholders had evaded their responsibility in controlling the behavior of their slaves.[65] Although the participants in and apologists for the mob executions in Missouri's Little Dixie in 1859 apparently supported slavery and evinced "prosouthern political views,"[66] their brutal actions nonetheless highlighted the limitations of formal law in sustaining a comprehensive white supremacy. Gestures of legal fairness and the efforts of slaveholders to protect their property investment could confound the will of a white community that demanded racial vengeance.

The antebellum lynching of African Americans forecast the wide-scale disavowal of formal law by many southern whites after emancipation. If formal southern legal systems existed to bolster slavery and left substantial space for the expansive personal authority of slaveholders, the collective killing of slaves and free blacks served to highlight divisions among whites in a vigorous republican polity organized around slaveholding and white supremacy, and to underline the tensions and contradictions of legal systems that attempted to control persons held as property, to protect the slaveholder's investment in them, and to extend them legal fairness. When emancipation and Radical Reconstruction dissolved slavery and its legal systems, conservative southern whites would seize and expand upon the precedent of the region's history of racial lynching as a template for how to impose white control independent of formal law.

The Midwestern and Western Frontiers

In September 1852, near Mora, New Mexico, an elderly man named Edward Conn, an unidentified boy that lived with him, and a woman, Paula Jaramillo, were found murdered in Conn's house, which had been robbed. U.S. deputy marshals soon arrested Jose de la Cruz Vigil, a Navajo Indian, and Gabriel Luhan, a Mexican, and turned them over to the alcalde of Mora. The arrested men reportedly confessed to the crime, and the alcalde had them conveyed to the jail in Taos for safekeeping. That evening, unknown persons broke into the jail, removed the two men and hanged them. Perceived as members of a borderland criminal underclass that included (but was not limited to) Natives and Mexicans, Vigil and Luhan were among the first victims of lynching in territorial New Mexico.[67]

Collective racial violence on midwestern and western frontiers in the mid–nineteenth century stemmed from white Americans' efforts to achieve a racial and cultural conquest of Native Americans and Hispanics that consciously supplanted recently established American criminal justice institutions as inadequate instruments for racial mastery. Recent histories of warfare with Natives and Mexicans made collective violence attractive; white frustration with complex questions of legal jurisdiction over Native populations inclined some whites to lynching violence when Natives and white communities came into friction. An elastic class and racial ideology of republicanism, through which many white Americans sought to confine citizenship and full civic participation to "respectable," productive white men, legitimized the exclusion of Natives, Mexicans, Chileans, and "disrespectable" whites from legal protections and institutions.[68] In nascent multicultural, transnational communities transformed by American expansion and resource extraction booms, white Americans found racial and class violence a powerful solvent for unsettled questions of political and cultural leadership.[69]

The antebellum lynching of Natives and Hispanics occurred within the broader context of concerns about widespread criminality, the effectiveness of newly implemented criminal justice institutions in an era of cultural conflict over legal change and reform, and the seemingly dangerous fluidity of social relationships in novel western settings. Substantial numbers of American whites and Anglo-Europeans, categorized by self-fashioned republican vigilantes as members of a parasitical criminal class that preyed on honest, independent, hardworking pioneers, were also lynched in the social flux of the resource extraction frontiers. Yet the cultural differences ascribed to a racial hierarchy proved especially compelling to mid-nineteenth-century western vigilantes, as white Americans sought to extend the genius of American republican institutions over indigenous and racially mixed peoples purportedly in thrall to primitive barbarism or despotic Latin cultural and political institutions.[70] In this racialized frontier context, slightly under half of the approximately 215 persons that died at the hands of lynchers in California between 1850 and 1860 were of Hispanic (primarily Mexican or Chilean) descent, whereas Natives contributed nearly 15 percent of total lynching victims in California in the 1850s.[71]

Racial violence varied significantly by geocultural context after the conquest and incorporation of Southwest borderlands from Mexico, settlement of political boundaries with the British in the Northwest, and the expansion of American settlement onto the lands of Native peoples throughout the West. White American gold-seekers quickly achieved a numerical dominance in Northern California that overwhelmed, sometimes through instrumental violence, the Natives and Mexican-descended Californios who already resided there, as well as the Mexicans (mostly Sonorans) and Chileans who arrived to participate in the Gold Rush.[72] The initial period of American settlement in the coastal Northwest in the 1840s and '50s witnessed substantial settler conflict with indigenous inhabitants, but by 1860, white Americans largely outnumbered Natives, from whom they had compelled major land cessions by treaty.[73] By contrast, the borderlands of Southern California, New Mexico, and South Texas saw a different pattern in which white Americans constituted a minority and shared power in the 1850s with Californios, Hispanic New Mexicans, and Tejanos, but also implemented notions and practices of criminal justice and collective violence that clashed and meshed with the customary legal ideas and practices of Natives and Hispanics.[74] In these fluid borderland contexts, Natives and Hispanics also sometimes initiated and participated in extralegal executions.

In a set of dynamics that would be transplanted to the edge of the continent with the arrival of Americans in the Far West, growing numbers of American migrants, including timber workers and farmers, had turned to lynching as they clashed with Natives over natural resources, legal jurisdiction, and criminal justice in the Upper Mississippi River Valley in the late 1840s. Whites typically resorted to collective violence in the heat of interracial conflict with Natives as federal authorities vainly sought to separate Native and white populations and local authorities hesitated at the uncertain legal jurisdiction they possessed over Native populations and the possibility of Native retribution for white violence. Paradoxically, both customary Native and popular white preferences for informal personal retribution were confounded by the antebellum American legal system's increasing emphasis on formal due process and its preference for the state's monopoly on the use of lethal force. This was the case in Chippewa Falls, Wisconsin, in July 1848, when a crowd of whites hanged an Ojibwa man who had stabbed a drunken lumberjack, Martial Caznobia, in an altercation over Caznobia's attempt to sexually assault the Ojibwa man's wife. A large group of Ojibwas came to the settlement demanding that the murderers be handed over to them or they would burn the town, a situation defused when a Native interpreter negotiated for the transportation of the ringleaders of the white mob downriver to authorities in Prairie du Chien for prosecution under American law.[75] Similarly, a group of whites in Gull Lake, Minnesota, in August 1857, seized and hanged three Natives—Joe Shambeau, "Jimmy," and Charles Gebabish—as the Morrison County sheriff conveyed them to jail in St. Paul after they were accused of murdering a German Catholic peddler. Sources indicate that local Ojibwas pondered and local whites feared retaliation for the triple lynching, but this never came off. In a familiar analysis that elided the deeper sources of conflict, the local Indian agent blamed the settler-Indian disputes on Natives' illicit access to an abundant supply of alcohol procured by whiskey runners.[76]

As white settlers arrived in the Northwest in significant numbers in the mid–nineteenth century, settlers' values collided with American and Native legal systems. In a pattern that would become common throughout the Far West in the 1850s, white Americans alternated extralegal hangings of individual Natives with more widespread lethal collective violence that targeted entire Native communities. White violence against Natives flowed from agrarian republican ideology that asserted that Natives squandered abundant natural resources and hindered virtuous settlers from putting the land to productive, individual use. In this context, Native offenses against settlers took on a larger meaning as violations of social order by members of a purportedly nonproductive class against pioneer producers seeking to extend the benefits of American civilization and liberty.[77] In a local context in which Natives were informally punished, typically through flogging, by settlers seeking to assert racial superiority and sovereignty over local resources, whites also collectively executed Natives outside of the legal process, often after accusations that Natives had murdered whites. A group of whites in northwest Oregon in the late 1850s hanged a Tillamook Native accused of burning to death a minister's wife and child. Similarly, around Puget Sound in 1853 and 1854, bands of settlers hanged at least three Indians accused of murder.[78] An editor in Olympia, Washington, characterized one such "summary" execution in Seattle as consistent with achieving "'indemnity for the past' and 'security for the future' to the white inhabitants along the

Sound."[79] The Indian agent for the Puget Sound District by contrast argued, "The practice of punishing Indians for supposed wrongs committed by them without sufficient evidence, is one frequently much abused."[80] The agent, M. T. Simmons, urged that settlers bring all complaints against Natives to him, instead of settling grievances privately, and stressed to settlers that "Indians have certain inalienable rights secured to them by law."[81] Small-scale retribution could easily spiral into mass hostilities. In an incident near Port Townsend, a posse of settlers pursued three Snohomish Indians they believed had killed a white man. One settler and nine Natives perished in the ensuing skirmish.[82]

Analogous patterns of Indian-white violence obtained after the implementation of American law and legal institutions in the vast regions taken in conquest from Mexico in the late 1840s, California and New Mexico, albeit within a social matrix of considerable racial, ethnic, and class complexity. Significant proportions of native-born Hispanics and Indians resided in the southern borderlands, to be joined in California by large numbers of American, European, Australian, Chinese, Mexican, Chilean, and Peruvian migrants that arrived with the Gold Rush. In this social maelstrom and its aftermath, at least twenty-nine Natives died at the hands of lynchers in California in the 1850s, most of them accused of murder.[83] Amid concerns of rampant criminality and a ubiquitous practice of informal collective violence (whippings and hangings) in Northern California mining camps and supply towns in the early 1850s,[84] white miners sometimes informally executed Natives that had been drawn into the social world of the mining camps. In March 1851, in Calaveras County, miners extralegally tried (with an empanelled jury and assigned defense counsel), convicted, and hanged Coyote Joe, an Indian accused of killing an elderly white man. Legal authorities had arrested and jailed Coyote Joe for the crime but had then released him, rousing local anger. Coyote Joe's ties to Americans were long-standing, as he had worked for Captain John Sutter for several years before the discovery of gold in the region, but this did not save him from informal execution.[85] In Southern California, where the arrival of white Americans was initially on a smaller scale that did not immediately overturn the regional social arrangements in which Californios had dominated Natives, American ideas and practices of informal justice may have interacted with customary indigenous practices of personal and communal retribution.[86] In April 1852, an American newspaper editor in Los Angeles reported a "lynching in San Gabriel," an incident in which persons living in the vicinity of the San Gabriel Mission extralegally hanged an Indian who had murdered an Indian.[87] In December 1853, the *Los Angeles Star* reported another summary execution at Mission San Gabriel in which Natives hanged an Indian that had killed an Indian. The

Natives that carried out the execution reportedly deliberated and decided to administer the punishment provided by American law, hanging.[88]

As elsewhere in the West, lynchings of Natives in California occurred within a continuum of formal (militia warfare, legal executions, judicially mandated floggings) and informal (extralegal collective executions and floggings) violence with sometimes ambiguous relationships to legal authority. Informal hangings were illegal but authorities usually took no action against the perpetrators; settler posses or militia were nominally legally constituted but their actions sometimes crossed the line into massacre. In the fall of 1850, for example, Indians in northwest California killed an English rancher, James S. Fryer. In retributive overkill, twenty whites from Humboldt and Eureka set out in pursuit of Fryer's assailants and killed seventeen Natives.[89]

American authorities, fearing the possibility of wide-scale hostilities with indigenous populations and sworn to uphold the rule of law, occasionally sought to prosecute settlers for collectively murdering Natives. In 1858, federal lawyers indicted local militia in Doña Ana County, New Mexico, for killing Indians they accused of stealing cattle. In an expression of racial ideology, some in New Mexico asserted that the thirty-six members of the Mesilla Guards should be acquitted because "the killing of Indians *non est crimenis,*" but others argued that under American law, "these Indians were as much entitled to that protection [of the laws] as the Mesilla Guard themselves."[90] A similar clash between racialized rough justice and due process commitments erupted in Taos, New Mexico, in 1852, after the lynchings of Jose de la Cruz Vigil, a Navajo Indian, and Gabriel Luhan, a Mexican. Urging a jury to identify and indict the individuals that had hanged the men, Judge John S. Watts stressed the sanctity of the right to trial by jury, which had been guaranteed from the promulgation of American law in 1846 (under the Kearny Code, imposed under American military occupation) and in subsequent enactments by the territorial legislature. Watts stressed that the lynchings had no justification and in legal terms constituted murder. "It is easy to perceive that the conduct of those persons, engaged in this business, is at war with, and in direct violation of, all the constitutional and legislative guards, thrown around the lives and persons of the people. These persons thus hanged were in the custody of the law, and entitled to its protection. In this case no necessity existed for the infliction of what is called 'summary justice' upon these men."[91] Intervening in a national antebellum debate over the legitimacy of popular violence under a republican form of government, Judge Watts argued that Americans pursuing Manifest Destiny in racially diverse Southwest borderlands must be especially vigilant to safeguard, not disregard, republican laws. "We, gentleman, should ever remember that, if law and justice should be banished from all other portions of the world, they ought to find a secure asylum in the bosoms of a free people, intrusted with the priceless privileges of a republican government."[92]

The vigilante violence of white Americans against Hispanics in the California Gold Rush took shape in the context of a heated contest for access to the most valuable mining claims, concerns about rampant criminality in the mines and supply towns, and pervasive ideas about work, character, and nationality influenced by antebellum republican ideology. In 1850, as they prepared to expel Hispanics from the community, white American miners in Sonora, Tuolumne County, adopted resolutions expressing their view of the relation between national identity and culture in the mines. "The laws and property of the American citizens are now in danger from the hands of lawless marauders of every clime, class and creed under the canopy of heaven, and scarcely a day passes but we hear of the commission of the most horrible murders and robberies . . . as we have now in our midst the Peons of Mexico, the renegades of South America, and the convicts of the British Empire."[93] In the profoundly multicultural, transnational landscape of the Gold Rush, the celebration of the virtuous, independent, white American prospector, defending his livelihood against the depredations of degraded and dependent foreigners and criminals, became a central way for white American migrants to think about the forging of a social order. This racial republican ideology, with its power to shape communal ties and social status, led state legislators to levy taxes on foreign miners and undergirded the ubiquitous lynching violence of the Gold Rush. Hispanics and Natives were hardly the exclusive victims of vigilante violence (which also targeted alleged criminals that included white Americans, African Americans, Englishmen, "Sydneys" from Australia, Europeans, and Chinese), nor were white Americans the only perpetrators of collective violence (evidence suggests that white Americans constituted the majority of vigilantes, but persons of various nationalities participated). Yet persons of Mexican descent, particularly large numbers of Sonorans who competed with white Americans for access to the mines, became the most significant recipient of white Americans' wrath. Derided as racially mixed "greasers" that spoke a foreign tongue and were beholden to backward political institutions, a servile labor system, a despotic church, and the episodic criminality of social banditry, dozens of Mexicans that were accused of crimes against the persons and property of white Americans were collectively murdered by Gold Rush–era lynchers in California.[94]

Allegations that Hispanics had committed murder were the most likely to inspire summary executions in California during the Gold Rush. In November 1851, a group of Mexicans fought with a party of Americans at Turnersville,

Calaveras County, resulting in the deaths of several American prospectors. Searchers captured one of the Mexicans, identified as Domingo, extracted a confession from him, and hanged him "by order of Judge Lynch."[95] Not prone to making careful distinctions with regard to Latin American nationality, Gold Rush crowds also collectively murdered Chilean miners. In July 1853, a posse apprehended an unnamed member of a party of Chileans that had allegedly murdered and robbed an elderly Chinese man. The next day, after giving him the opportunity to ask for "pardon," a crowd hanged the Chilean suspect at Jackson before a group reported at "about 1,000 persons."[96] Allegations of transgressions against property by Mexicans also stirred Gold Rush vigilantes to action, with particular anger directed at horse theft and the organized criminality of banditry with its overtones of Mexican resistance against assertions of Anglo-American dominance.[97] Eschewing the elaborate ritual with which some Gold Rush–era crowds had mimicked formal legal procedures, "Judge Lynch and a goodly number of his b'hoys" at Jackson also hanged an unidentified Mexican accused of stealing two horses and a mule from miners in July 1853.[98] Interpreting the history of vigilante violence in California, a San Francisco editor argued that this lynching would not have been acceptable in the early years of the Gold Rush, as the summary hanging occurred "without a fair trial by an informally constituted inquest." Signaling a shift in attitudes as the mining boom wound down amid the elaboration of urban society in Northern California, the *Alta California* asserted that the lynching of the Mexican at Jackson had no justification, for the administration of criminal justice had improved substantially in the ensuing period, and "now . . . the legal authorities are not only able but willing to do their duty faithfully and promptly."[99]

Vigilantes employed more elaborate informal procedures in Southern California in October 1853, when militia staffed by Anglo-American settlers, the American Rangers, captured four Mexican "bandits" accused of horse theft and murder at San Luis Obispo. At the courthouse in Los Angeles, an informally appointed jury tried and condemned Anastacio Higuerre, Manuel Olivas, Ramon Espinosa, and Cayetana Espinosa to be hanged, and this verdict was ratified by "the people." However, some argued that the men should not be hanged in Los Angeles, as they had committed their crimes elsewhere.[100] Conveyed by steamer to San Luis Obispo, three of the Mexicans were hanged on the beach there by "the people" assembled. The mutual ethnic antagonism between Mexicans and Americans permeated the entire episode, and those who executed Anastacio Higuerre ignored his final request "that he would die happy if he could be freed long enough to flog one yankee."[101] In a reflection of white Americans' efforts to downplay the ethnic overtones of the violence amid a multicultural social landscape, the Anglo press lauded the "uniting efforts" of the Rangers and reported that Californios in San Luis Obispo joined Americans in endorsing the summary execution.[102]

The Southwest borderlands, home to Natives dominated by local Hispanic elites, and mining and ranching frontiers that attracted not only white American but also Mexican migrants, offered an intricate landscape for the lynchings of Hispanics in the decade after incorporation by the United States. American migrants, a minority of the population, led and shaped collective violence with ideas and practices forged in earlier decades in the American backcountry, but Hispanic elites sometimes collaborated with or participated in the violence. In this context, Americans and Hispanics sometimes cooperated to lynch Hispanics, but an allegation that a Mexican had violated emerging boundaries of power and race by murdering an American was most likely to precipitate the lethal retributive violence of lynching.[103] In November 1858, lynchers extricated Pancho Daniel, a Sonoran bandit who had participated in the assassination of Los Angeles County Sheriff James R. Barton, from the Los Angeles jail and hanged him. Criticizing the slow and unpredictable pace of due process law, the defenders of the lynching of Daniel cited the nearly year-long delay in bringing his case to trial, arguing that "the technicalities of law . . . may have been taken advantage of to defeat the ends of justice."[104] In January 1858, in Brownsville, Texas, a Mexican stabbed to death an American magistrate, Edward J. McLane, who had intervened after the man had stabbed his wife after failing to persuade her to return with him to Mexico. A Corpus Christi newspaper reported that the Mexican from near Matamoros "was set upon by his Honor, Judge Lynch," that is, taken from the Brownsville jail and hanged from a large tree.[105]

In short, the antebellum lynching of Natives and Mexicans flowed from the combustive combination of the racial republicanism of white Americans with diverse and unfinished frontier social orders, where nationalities and ideas and practices of crime and punishment mixed and clashed. In novel multicultural landscapes seemingly marked by conflict and crime and imbued with antebellum ambivalence and discord over the growth of due process law, where white Americans could not yet take their dominance for granted, the lynching of Indians and Hispanics became a means of asserting the authority of white migrants' values. Despite their relatively brief duration, the antebellum racial and class frontiers bequeathed a lengthy legacy. Lynching violence against Indians and Mexicans would persist for decades, albeit at a reduced level, after Americans consolidated control across the West.[106]

4. Lynchers versus Due Process

The Forging of Rough Justice

By the early 1850s, due process and rough justice sentiments had competed for cultural supremacy in American life for several decades. The cultural conflict over the direction of criminal justice took on particular intensity at midcentury, however, as a result of reformers' success in modifying criminal law, increasing attention to and concerns about perceived threats to sectional identity, and the challenges posed by the rapid growth of a novel, multicultural social landscape with the American incorporation of California and the ensuing Gold Rush. Within these dynamic southern, midwestern, and western cultural and legal contexts, lynchers performed collective violence that protested the administration of criminal justice, particularly the adjudication of homicide cases. Rejecting reformist sensibilities that sought fair and humane criminal justice, lynchers instead sought harsh and swift punishment for crimes, especially homicide, which transgressed deeply held communal values.

The Upper South and the Lower Midwest

On November 25, 1856, a large mob seized an African American river laborer, Bill, from the jail at West Union in southern Ohio and conveyed him ten miles to an island in the Ohio River near the town of Manchester, Ohio. Accusing their victim of "ravishing" a white woman identified as Mrs. Morris, the mob, apparently led by several of the white woman's male relatives, hanged Bill from a tree. The lynching of an African American man for rape on the north side of the Ohio River, within sight of Kentucky, provoked a conversation about the differences between northern and southern systems of criminal justice. Local observers pointedly contrasted the law in Ohio, which punished a conviction for rape with a penitentiary sentence of twenty-one years, with the statute in Kentucky, which made the rape of white woman by a negro a capital crime. Some locals argued that if the punishment in Ohio for the alleged offense had been the same as in Kentucky—death—the lynching would not have come off. Their argument that a criminal justice system arranged around ideas of free labor and due process could not effectively police the color line anticipated the notions of northern and southern lynchers of African Americans during the Civil War and Reconstruction, as will be seen in chapter 5.[1]

As the 1856 lynching in Adams County, Ohio, starkly revealed, the border states of the Ohio and mid–Mississippi Valleys were key staging grounds for contests over the nature of law, criminal justice, authority, and community in the late antebellum United States. Border regions were the sites where expanding Yankee notions of free labor, centralized authority, individual rights and humanity, and regularized legal process collided with the southern institution of slavery and backcountry understandings that prioritized local authority, community, honor, and the uses of informal violence. In the 1860s and '70s, in a reflection of how the Civil War and Reconstruction had intensified local contests over the proper bounds of the state and criminal justice, southern Indiana and the varied regions of Kentucky and Missouri would emerge as the most lynching-prone areas of the country outside the Deep South.[2] But this only continued a prolonged cultural contest stemming from the antebellum era in regions where the very meanings and implications of sectional identities and differences were most obvious and in the process of definition.

On January 27, 1838, in his Address to the Young Men's Lyceum of Springfield, Illinois, the young lawyer Abraham Lincoln deplored recent mob killings in Vicksburg, Mississippi, and St. Louis, declaring that the chaos of mob violence imperiled American social and political institutions.[3] Lincoln's speech responded to the November 7, 1837, mob assassination of abolitionist editor Elijah P. Lovejoy in Alton, Illinois. Lovejoy had been driven out of St. Louis by a mob infuriated by his denunciation of the legal proceedings that had exonerated the lynchers that had burned to death Francis McIntosh, a "mulatto" boatman from Pittsburgh who had killed a deputy sheriff.[4] Abraham Lincoln's insight that lynching violence embodied a cultural conflict over the nature and function of law had particular relevance in the border regions of the Upper South and Lower Midwest, regions where Lincoln was born and raised and began his political career. Constituting the northern boundary of an increasingly defensive Peculiar Institution troubled by northern hostility to the expansion of slavery and populated by diverse whites with varying

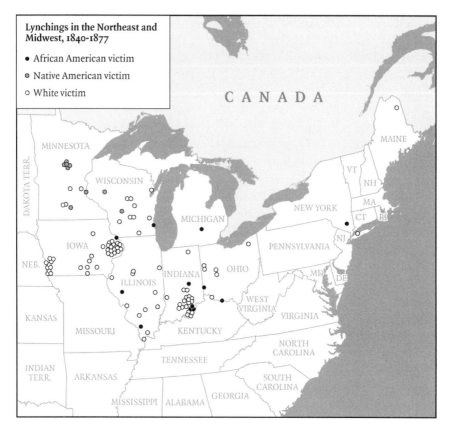

Lynchings in the Northeast and Midwest, 1840-1877

• African American victim
⊙ Native American victim
○ White victim

attitudes toward slaveholders and slaveholding, portions of the polities of the upper southern states of Kentucky and Missouri also embodied traditional backcountry preferences for localism and ambivalence toward state authority.[5] The southern counties of the lower midwestern states of Ohio, Indiana, Illinois, and Iowa had been populated in the early to mid–nineteenth century by migrants from Virginia, Maryland, North Carolina, Kentucky, Tennessee, and Missouri that brought traditional preferences for local authority and racial hierarchy but competed in their states' political and legal cultures with Yankees from New England and the Mid-Atlantic that dominated northern counties and sought reformist solutions that posited an important role for an expanding state in solving social problems.[6] Clashing understandings of the efficacy of the law and the state in administering criminal justice provided an important context for antebellum lynching violence in the border states of the Upper South and Lower Midwest. Cultural conflict over the nature of criminal justice and recourse to "mob law" was particularly pronounced in border regions, for this was a middle ground where competing legal cultures and systems, slavery versus free labor, and rough justice versus due process law constitutionalism, met and clashed in the antebellum era.[7]

If slavery seemed most tenuous in the Upper South, and divisions among whites over the role of bond-holding and the law in the maintenance of racial control were most profound in the border states, race was not always a factor in communal violence in border regions. For instance in the years between 1856 and 1860, mobs in the Upper South and Lower Midwest collectively killed at least thirteen white men following allegations that they had committed murder. The lynching of whites accused of murder reflected community tensions over the adjudication of homicide cases and concerns that the formal legal system might not impose punishments that reflected neighborhood preferences for the local supervision of criminal justice and the timely execution of murderers. For example, in the early 1860s in Union, Missouri, a mob of fifty undisguised men seized William Hall from a preliminary examination at the courthouse and hanged him from an elm tree. Hall had been convicted of murder after a change of venue to an adjoining county in 1858 and had served time in the penitentiary and in an insane asylum, but was then released and returned to Franklin County where he shot his sister to death, an offense for which he was being arraigned when captured and then executed by the mob.[8] In another example, in July 1857, William B. Thomas was tried in Poweshiek County in south central Iowa for murdering Andrew and Mary Casteel. When the judge ended the trial by granting a change of venue to another county, a mob descended on the court room and removed Thomas to the outskirts of Montezuma, where they hanged him. The mob was apparently inspired and led by relatives of the murdered couple.[9] Similarly, in February 1856, in Charleston, Illinois, a crowd estimated at five hundred gathered to watch the legal execution of A. F. Monroe. When the crowd, lubricated with whiskey, learned that the governor had issued a stay of execution, it transmogrified into a mob that attacked the jail, dragged out Monroe, and hanged him from a tree.[10]

Border state lynchings derived particular meaning and context from the importance of kin, clan, and neighborhood as the foundation of social relationships and the means for the resolution of conflict. Though they at times perceived the formal law as useful in controlling crime and resolving disputes, border region residents sometimes viewed the retribution afforded through informal collective violence as a more satisfying means of resolving serious dilemmas of community conflict and social order. For instance, in July 1856, in Morgan County, Missouri, community members accused Jim Ray of poisoning twenty school children and their teacher. A letter writer to a newspaper described the "lynch law" procedure by which Ray was collectively executed. Addressing a large crowd, a Baptist preacher drew out from them "those who have been immediate sufferers by the late tragedy," fifteen farmers who stepped forward and then voted to hang Ray. The fifteen male relatives of the victims of the poisoning afforded Ray the opportunity to pray and to make a final statement (in which he proclaimed his innocence), and then hanged him from the limb of an oak tree.[11]

Some border-state lynchings of whites reflected neighborhood anger at crimes that were perceived as particularly offensive to community mores. The murder of a law officer or the murder of multiple members of a single family could implicate deeply held notions of social order and the sanctity of the family, catalyzing the formation of communal mobs. In July 1858, a large mob in Lexington, Kentucky, hanged William Barker several hours after he had murdered the city marshal, Joseph Beard. Newspaper reports stated that townspeople were summoned to the courthouse through the ringing of the courthouse and fire bells. Members of the crowd motioned that Barker should be hanged immediately and the mob overwhelmed the jailer and pulled out their victim; speeches by a judge and other prominent men pleading that Barker should be "tried and hung by the action of the law" were overcome with shouts of "Hang him! Hang him!" The mob hanged Barker from the courthouse window, and the crowd then took up a collection for the murdered city marshal's widow and children.[12]

Another lynching inspired by outrage at a crime that offended deeply held notions of moral order occurred in July 1860 in Jefferson County in southeast Iowa after John Kephart had murdered Mrs. William Willis and her daughter, Mary Jane. Kephart had aided the Willis family as it journeyed west into Missouri, and it was rumored that he had also poisoned the family patriarch, William Willis. After the bodies of the mother and daughter were discovered in the Skunk River in the vicinity of Batavia, law officers and a posse captured Kephart in Missouri. On July 5, a large mob, reportedly composed of one thousand persons, attacked the jail in Batavia and seized Kephart from it. The mob took Kephart to the location on the Skunk River where the bodies of the Willises had been found and built a scaffold and dug a grave for him. Before the mob hanged Kephart, one of the lynchers, John Beach, addressed the crowd with an argument asserting that the collective killing of Kephart was wholly consistent with constitutionalism, a faithfulness to the law, even as the mob execution itself dispensed with the formalities of the law. Stressing the imperative of the performance of rough justice, Beach asserted "that he had always been a peaceable and law abiding citizen and was so yet. That the prisoner deserved hanging. That they would observe the substance of the law and dispense with the form."[13] However, others in southeast Iowa vigorously rejected this rationale for rough justice constitutionalism, echoing instead Abraham Lincoln's use of due process constitutionalism to criticize the lethal actions of mobs. In a column headlined "How the Lynching of Kephart is Looked Upon," the *Fairfield Ledger* reprinted the opinion of the *Mt. Pleasant News*. The Mt. Pleasant editor passionately opined that the mob members who killed Kephart must be prosecuted or the law would be rendered ineffectual and the rights of all American citizens would be endangered:

> We care not how respectable the men were who killed Kephart, or how great a villain he was, it does not form the least semblance of an apology. He was an American citizen—their peer, under our constitution and laws, and in the eyes of the law he had the same right to kill them that they [the mob] had to kill him; and the spirit that murdered Kephart would destroy our press, and take our lives for rebuking it—would break into our Penitentiaries, and turn loose upon society horse thieves, and murderers and counterfeiters. There would never be a criminal brought to justice; the laws would prove ineffectual, and fall powerless. The respectable citizen, and as one remarked, God fearing citizens, should remember that all they possess is theirs by the protection of the law which they have so wantonly violated.[14]

As the lively debate between rough justice and due process constitutionalists over the lynching of John Kephart illuminated, the antebellum border regions of the Lower Midwest and Upper South were highly contested landscapes where diverging understandings of law, authority, and the state competed for primacy within the popular discourse. Border state lynching stemmed from backcountry skepticism of the efficacy of the law and the state in the control of white and black criminality; the proximity of slavery highlighted the very freedom of whites to seek to define the proper contours of criminal justice and the protection of neighborhoods. Yet border region lynchers and their defenders, who argued that communal mobs could better impose justice and the "substance of the law" than could courts, never had the field to themselves. Their reformist neighbors, beginning with Abraham Lincoln, retorted that the lawlessness of lynching endangered "the rights and liberties of the citizen."[15] While this conflict over law and lynching flared throughout the antebellum United States, it was waged especially strenuously in the border states, for this was the setting where southern backcountry and northern reformist cultures met and clashed head on, and where their forces were most evenly matched.

The Upper Midwest

The antebellum movement for the abolition of capital punishment emanated from concern over the effects of public executions on the masses that avidly viewed them, particularly the presumed coarsening of impulses that occurred when large crowds avidly observed the suffering of the condemned. The movement, which began in the Northeast, was backed by middle class reformers as one of a panoply of measures (such as the abolition of slavery and women's suffrage) that sought to ameliorate human cruelty and suffering and to thus create a more just and humane social framework. The movement eventually reached the growing Midwest, where antideath penalty forces achieved their legislative aims in Michigan (1846) and Wisconsin (1853)—young upper midwestern states with political cultures that included substantial numbers of Yankee reformers. Several thousand had watched the public hanging of John McCaffary in Kenosha, Wisconsin, in 1851, leading a Madison editor to bemoan, "Murder before the people, with the horrors removed by the respectability of those engaged in its execution." Assemblyman Christopher Latham Sholes, who published the *Kenosha Telegraph,* led the legislative campaign for abolition with Waukesha County farmer-legislator Marvin Bovee. The reformists' worldview entailed a conception of human nature and the prospects for human relationships quite at odds with those opposed to the abolition of the death penalty. For advocates of abolition, human nature and society were pliable and perfectible and society could be guided, through good laws, to a more advanced and enlightened state in which people treated each other according to principles of reason and humanity. Their opponents, who were often rough justice advocates, argued by contrast that human nature was sometimes intrinsically inclined to evil, that it was unrealistic to believe that individuals or society could be reformed or perfected, and that only the expectation of harsh punishment for serious crimes, of capital punishment for murder, could deter criminals from killing. To them, a society without a formal death penalty was a society asking for murderous crime and disorder.[16]

In the months after the abolition of capital punishment in Wisconsin, several lynchings helped to shape an intense cultural debate over whether a state criminal code that lacked a death penalty offered sufficient deterrence to criminals and met public expectations of harsh consequences for homicide. In July 1855, David Mayberry, a Mormon from Tennessee, allegedly robbed and murdered Andrew Alger, a settler originally from New York State who labored as a raftsman on the Rock River. A jury in Janesville tried and convicted Mayberry of murder, but a mob of several thousand seized and hanged him after he was sentenced to life imprisonment, ignoring speeches by prosecuting attorneys and the presiding judge urging that the majesty of the law be respected.[17] Mayberry's trial had incorporated the cultural division in Wisconsin over the recent abolition of the death penalty. The state attorneys that prosecuted Mayberry used competing arguments to persuade jurors and potential lynchers to accept the legitimacy of a murder trial that could not legally culminate in a death sentence. In his opening statement, prosecuting attorney George P. Ely asserted that the legislature had foolishly disregarded the natural law of lethal retribution for murder, but that it was the duty of citizens to accept the law as it now existed.

> But in these days of cavil and selfish intriguing, men have in their legislation deemed that the law thundered from Sinai's top was no longer binding upon them. They have, and do by their acts say, "we are above all law except our own—away with a higher law." However much I might wish that our law at this time were different, as an ardent lover of good order and society, I shall feel it my duty to abide by it until experience shall teach our Legislature that chains and prisons are but idle mockery to the man, who will, for the glittering dust of earth, take the life of his fellow-man.[18]

Another prosecuting attorney, David Noggle, took an opposing stance, arguing that Wisconsin's revised criminal code offered more reliable and fair punishment than atavistic criminal statutes that relied on capital punishment, which juries were often reluctant to inflict and which risked the execution of innocent persons. Noggle argued that lynching Mayberry, which was rumored to be in the offing, would constitute a destructive act that would damage the locality and possibly lead to repeal of Wisconsin's progressive homicide statute.

> Such an act would disgrace our State, our County, and would be an endless disgrace to our city; besides it would have the tendency to repeal the law we now have, which, in my humble opinion, is the best law in the land, and it would have the tendency to re-enact that law which is befitting the dark ages and barbarous nations—a law that has hung scores of innocent men, and a law that would do more to clear the guilty than could be done by all the lawyers in Wisconsin.[19]

Wisconsin editors opined over what the mob execution of Mayberry meant in a state that lacked a death penalty. The *Janesville Democrat Standard,* after laying the blame for a climate of lawlessness on Free Soilers who incited resistance to (and illegally rescued slaves from) the Fugitive Slave Law, argued that the mob killing of Mayberry demonstrated that Wisconsin needed to restore capital punishment.

> This was the man who was lynched by the "Janesville mob"; and if any set of circumstances could justify men in violating law, and taking its administration in their own hands, (and not for the purposes of *revenge,* but for the ends of justice,) these circumstances and these motives go far in justifying the execution of MAYBERRY. . . . We believe that the times in which we live, demand

the restoration of the death penalty, and that public sentiment, throughout the State, clamors for its re-enactment. Those who are opposed to it, are ahead of the age, are misguided, as we believe, by a false philanthropy, and are the advocates of a doctrine, which, in the present condition of our race, is productive of immense injury to the social well being of man.[20]

Less polemically, the *Janesville Gazette* agreed that the lynching of Mayberry demonstrated that the death penalty ought to be restored, but asserted that some of the problems that hampered the administration of capital punishment could be averted by giving juries the option of whether or not to impose the death penalty after a murder conviction.[21]

Less than a month later, a mob in West Bend, Wisconsin, hanged George DeBar, a nineteen-year-old farmhand who had attacked a German farmer, John Muehr, and his wife and had murdered a boy employed by them as a farm laborer, Paul Winderling. DeBar had worked for Muehr as a hired hand and claimed Muehr owed him wages and had struck him in an election-night dispute several months earlier. The German Catholic crowd roused by DeBar's attack on members of their community was catalyzed by DeBar's identification as a member of the nativist Know-Nothing political party. The German Catholic mob of several hundred seized DeBar from his trial, which had been expedited to avoid the possibility of mob violence. German American militia companies looked on as the crowd seized DeBar but failed to intervene.[22]

The Yankee abolitionist editor of the *Milwaukee Free Democrat*, Sherman Booth, who had led the highly controversial mob "rescue" of fugitive slave Joshua Glover the previous year, decried the mob killing of DeBar, arguing that it positioned Wisconsin not in the forefront of social advancement but instead in the vanguard of lawless lynching.[23]

> Has it indeed come to such a pass, that in this nineteenth century, in an age claiming to be enlightened and progressive, in refined and civilized communities, such scenes as these are to be of frequent occurrence? Are the laws of our Land, to which we owe our present prosperity, and future stability, to be broken with impunity, and with impious hands? Heaven forfend! Yet so indeed it would seem, and Wisconsin bids fair to take the lead of the Northern States in allowing Lynch Law to overrule the Courts of Justice, and permitting the wild rage, or excited fury of a mob, to trample down legal barriers, and adjudge life or death to the criminal.[24]

Positing that adherence to law offered the only reliable path to social and economic progress, Booth emphatically rejected the notion that the death penalty discouraged lynching. The reformist editor scoffed at standard rough justice arguments that scorned the credulity of juries at the hands of skilled defense lawyers and that asserted that murderers could easily get off with the insanity plea. Booth instead placed his faith in the rationality and common sense of juries.

> That the existence of capital punishment in a State acts as an antidote to lynch law, we do not believe. For, though without definite knowledge of facts, we venture to say *more cases of lynching have occurred in States where the death penalty is in force, than where it has been abolished.* The argument . . . that "had Mayberry and Debar lived, pleas of insanity would have been put in for them, and probably or possibly thwarted the ends of Justice," is entirely gratuitous. They might or might not. Juries, with some lamentable exceptions, generally render just verdicts, and are not so credulous as to be always imposed upon by the cunning of unscrupulous lawyers.[25]

A letter writer in the *Milwaukee Sentinel* styling himself LEX parried Booth's thrusts, insisting that the death penalty was not a relic of a barbaric age but rather a mode of punishment preferred throughout history by "enlightened nations." LEX dismissed the humanitarian perfectionist assumptions underpinning the abolitionist editor's views, asserting that in Booth's reformist penology, "The crime is lost sight of in sympathy for the 'poor wretch lingering out his life in the cold walls of a prison.'"[26] Finally, another letter writer to the *Sentinel* argued that the Janesville and West Bend lynchings were in fact a healthy manifestation of popular constitutionalism, with the people stepping in to fill the breach left by a reformed criminal justice system that did not offer adequate security to citizens. "The want of protection on the part of the government and the laws, and their worse execution, has thrown the necessity, deep, imperative necessity, upon the people to protect themselves. It is their clear right to do so in such extreme cases, and their clear duty."[27]

Although some called for the restoration of the death penalty in the wake of the two mob executions, Wisconsin legislators resisted the clamor for restoration. Debate over whether the death penalty should be restored or not would flare periodically amid twelve lynchings for homicide in Wisconsin over the next four decades, but the state did not reinstitute capital punishment.[28] Wisconsin was not alone in the cultural paroxysms it experienced after abolishing the death penalty. The neighboring upper midwestern state of Minnesota witnessed a similarly prolonged debate over the death penalty in the last decades of the nineteenth century, one punctuated periodically by lynchings. Minnesota lawmakers effectively placed a moratorium on executions in 1868, but this measure was reversed in 1883. Contention in Minnesota over the effects and efficacy of executions continued until 1911, when the legislature and Governor Adolph Eberhart abolished capital punishment.[29] In another example, the lower midwestern state of Iowa, where rough justice sentiments held nearly equal sway with due process perspectives, abolished the death penalty in 1872, but restored it in 1878 after several well-publicized lynchings for homicide.[30]

The Far West

In the first years after Americans, Latin Americans, Europeans, Australians, and Chinese flocked into California in the wake of the news of the discovery of gold, lethal and nonlethal vigilante violence, some of it quite organized and some quite spontaneous, became a seemingly ubiquitous feature of Gold Rush society. Even after the full implementation of legal institutions with statehood in 1850, some argued, refashioning rhetoric from earlier southern and midwestern frontiers, that overstretched law officers and courts could not handle a proliferating criminal class, racially and ethnically diverse in composition, that exploited the distances between mining camps and towns in California's vast and remote spaces. In columns that were reprinted in newspapers throughout the United States, defenders of California lynchers asserted that virtuous communities of honest prospectors banded together to perform collective violence that expunged the threat posed by criminals that exploited the gaps in the administration of criminal justice. Some also avowed, in instrumentalist republican tones, that vigilantes stepped in for fragile local criminal justice threatened by the susceptibility of officials and trial witnesses to corruption in a newly formed, highly acquisitive society where individuals were only as good as their actions or their reputation. Arraying against California's governor in an extended, nationally publicized contest over the proper nature of the state's criminal justice system, Gold Rush–era lynchers and their apologists declared that the careful legal procedures of due process law could not offer sufficient protection to communities endangered by mounting criminality.[31]

California newspaper editors sought to interpret the meaning of rampant lynching violence for local residents and for distant readers that absorbed detailed accounts reprinted in eastern newspapers. As they did so, California editors sought to craft their own understanding of an emerging regional style of law and violence, to defend the reputation of their nascent region, and to reassure family back home along with potential immigrants and investors in the eastern United States. In February 1851, the *Alta California* conceded that "doubtless many of our good friends at home read with horror the accounts of the execution of summary justice which are continually occurring in the mining region of California, and they probably regard those who assist or countenance such movements as but little better than their victims."[32] The San

Francisco editor insisted that the newspaper fully backed "respect for law," but asserted that the collective violence flowed naturally from the unusual legal and social conditions extant in California and that "people's courts" typically sought to administer informal justice scrupulously and fairly.

> But it must be remembered . . . that in the wild, mountainous, golden region of California, seats of justice are often few and far between, that the character of the country itself forbids the conveyance of criminals, to any great distance, that in the present incipient stage of our organization no jails have been built, and no mode provided for keeping criminals with any degree of safety until they can be remanded to the proper authorities at a distance. When in addition to these considerations it is remembered that in our gold mines there is every inducement for the thief, the robber, and the murderer to commit wrong, and that the lives and properties of whole neighborhoods are sometimes placed in jeopardy by the presence of wrong-doers, it is not strange that where a villain is caught and after a fair trial, which is usually given him, if found guilty, a sure and speedy punishment is administered.[33]

The *Alta California* believed that lynch law would fade away as "the mining portion of our state becomes more permanently settled, and the usual forms of law more easily arrived at."[34] Unimpressed with such arguments, the *New York Tribune,* a few months later, scored California for sliding backward into an orgy of "Lynch Law" that it felt set a "hazardous" course that jeopardized law and order in the state. The *Alta California* reprinted the *Tribune*'s criticisms but categorically rejected them, insisting that California vigilantes had never sought to "'*ignore* the laws.'" The San Francisco editor cast the intentions of the state's lynchers in a more benign, indeed, exemplary light. "Temporarily, only, have they assumed the power to direct speedily the ends of justice, and this has been, as it is very well known, when crime of the most aggravated character lay beyond the reach of law and the constituted authorities."[35]

Cultural conflict over criminal justice in Gold Rush–era California came to a head over Governor John McDougal's use of executive authority to reprieve individuals sentenced to capital punishment. McDougal, an Independent Democrat, had been born in Ohio, arrived in California as a forty-niner, was elected lieutenant governor after the state's constitutional convention, and succeeded to the executive office upon the first governor's resignation due to popular dissatisfaction. In April 1851, Governor McDougal postponed the execution of Hamilton McCauley, who had been sentenced to hang in Napa for murdering a magistrate. Local residents prevented the governor's emissary from crossing the Napa River by ferry to deliver the reprieve, while a small group of lynchers broke into the jail at Napa and hanged McCauley in his cell.[36] In August 1851, McDougal reprieved William Robinson, who was sentenced to be executed with two other convicts in Sacramento. When the sheriff read the governor's proclamation of reprieve to the large crowd assembled to watch the triple execution, the crowd responded by shouting: "Hang the rascal," "String him up," and "Lynch him." Taking Robinson from law officers, "the people" turned him over to a "committee" that hanged him on the scaffold immediately following the two legal executions. The Sacramento crowd then hanged Governor McDougal in effigy, and a mass meeting adopted a resolution demanding his resignation, asserting that the reprieve of Robinson demonstrated the governor's incapacity for his office's "sacred duties."[37] The *Alta California* argued that the governor's attempt to ensure the fairness of legal process by delaying execution recklessly undermined popular confidence in the efficient administration of law. "Governor McDougal committed a great mistake in stepping between the people and a lawfully tried, convicted and sentenced criminal, just at the moment when they demanded the severest example, and expected in good faith of the law's efficiency, the execution of the self-confessed robber."[38] The San Francisco editor found the explanation for the governor's reprieve in a cultural chasm that separated advocates of the harsh and rapid punishment of criminality from an influential social element that placed undue emphasis on the humanity and rights of the defendant. "There is always in every community a class of individuals whose sickly fears and distressful fancies are ever picturing some horrible injustice as likely to befall men accused of crime, and whose false sympathies are readily enlisted whenever professions of penitence and solemn promises are wrung from criminals by the terrors of approaching punishment."[39]

John McDougal's term as governor was plagued by wrangling with lynchers and their defenders, and he denounced the San Francisco vigilantes' hangings of four men in the summer of 1851, asserting that "No security of life and property can be guaranteed, except the constitution and law are observed."[40] The governor's defense of due process law against vigilantes who usurped legal authority to lethally punish their social enemies registered the depth of antebellum cultural conflict over criminal justice amid the sweeping social transformation of the far western edge of the American continent. While the scale of lynching violence stemming from the debate between rough justice and due process waned in California by the mid-to-late 1850s, the well-publicized rhetorical defense of Gold Rush lynching as justifiable violence perpetrated by virtuous communities seeking to defend themselves against criminals who exploited gaps in law would help to frame the self-image of subsequent generations of lynchers and their apologists in the West, Midwest, and South.[41]

5. The Civil War and Reconstruction and the Remaking of American Lynching

The remaking of the nation during and after the Civil War was a national process, not merely a southern one. Northerners and westerners, along with southerners, responded to and remade social, political, economic, and legal arrangements in the wake of emancipation, the extension of rights to African Americans, and the expansion of federal and state authority in the 1860s and '70s. The transformation of the United States during the Civil War and Reconstruction was a complex, fitful process, with interconnected local, regional, and national dimensions.[1] Violence, including the collective violence of lynching and vigilantism, was an important aspect of this process, a visceral means of seeking to resist and to redirect the dynamics of social, political, and legal change. Historians have long interpreted Congressional Reconstruction as an era in which white southerners unleashed collective racial violence in resistance of an expansion of governmental authority that sought to promote racial equality.[2] Yet collective violence that responded to the war's social and legal alterations had emerged soon after Ft. Sumter, and it transcended regional boundaries in the Civil War and Reconstruction, occurring in both the South and in the North. American lynching had arisen in the decades before the Civil War in the regions beyond the Alleghenies as localized conflict pitting the state's efforts to extend the protections of due process law versus the claims of neighborhoods committed to defending notions of race, ethnicity, class, kin, honor, and crime control. The Civil War's myriad transformations of legal and political structures and social relationships, not least of them emancipation, led some northerners (most notably Irish Catholic immigrants) and white southerners to further recast lynching into a central weapon of reaction against an emergent state, championed by Republicans, that sought to extend the promise of racial equality. With the retreat from Reconstruction, the lesson seemed clear, particularly for the white southerners who had employed massive lethal violence to reclaim political power in "Redemption" and who had turned lynching into a familiar means of policing the everyday racial conflicts of postemancipation life. The lesson of Reconstruction, especially for the postbellum white South, was that lynching violence was a more reliable instrument for the perpetuation of racial control than a fragile and unreliable state that made abstract promises of legal fairness.

The Upper Midwest and the Northeast

Historians have charted the rise of racial ideologies among working class whites, particularly Irish Catholics, in tandem with class and political formation in the antebellum North, and their participation in large-scale racial violence in the 1863 New York City Draft Riots. But the Draft Riots, which included numerous mob beatings and hangings of African Americans, constituted merely the highest tide of reactionary racial violence in the North during the Civil War and Reconstruction.[3]

Analysis of wartime racial lynchings[4] in Milwaukee and Newburgh, New York, offers an additional vantage point for apprehending the dynamics of racial violence in the urban North in the Civil War era. In Milwaukee and Newburgh, Irish Catholic ethnic solidarity was as pivotal as a developing concept of "whiteness."[5] Competing with African Americans for social status and jobs at the lowest rungs of northern society and influenced by the racial slogans and ideology with which the Democratic Party sought to link southern planters and northern workers in defense of white supremacy, Irish Catholic communities in the North enacted homicidal collective violence that sought to avenge Irish kinfolk victimized by alleged African American criminality. In the process, Irish American lynchers sought to vindicate Irish immigrant communities that viewed themselves as diminished by nativism and racial egalitarianism that sought to elevate blacks. Reflecting the profoundly hybrid, transnational characteristics of the northern United States in the mid–nineteenth century, Irish American lynchers reinterpreted Old World practices of communal violence in an unfamiliar and seemingly hostile American legal and social context by resorting to collective murder as retaliation for crimes against fellow Irish. As they did so, Irish Americans transposed traditions of community violence that had been manifested in Ireland in highly localistic legal cultures that distrusted and sometimes nullified British laws.[6] Perhaps influenced by knowledge of white southerners' collective burning and hanging of slaves and free blacks in the antebellum era, Irish Americans used lynching in the era of the Civil War and Reconstruction to avenge slights by blacks to Irish communal honor, eschewing Republican efforts to create an omnipotent state that might override local preferences and guarantee rights to African Americans.[7]

Yet ethnic solidarity was not always the decisive factor in racial lynchings in the North in the Civil War and Reconstruction. In Ingham County, Michigan, in 1866, rural white Democrats unleashed collective violence that signaled resistance to Republicans' advocacy of racial equality during Presidential Reconstruction. Midwesterners differed markedly in their stances on the legitimacy of the mob violence in Ingham County, but consistently interpreted this lynching as an aspect of a broader national, cross-regional conversation over the direction of President Andrew Johnson's Reconstruction policies.[8]

Racially motivated lynching of African Americans was certainly not new in the 1860s. As discussed in chapter 3, white southerners had collectively murdered African Americans during slavery, informally executing by hanging and burning at least forty-four, and possibly many more, slaves in the South in the years 1824–62. Beginning in the antebellum era, Americans began to call this practice of southern racial violence *lynching,* a term they also used to describe lethal and nonlethal summary collective violence that targeted whites in the South, and whites, blacks, Indians, and Mexicans in regions outside the South.[9] Southern extralegal executions of African Americans were frequently reported in the northern and abolitionist press, sometimes with editorial comments asserting that informal collective executions of slaves were an inevitable by-product of the inhumanity and barbarity of the social relations of Southern slavery.[10] Racial violence was also a familiar phenomenon in the North. Groups of Northern whites, often working class, had rioted against blacks in a variety of urban settings in the early republic and, especially, in the antebellum era, as social tensions arose in the wake of agitation for immediate abolitionism after 1830.[11] Yet, given the particular context in which they occurred, northern lynchings of African Americans during the Civil War and Reconstruction had special significance. They revealed substantial resistance among some white northerners to the war's implication of racial egalitarianism and the extension of rights to African Americans. They indicated that portions of the northern populace rejected Republicans' advocacy of an expansive, activist state and legal system that might guarantee and protect the rights of blacks, favoring instead limited government responsive merely to the needs of their particular, racially defined communities. The northern lynchings diverged in practice from antebellum racial rioting,[12] as the crowds in Wisconsin, New York State, and Michigan collectively murdered individual blacks accused of particular crimes. Each of these lynching cases involved portions of white communities that refused to leave the adjudication and punishment of African American criminality to courts, insisting that the formal legal system with its ostensible fairness and neutrality could not be trusted to harshly punish black miscreants. The lynchings in the early-to-mid-1860s indicated that some northerners viewed illegal collective murder as a legitimate strategy for resisting racial equality and subordinating African Americans. In each of these respects, white northerners in the Civil War and the early portion of Reconstruction participated in strategies and practices of racial violence that would also be employed by white southerners in Reconstruction.[13]

Urban Irish and rural Democrats were, then, in a sense, innovators, as they were among the first white Americans to lynch free blacks in a society organized around principles of free labor; their resort to a ritual of collective murder of African Americans was not shaped by the limitations and tensions inherent to the sustenance of racial and legal order within a slave society, which had been the context for the lynching of African Americans in the antebellum South. Rather, racial lynching in the North stemmed from the competing claims of an ascendant legal order in the early-to-mid-1860s that was avowedly racially neutral, versus the demands of a localistic, aggrieved, racially defined community protective of what it viewed as its social prerogatives. In this respect, despite important differences in contexts, northern white workers and rural white Democrats paralleled, and indeed slightly anticipated, the practice and ideology of white southerners who would seize upon lynching as a means of rejecting the Reconstruction state's insistence on color-blind law. In 1860s northern print culture, characterized by sharply defined political party allegiances that shaped ideological stances and perspectives on race, slavery, secession, the war, and Reconstruction, the discourse surrounding northern lynching violence punctuated a vigorous conversation over the prospects and legitimacy of the emerging racial and legal order of the post–Civil War nation.[14]

The understanding that white northerners helped to fashion a practice of racial lynching contributes complexity and nuance to long-held notions of the nature and character of particular American regions, and also helps to reconfigure the history of race in the twentieth-century United States. The vexatious northern encounter with race in the decades after 1900, including occasional northern racial lynchings,[15] brutal race riots,[16] and concerted northern white working class resistance to school and housing desegregation,[17] may seem less novel in light of the North's mid–nineteenth century experience with murderous racial violence that spurned the extension of racial equality in the Civil War and Reconstruction. Like slavery in the northern colonies in the seventeenth and eighteenth centuries, mid–nineteenth century northern racial lynchings can be understood as a formative but subsequently sublimated aspect of the history of the construction of northern white racial identity, an erased episode in the creation of a bifurcated racial self-conception that in later decades professed a commitment to the elevation of the status of African Americans and pointedly contrasted the region's relatively benign race relations with those in the South, yet also blanched at the physical proximity of African Americans and at times fiercely resisted meaningful racial integration. During the Civil War and Reconstruction, rural and urban working class whites in the Upper Midwest and the Northeast, many of them from Ireland, helped to craft a practice of racial lynching that in some ways resembled white southerners' adoption of racial terror in the postbellum era.[18]

Prior to their arrival in the United States in the 1840s and '50s, the Irish had developed practices of extralegal violence in ambivalence and opposition to the British state. One analyst has argued that as a consequence of British colonial rule, the Irish regarded "the law not as a manifestation of abstract 'justice' but as a manipulable vehicle of group interest." Another scholar has asserted that "the normalizing of violence in Ireland was a direct product of the English refusal to attend to Irish grievances unless they were expressed violently."[19] Reflecting the colonized context, Irish society saw a relatively low homicide rate, but extensive amounts of personal and recreational violence, which was not punished by the Irish juries that often ignored the instructions of judges. In eighteenth- and nineteenth-century Ireland, personal and communal extralegal violence sometimes punished, even lethally, those accused of sexual offenses. Communal violence in Ireland also took the form of "moonlighting," nocturnal extralegal violence perpetrated by groups of men. In moonlighting, agricultural laborers sought to punish their class antagonists, farmers, and local men sought to police community standards.[20]

Irish Catholic immigrants to the urban northern United States reworked older patterns of extralegal violence that expressed alienation from the formal legal system in the American context of anti-Irish nativism, the divisive politics of the sectional crisis, and tensions surrounding the onset of the Civil War. On September 6, 1861, in Milwaukee, a crowd of fifty to seventy-five Irishmen forced their way into the city jail and seized an African American, Marshall Clarke. Clarke and another African American, James Shelton, had exchanged insults and blows with two Irishmen, Darby Carney and John Brady. During the altercation, which was precipitated by the offense Carney and Brady took at the two African Americans' interaction with white women on the street, Shelton apparently stabbed Carney, who soon died from the wounds. The *Milwaukee Sentinel* noted that "the preparation for the lynching"[21] was discussed openly in the city, but that authorities did little to head off the impending mob attack on the jail. Shelton escaped as the crowd stormed the jail, but the mob dragged Clarke, beating him brutally along the way, to the fire engine house in the predominantly Irish Third Ward, where they questioned him and then hanged him from a pile driver. Thousands reportedly flocked to the scene of the lynching and the station house where Clarke's body was taken, some carrying away pieces of the rope as mementoes of the event.[22]

The collective murder of Marshall Clarke in Milwaukee drew substantially from the solidarities, grievances, and institutions of the upper Midwestern city's Irish community. By 1861, most of Milwaukee's Irish population was Catholic, with roots in the emigration from impoverished rural districts of Ireland in the 1840s. Milwaukee, a metropolis numbering more than 45,000 on the eve of the Civil War, was distinctive because its German population, many of whom had also arrived in the 1840s and '50s, outnumbered its Irish. In 1860, Germans composed just over one-third of the city's population, whereas the Irish constituted less than 7 percent of city residents. By 1861, Germans enjoyed a foothold in skilled trades and the professions and had developed an extensive network of social and cultural institutions, whereas most Irish remained in unskilled and semiskilled work. The majority of Milwaukee's Irish lived in the densely concentrated Third Ward, a neighborhood that lacked a parish church and that was reputed for its extensive concentration of saloons and the frequency of personal violence. Irish Milwaukee had been devastated in September 1860 when the steamboat *Lady Elgin* had sunk in Lake Michigan. The *Lady Elgin* had sailed on an excursion to Chicago conveying Irish Milwaukeeans to attend a speech by Democratic presidential candidate Stephen Douglas. The excursion was a means to raise money for arms for the Irish militia, the Milwaukee Guards. The governor of Wisconsin had seized arms from the guards when the Irish militia captain had stated that he would uphold federal rather than state authority in a dispute that pitted Wisconsin abolitionists versus the federal government. On the return trip to Milwaukee, the *Lady Elgin* sank, killing approximately 75 percent of the four hundred passengers aboard. Around one-third of the households in the Third Ward lost kin in the tragedy, and Irish community leadership was depleted.[23]

Social ties and a sentiment of ethnic grievance among Milwaukee's Third Ward Irish were key ingredients in the mob killing of Marshall Clarke. The Third Ward's Irish fire company helped to coordinate the mob violence, summoning the community by ringing fire bells when news of the death of the murdered Irishman, Darby Carney, arrived, and offering the fire engine house as the site for an interrogation and informal trial of Clarke after he was seized from jail. These events also precipitated ethnic divisions, as German members of the fire company objected to Irish firemen dragging the hose cart through the Third Ward to gather men to participate in the mob, and Irish and Germans exchanged blows.[24] One source suggested that most of the Irish mobbers were "low, desperate boys and young men," some with rural origins, and that the more established Irishmen in the Third Ward did not participate.[25] Observers sympathetic to the Irish argued that the act of collective murder took shape from the Irish community's resentment of its marginalization in Milwaukee's social and political life, with the first anniversary of the sinking of the *Lady Elgin* a vivid reminder of Wisconsin abolitionists' and Republicans' long-standing nativist disdain for Irish Catholic culture and Republicans' elevation of the status of African Americans even as they denigrated Irish Catholic Democrats. By this reasoning, the Irish in Milwaukee's Third Ward believed that Republicans in Wisconsin would come to the aid of the two African Americans that were alleged to have murdered Darby Carney, just as they had "rescued" a fugitive slave, Joshua Glover, from federal authority in 1854, meaning that justice was unlikely for the Irish Milwaukeeans reeling from the death of a countryman at the hands of African Americans.[26] A Chicago editor interpreted the events in a column reprinted in a Democratic newspaper in Milwaukee, highlighting the ethnic, racial, and political dynamics underlying the Irish Third Ward's resort to lynching.

One year precisely from the time of that calamity, or as was stated in the account we published yesterday, at almost the same hour of the night in which the *Lady Elgin* sunk, an Irishman of Milwaukee was stabbed to the heart by a drunken, insolent, pampered negro. To those who know anything of the feeling with which Irishmen remember the dead—with what reverence they observe the anniversary of the death of their kindred and friends, it will not seem surprising that on that eve of the anniversary of the untimely death of so many of their kindred neighbors and friends the ball that announced the death of Carney at the hands of the negro, sounded upon many wakeful ears. Nor is it surprising—illegal though it was—that with the recollection that in Milwaukee mob-law had been declared supreme over the constitution; that as mob-law had rescued men for violating federal law; that as mob-law had made men judges, governors and State dignitaries; that as Carney was only another "Irish democrat," his murderer, particularly as that murderer was a negro, would be rescued and liberated. We say that it is not surprising that men whose minds were filled with the mournful, if not bitter, memory of their kindred and friends, sacrificed one year previously while engaged in procuring arms of which they had been stripped because of their devotion to the laws of the Union, rushed forth, seized that negro, and made vengeance sure.[27]

All observers cited the central role of race in the lynching of Clarke, even as they differed in their perspectives on whether the Irish mob's racial sentiments were understandable (the Democratic press) or deplorable (the Republican press). Prewar social relationships, the recent secession crisis, and the onset of Civil War shaped the discussion, even as long-held views of race, slavery, and the sectional controversy provided context. Both Marshall Clarke and James Shelton, the African Americans alleged to have participated in the murder of Darby Carney, had well-established ties to Milwaukee's small black community, which the census numbered around a hundred in 1860. Clarke was the son of a barber in the city, and Shelton was a waiter at a "confectionery [*sic*] saloon" who was boarding with an African American named Brown, who had gone to war with the First Regiment as a servant to a colonel. Free blacks and fugitive slaves residing in Milwaukee in the 1850s often lived in the First Ward, near the households of wealthy whites, where they were employed as servants. The Republican press reported that Clarke and Shelton were well-known and liked by the middle and upper class whites who patronized the service establishments with which they were connected.[28]

Competing narratives that emerged over the circumstances of the clash between the Irishmen, Darby Carney and John Brady, and the Africans Americans, Clarke and Shelton, revealed diverging racial ideologies in wartime Milwaukee. From all accounts, the confrontation between the African Americans and the Irishmen, which may have occurred under the influence of alcohol, revolved around the Irishmen's response to the African Americans' interaction with two white women on the street. Those partial to the Irish Americans claimed that the blacks had insulted the white women and that Carney and Brady came to the defense of the women. Those sympathetic to the African Americans argued that the white women were actually walking with Clarke and Shelton and that the Irishmen chose to start a fight, with the African Americans defending themselves with knives, which led to the stabbing of Carney.[29] Accounts emphasized that the confrontation revolved around the African Americans' assertion of their right to freely mix in Milwaukee's polyglot public spaces, reporting that Clarke and Shelton had declared, "We are as good as any d——d Irishman, or any Yankee either!"[30] By contrast, the lexicon of the mob that seized Clarke from jail expressed Irish rage at the death of Carney but also frustration at the ways in which the liaison between abolitionists, Republicans, and blacks seemed to thwart the aspirations of Irish in Milwaukee's polity. In the oral expressions of Irish Milwaukeeans, only the degradation of blacks through the ritualistic collective killing of one of the African American assailants could satiate Irish communal anger. The mob reportedly shouted "We must have revenge! kill the d—— niggers!" and "D——the niggers and abolitionists!"[31] A Democratic newspaper, the *News*, and members of the Irish community repeatedly referred to Clarke, Shelton, and other African Americans in the city as "contraband," a usage that sarcastically referenced Union Army General Benjamin Butler's recent classification of escaped slaves in Virginia as "contraband of war" that would not be returned to their former owners under the Fugitive Slave Law. The Democrats' language implied that Republican policies had dangerously elevated the status of African Americans in both Milwaukee and in the areas of the South that had come under Union control, but also suggested that the fact of racial slavery in the South should continue to define the status of blacks in a northern city, even as northerners fought to restore the seceded southern states to the Union.[32]

Milwaukee's Republicans, largely Yankee and Protestant, interpreted the lynching violence in ways differing markedly from Democrats, with their ties to the Irish community. Both sides emphasized their commitment to constitutionalism,[33] that is, the importance of adherence to a legal order rooted in representative political institutions, but Democrats did so by arguing that abolitionists and Republicans had incited a breakdown in law and order by disregarding the rights of Irish and German Catholics and by hypocritically ignoring and violating laws that preserved the institution of slavery. Democrats argued that the violence was an understandable response to the Republicans' nativist denigration of Irish Catholics, and the Republicans' willingness to resort to lawlessness (for example, "rescues" of fugitive slaves, in defiance of federal law) that elevated unlawful and disorderly blacks, a congenital Republican disrespect for law that had ultimately resulted in the recent secession of the southern states.[34] Republicans parried by arguing that the Irish community had proven itself unfit for American laws by refusing to accept the concept of due process of law when it applied to blacks, and that Democratic officials obeisant to Irish constituents were sorely derelict in their duties in failing to prevent the mob execution. Republicans decried the Irish mob's disregard for the legal rights of an African American who was merely culpable as an accomplice to a murder (James Shelton, not Marshall Clarke, had actually stabbed Darby Carney). Republicans assailed the lynching as a dangerously overwrought expression of atavistic ethnic grievance in a burgeoning midwestern city, an index of Irish incapacity for the responsibilities of American citizenship. Republicans also criticized Milwaukee's Democratic officeholders, Sheriff Charles Larkin and Mayor James Brown, for letting the Irish community carry off the mob execution, despite widespread knowledge that the lynching was impending, and demanded that Democratic city authorities reimpose law and order on Milwaukee's streets, even as northerners fought to bring lawless southerners back into the Union.[35]

The aftermath of the lynching of Clarke would prove more ambiguous, as Milwaukeeans sought to demonstrate that due process law, not mob law, would prevail in the city. Legal process failed to yield results that satisfied either the Irish lynchers and their defenders or those who lambasted their actions. Authorities energetically headed off any possibility of another lynching when James Shelton was captured and tried for the murder of Darby Carney. Law officers spirited Shelton to Chicago for safekeeping, but when the African American defendant was brought back to Milwaukee for the trial, a jury acquitted him on a self defense plea.[36] A month later, six Irishmen were tried for their alleged participation in the lynching of Marshall Clarke, but the jury could not agree and failed to convict them.[37] Milwaukeeans struggled to make sense of the dual acquittals of Sheldon and the alleged lynchers. The editor of the *Milwaukee Daily Wisconsin* attributed the acquittals to the defects of the jury system, namely the requirement that jurors reach a unanimous verdict for a conviction, a high barrier given the likelihood that at least one person on a jury would be sympathetic to a defendant due to personal relationship, kinship, or ethnicity.[38] However, the Democratic *Milwaukee News* scored the *Wisconsin*'s failure to criticize the acquittal of Sheldon even as it lamented the acquittal of the alleged lynchers. Noting that three of the same jurors had sat at both trials, the *News* argued that the *Wisconsin*'s position signaled that it perceived the murder of a "negro" to be of greater significance than the murder "of an Irishman." In a reiteration of the lens of ethnic and racial grievance through which Democrats had interpreted the entire lynching affair, the *News* castigated the *Wisconsin*'s criticism of the acquittal of the alleged lynchers as "the last run of Know-nothingism."[39] Thus, even as legal process prevailed in Milwaukee in the months after the mob murder of Clarke, perspectives on the criminal justice system's adjudication of the events surrounding the lynching continued to cleave along lines shaped by ethnicity, race, class, and political identity.

Two years later, in June 1863, social bonds among Irish and the Irish community's pursuit of racial vengeance spiraled again into collective murder in Newburgh, New York, a town along the Hudson River in the Catskills Mountains sixty-five miles north of New York City. After law officers arrested an African American, Robert Mulliner, for the alleged rape of a recently arrived Irish woman, Ellen Clark, a mob of fifty Irishmen, supported by a crowd of several hundred Irish, surrounded the courthouse and demanded that Mulliner be turned over. Overwhelming the sheriff, the mob rejected the entreaties of the parish priest, Father E. J. O'Reilly, two judges, and the district attorney that the law be allowed to take its course. Forcing their way into the courthouse jail with axes and sledges, the mob pulled out Mulliner, kicking and pounding him as they carried him to a tree in the courthouse yard, from which they hanged him. Hundreds reportedly visited the scene of the lynching the next day.[40] In the aftermath of the racial mob execution,

many African Americans fled Newburgh, fearing a more general racial po-
grom. Father O'Reilly and a Democratic newspaper with close ties to the
Irish community, the *Telegraph*, spoke out to quell talk of further violence,
and none apparently occurred, even as the Draft Riots erupted in New York
City three weeks later.[41]

In Newburgh, as in Milwaukee, Irish Catholic ethnicity and contending
racial ideologies and political affiliations influenced by the cultural politics of
nativism and the social tensions of the early years of the Civil War provided
the context for racially motivated lynching. Newburgh, a city numbering
more than 15,000 in 1860, was connected by the Hudson River to industrializing New York City and its hinterland. In 1860, the U.S. Census tallied African
Americans as 3.5 percent of Newburgh's population, an African American
community composed of blacks whose ancestors had been slaves in colonial
New York as well as African Americans that had fled from southern slavery.[42]
Robert Mulliner, the African American murdered by the Newburgh mob,
had lived intermittently in a black settlement outside of the city, and had
worked in surrounding communities and served a jail term in Newburgh for
theft.[43] In 1870, the census enumerated 25 percent of Newburgh's population
as foreign-born, including substantial numbers of Irish.[44]

Irish solidarity and collective grievance at the perceived slighting of the
Irish by African Americans and their political allies were instrumental in
the Newburgh lynching. Irish laborers who worked along the city's docks
provided the leadership and ranks of the mob, joined by Irish who came in
from nearby towns along the Hudson River. Ellen Clark, the Irishwoman
from County Meath allegedly raped by Robert Mulliner, had been drawn
to Newburgh by ties to acquaintances that lived in the region, and some of
the mobbers from the other side of the river reportedly had known Clark's
parents in Ireland. The Irish community in and around Newburgh was not
homogeneous. Several leaders of the Irish community, Cornelius McLean,
a member of the board of trustees, William Cleary, proprietor of an inn,
and the Rev. E. J. O'Reilly, sought to dissuade the mob from its intentions.
Respecting the Catholic priest but not his counsel, the mob leadership staged
an apparent acquiescence to Father O'Reilly by a portion of the crowd that
included his Newburgh parishioners, even as they orchestrated the rest of
the mob to surge behind him into the courthouse. [45] After hanging Mulliner,
the mobbers adopted a resolution to "stand by each other" in the event of
any legal proceeding against the lynchers.[46]

For the Newburgh lynchers, anger at Robert Mulliner's alleged crime against
"one of their countrywomen" melded with an insistence on the inferiority of
blacks and a rage at political relationships that seemed to lessen Irish and elevate
African Americans. Rejecting the speeches of local officials who argued that

the law should be allowed to take its course because Mulliner would most likely receive an extended prison term of at least ten years for his offense, the mob shouted "d—— nagur." Rebuffing a judge who sought to halt the mob's attack on the cell door, the mob decried him as "a d—— Abolitionist, for whom they had not respect."[47] Others in Newburgh interpreted the lynching as a product of Irish grievance and racial prejudice. In a sermon delivered in Newburgh one week after the lynching, the Rev. C. S. Brown, a Methodist Episcopal minister, found an explanation for the mob execution of Mulliner in Irish resentment of nativism, hatred of blacks, and partisan political animosities exacerbated by the war. Brown argued that as a victim of nativism, "the Irishman" had acquired an attitude of "semi-hostility" toward native-born Americans and a corresponding perception "that the law was for him, and not for those who committed offences against him."[48]

The Newburgh mob's explicit rejection of the formal law recapitulated Irish rejection of the legitimacy of British laws, and it initiated a conversation about American constitutionalism, the limits and the legitimacy of the legal order, and popular collective violence that might usurp legal processes. As in Milwaukee, the dialogue over constitutionalism had strong political overtones as Democrats expressed sympathy for the Irish Catholic mob's resort to violence, whereas Republicans unequivocally condemned the racial violence. Some, including a coroner's jury that investigated the death of Mulliner, believed that the city's Democratic newspaper, the *Telegraph,* had actually incited the mob execution by declaring in its reporting of Mulliner's alleged rape of Ellen Clark that the African American "should be hung without a judge or jury as soon as taken."[49] The *Telegraph*'s editor retorted that these critics were partisans allied with the city's Republican newspaper, the *Journal.* The *Telegraph* admitted, however, that its original language had been "injudicious" in light of the violence that followed and expressed regret at the "violation of the public jails and the defiance of the law."[50]

Amid the partisan skirmishing over the lynching, ideological divisions emerged concerning the sanctity of the legal process and under what circumstances lynching violence might be justifiable. The Democratic *Telegraph* argued that, given the severity of Mulliner's crime, a resort to collective murder might have been acceptable if Mulliner had been summarily executed before he had fallen into the hands of the law: that is, before he had been arrested, as this would not have involved an overt rejection of the authority of the criminal justice system.[51] The *Telegraph* asserted that it understood the mob's distrust of the legal process, finding it rooted in a frustration over "the inadequacy of our laws." The Democratic editor explained that "seduction, and rape, and many kindred crimes, are not adequately punished by the laws of this State—that even the Statutes which we have are too frequently practically evaded, by the infliction of the lightest punishment provided or escaped entirely through disagreeing jurors."[52] The Republican *Journal* by contrast could find no palliation for lynching. The *Journal* asserted that "respectable men of all parties" in Newburgh joined in condemning the collective murder and seeking the prosecution of those responsible so that "the majesty of the outraged law shall be vindicated." Emphasizing the importance of adherence to due process law for the protection of society, the Republican editor opined that the aggressive prosecution of the lynchers was the only means to protect the community from a descent into "lawless anarchy."[53]

Just over three years later, the rural Upper Midwest would become the setting for a lynching similarly shaped by the war's social transformations along with the racial politics of Reconstruction. On August 27, in Mason, a village south of Lansing, Michigan, a mob of approximately three hundred white men seized an African American, John Taylor, from jail and hanged him. Taylor had quarreled over wages with the white farmer, John Buck, who employed him and had left to work for other white farmers in the neighborhood, but allegedly returned one night to attack Buck's wife, mother-in-law, and daughter with an axe. Subsequent press reports suggested that all of the women recovered from their wounds and asserted that the lynchers came from "intensely 'Democratic' and anti-negro" districts south of Lansing.[54]

John Taylor was an eighteen-year-old "mulatto" African American whose life had been fundamentally altered by the Civil War and Reconstruction. Taylor had been born into slavery in Kentucky, to a slave mother impregnated by her owner, but during the Civil War had been "captured" by Northern troops and had become a servant to a chaplain from Hillsdale, Michigan. Building on the ties to Michigan that he had formed through his association with the Union Army, Taylor served in a Michigan negro regiment, and then returned to Michigan to work in Jackson County for a guardian appointed by the Union Army. The guardian was to hold the bounty of five hundred dollars that Taylor had received for his military service until Taylor reached the age of twenty-one. However, Taylor did not get along with his guardian's sons and left his employ to eventually "hire out" to a white farmer, John Buck. Taylor quarreled with Buck over wages, with Buck refusing to pay him the full amount owed after he quit, a dispute that precipitated Taylor's alleged attack on Buck's female relatives and his ensuing death at the hands of a mob of white lynchers.[55]

The lynching of John Taylor exposed ideological fault lines in a central Michigan community recovering from the war and deeply divided over race, law, and Reconstruction politics.[56] In 1860, the U.S. Census had enumerated thirty-seven "free colored persons" in Ingham County, the majority of them residents of the city of Lansing, comprising a mere 0.2 percent of the county's population.[57] Over the next decade, under the influence of the war's transformations, Ingham County's African American population expanded modestly to include a meaningful black presence in rural farming areas outside of Lansing. By 1870, the U.S. Census tallied 158 blacks in the county, just under half of them residents of Lansing, comprising 0.6 percent of the county's residents.[58] Many of the lynchers were apparently from lilywhite Delhi Township, the community nearest the Buck farmstead. John Buck himself participated in the mob's interrogation of Taylor before the execution, forcing the African American to state that he had been compensated fairly for his labor and demanding that he tell what had led him to "chop my family to pieces."[59] As the mob manhandled Taylor before lynching him, it shouted racial epithets, such as "d——d nigger."[60] The Republican press in Michigan deplored the actions of the lynchers, finding an explanation for the mob's actions in the deep-seated racial prejudices of the "Copper Johnson" Democrats (supporters of anti-Lincoln Copperheadism during the war and now President Andrew Johnson's conciliatory Reconstruction policies, against which Republicans were coalescing) living in the vicinity. Delhi Township would indeed prove a stronghold for the Democrats in the November 1866 election, sustaining Democratic majorities despite a state- and county-wide Republican tide. However, the lynching hurt Democrats in Ingham County. The Democratic candidate for sheriff, allied with the outgoing Democratic sheriff who some had argued had done little to prevent the mob killing, lost to a Republican in the November election.[61]

White Michiganders' perspectives on the mob murder of Taylor cleaved along cultural and partisan lines, evincing ideological stances on race, class, and law forged by intense Reconstruction politics. Republican editors opined that the lynchers were, generally, lawless and bigoted ne'er-do-wells, at one with President Johnson's policy of "sustaining rebels in opposing the law," an approach to Reconstruction that they argued had recently resulted in murderous race riots targeting the African American populations of Memphis and New Orleans, and which had now precipitated racial violence in the rural North.[62] Republican editors asserted that the mob had little reason to believe that Taylor would not serve the full legal penalty for his crime, and that the lynching constituted a damaging, embarrassing, and uncivilized "defiance of all law."[63] A day after the collective killing, a meeting of citizens of Mason, the village where the mob had seized Taylor from jail, adopted resolutions condemning the lynching for its "disregard of law" and violation "of all law and good order."[64] Defenders of the lynchers argued differently, insisting that the gravity of the crime and Taylor's status as a "negro" demanded a harsher punishment than Michigan law provided. The editor of the *Eaton Rapids Journal* asserted that the legal punishment for Taylor's alleged crime, perhaps twenty years in prison, was not sufficient given the heinous nature of his attack on the women, particularly in light of Taylor's youth and the possibility that he might commit further crimes after serving a prison term. Given these circumstances, the Eaton Rapids editor found the lynchers' actions justifiable.[65] Refuting the Eaton Rapids journalist, a Grand Rapids editor retorted that the lynching had disgraced Michigan, displaying a low cultural level in which the lynchers had been no more able to control their "passions" than had their victim, John Taylor. Indulging the humanitarian perfectionist ideals that had informed antebellum reform movements and that would soon fuel the egalitarian thrust of Congressional Reconstruction, the Grand Rapids editor expressed sympathy for the "poor, ignorant boy" who had been lynched, arguing that Taylor was more understandably prone to passionate violence than the adult white men who had lynched him.[66]

The lynchings in Milwaukee in 1861; Newburgh, New York, in 1863; and Ingham County, Michigan, in 1866, indicate how the sectional crisis, the Civil War, and the early years of Reconstruction had destabilized and reconfigured northern political culture and social relations. Even as Republicans argued for a more powerful, activist state that might halt the expansion of slavery and then extend rights to African Americans, working class Irish and rural Democrats in the North resisted a government that might use legal authority to weaken white supremacy in a society organized around principles of free labor. In events that paralleled in miniature southern whites' resort to racial terror against African Americans in Reconstruction, working class and rural northern Democrats turned to the racial violence of lynching as they sought to reject Republican racial egalitarianism and to reassert racial hierarchy. The Lower Midwest, a cultural and political borderland of the South that shared some of its racial and antistatist views, would witness a similar reaction against the racial equality espoused by the expanding Reconstruction state. Whites lynched seven African Americans after accusations of murder and rape in central and southern counties of Illinois, Indiana, and Ohio from 1871 through 1877.[67]

The South

Historians have perceptively interpreted the emergence in the South of highly organized, often politically motivated terrorist violence that sought to wage a "Counterrevolution" against Congressional Reconstruction. Such terrorist violence was often perpetrated by vigilante groups such as the Ku Klux Klan.[68] Scholars have done less to analyze the emergence of less orchestrated, everyday collective violence by whites against African Americans across the South in the 1860s and '70s, although important studies of Kentucky, central Texas, South Carolina, Mississippi, and Louisiana have begun to fill in the picture.[69] The historian Gilles Vandal has exhaustively documented the ubiquity of collective homicide in Reconstruction Louisiana. Vandal has charted 402 cases of collective murder between 1865 and 1876, locating geographic concentrations of lethal collective activity in the Red River Delta of northwest Louisiana and in the Sugarland of south Louisiana, and particular temporal concentrations in 1868 and 1874, years of highly racialized politics in which conservative white Democrats sought to dislodge ruling white and black Republicans. Vandal finds that whites committed most acts of collective violence (85%), and that in two-thirds of cases of Reconstruction-era collective killings, whites murdered blacks (68.7%). Political motivations underlay more than one-third of collective killings in Louisiana in Reconstruction, whereas just under one-third of collective murders in Reconstruction entailed a response to criminal activities.[70] Lynchings that targeted individual blacks accused of criminal offenses[71] were an important manifestation of endemic collective violence during Reconstruction. Vandal documents that 124 blacks and 46 whites died at the hands of lynchers from 1866 through 1876, a far higher rate of lynching than occurred in the succeeding years of the early Redemption era, when 47 blacks and 22 whites died at the hands of mobs from 1877 through 1884. As with the more general geographical distribution of Reconstruction violence, lynching was particularly concentrated in the Red River Delta and in the Sugarland.[72] Vandal also identifies thirty-three vigilance committees that employed coercion and violence against purported criminals during Reconstruction in Louisiana, with vigilantism concentrated in the Sugarland as a response to cattle thievery.[73] Vandal convincingly argues that lynching became a means by which whites responded to the challenges African Americans made to white supremacy in Reconstruction, and that lynching violence became "an important political instrument in insuring that Louisiana remained a 'white-man's country.'"[74]

Informed by Vandal's deep and valuable excavation of lynching and collective murder in Reconstruction Louisiana, the analysis that follows examines the transformation of lynching violence in Louisiana from 1866 through 1876, exploring how contemporaries sought to interpret the function of rampant collective violence in the context of emancipation and Reconstruction. The transformation of social and political relationships in Louisiana in the Civil

War and emancipation led Louisianans to draw upon significant traditions of collective violence within new circumstances and to recraft collective murder as a weapon in what would become a prolonged contest for political, legal, and racial authority. In the antebellum era, mobs of white Louisianans had occasionally killed slaves.[75] Antebellum Louisiana experienced additional varieties of vigilantism. For example, near Shreveport in 1859, slaveholders' anxiety over the theft of slaves led to the mob hanging of a white man identified as "Etherington or Henry." Shreveport-area planters had transported the alleged slave thief back from New Orleans, where he had been arrested for seeking to sell slaves that had disappeared from Caddo Parish.[76] Late antebellum vigilante violence sometimes displayed a more intricate pattern. In an Acadian variation on the intracommunal conflicts for power and social status that plagued the southern, midwestern, and western frontiers in the antebellum era (which were analyzed in chapter 2), an extensive vigilante movement led by Acadian landholders in southwest Louisiana in 1859 targeted lower class white deviants and sparked "antivigilante campaigns" by landless and yeomen whites and an ensuing bloodbath in 1859–60. Eventually local vigilantes also directed their efforts against free persons of color. But patterns of collective violence began to shift significantly with the Civil War and emancipation. During the war, the region saw prolonged guerilla violence between "Jayhawkers," who supported the Union and allied with Creoles of Color and ex-slaves, and Confederate supporters.[77] Significantly, during the war and after, vigilante bands also made freed people their targets throughout Louisiana, seeking to reassert the racial control altered by emancipation.

The emergence of systematic postwar antiblack violence can be seem most vividly in Franklin Parish, where in October 1866 ex-Confederate guerillas organized as the "Black Cavalry" to discipline black labor upon plantations and to regulate the movement of African Americans. When freed persons retaliated by murdering a vigilante named Mr. Price, who had on several occasions "in disguise with a blackened face" taken blacks from "negro quarters" on a plantation and flogged them, a disguised band of white regulators "lynched" eight blacks, hanging two of them and removing the rest from the vicinity, apparently killing them.[78] A Union Army colonel, S. M. Quincey, investigated conditions in Franklin Parish and reported that African American lives were "much less safe throughout this section of the country since emancipation than during the existence of slavery." Quincey related a conversation with a Black River planter who had whipped a freedman for running away, and then had flogged him again for threatening to "tell the Yankees." The planter said he had told "his negroes that while they were slaves he would not kill even on great provocation, as he thereby destroyed his own or another's property—'But now' said he 'you are nobody's property' and damn you 'look out.'"[79]

In Presidential Reconstruction, as Union troops and Freedmen's Bureau agents sought to supervise an uneasy transition from slavery, planter vigilante intimidation of black laborers worked in tandem with courts to control African American lives and labor. Colonel Quincey interviewed Judge Thomas Crawford, who had recently held session at Winnsboro and who would later be assassinated by white conservative vigilantes. Crawford acknowledged that no jury in the parish would convict a white man accused of assaulting a black man, and that legal authorities had taken no action in response to the "many instances of the murder of freedmen" in the parish, but the judge asserted that the theft of African American property would be punished as swiftly as the theft of the property of whites.[80] Similar dynamics were at work in Bienville Parish in August 1866. A Union Army captain, N. B. Blanton, reported numerous "outrages" committed by whites against freed persons, including severe floggings administered by vigilantes known as "nighthaulkers" in the western portion of the parish in the vicinity of Ringgold and Lake Bastineau. An African American victim of a vigilante whipping, Green Jones, told Blanton that the Regulators had said that "they would not allow negroes to live off by themselves" or to possess horses. Blanton attributed the violence to the nearly complete failure of the crops, and noted that white public opinion was against enforcement of "the laws against the whites for the protection of the colored people" and thus beatings of African Americans were ignored.[81] Although some of the patterns were similar, racial violence could take on more complex meanings in Acadian districts of southwest Louisiana. In St. Landry Parish in 1867 and 1868, for example, outlaws Benjamin and Cyriaque Guillory orchestrated collective murders of freedmen with ties to planters that they viewed as their social enemies.[82]

As conservative Louisiana whites initiated collective violence against freed persons to reverse the fact of emancipation, Louisianans also reworked practices of lynching violence embodying antebellum notions of communal order, honor, skepticism of law, and neighborhood sovereignty amid an atmosphere of postwar social disorder and legal uncertainty. For example, in April 1866, in Morehouse Parish, a man named Carrigo stabbed his wife to death. A mob seized Carrigo from jail and hanged him.[83] In another example, on September 1873, a vigilance committee reported to include three hundred members hanged twelve alleged cattle thieves in Vermilion Parish. Press reports asserted that the lethal vigilantism was a response to endemic stock theft in Vermilion and the inability of "the people . . . to obtain redress by process of law." [84] Though nonracial lynchings, instances of whites lynching whites and blacks lynching blacks,[85] would persist in postbellum Louisiana, in the context of emancipation and Reconstruction, white Louisianans shaped a praxis of lethal collective violence that was predominantly racial in motivation, seeking to use lynching violence to demarcate the boundaries of African American autonomy, assertion, and resistance within a novel and complex political and legal order.

Louisiana's political landscape shifted dramatically in 1868 with the adoption of a Radical constitution and the election of a Republican governor, the Yankee migrant Henry Clay Warmoth. The transfer of power to the Radicals and the contest over the impending November presidential election precipitated a wide-scale "Counter Reconstruction" across the state as conservative white Louisianans mobilized against the Radical Republicans by forming paramilitary organizations that included the Knights of the White Camelia, the Ku Klux Klan, the Swamp Fox Rangers, the Seymour Knights, and the Hancock Guards.[86] Conservative whites unleashed a vast wave of violence against African Americans and white Republican Unionists in 1868, murdering hundreds, and perhaps more than a thousand persons.[87] On August 1, Warmoth fruitlessly beseeched President Johnson to dispatch more federal troops for the purpose of suppressing "disorder and violence, arresting criminals, and protecting criminals, and protecting the officers of the law in trying them" as well as for "the breaking up of all secret political organizations."[88]

White conservatives interpreted the violence differently, through a lens of racial republicanism that argued that the Radicals, elected through the enfranchisement of African American men, had taken power illegitimately and that resistance to them by native white citizens was valid. The *New Orleans Daily Picayune* voiced the white conservative stance in response to Governor Warmoth's letter to President Johnson. Flatly denying the extent of the political and racial violence that was occurring across Louisiana, the *Picayune* nonetheless articulated a white conservative rationale for extralegal collective violence that might accomplish purposes that could not be achieved through formal legal and political processes. In an editorial headlined "Radicalism Is the Fomenter of Lawlessness," the *Picayune* asserted that virtually all violence occurring in the state stemmed from private quarrels, not political differences. The *Picayune* argued that rampant lawlessness in Louisiana resulted from the fact that white Louisianans simply could not respect and support law and government as it existed under Radical rule.

> The fact is, the law and its administrators must be respectable, to be respected.
> If it be without warrant, or be imposed by force, it cannot expect to be regarded

with favor. If in addition to this it is imposed and exercised by men of low moral
character, be used to fill the pockets of strangers with the hard earned gatherings
of increased toils and diminished gains, and if the perpetual taunt of treason
and continued threat of further confiscation and debasement be the only reply
to complaint of these exactions and wrongs, it is no wonder that men will stand
aloof when law thus enacted and administered calls for aid to support it.[89]

As political violence ebbed and flowed in Reconstruction, surging significantly, for example, with the Colfax Massacre of black Republicans in April
1873 and again in 1874 with the homicidal campaign of the White League
against black and white Radicals,[90] lynching violence in Louisiana moved in
parallel, becoming increasingly racialized and routinized. As emancipation
had erased the formal controls whites had exercised over blacks in slavery,
whites turned to regulator violence that reasserted white authority over African American labor and mobility. As Radical Reconstruction supplanted
conservative native white control of political offices and courts, conservative
Louisiana whites deployed individual and collective violence that sought to
destroy the Radicals and their goal of racially egalitarian political administration and courts. The Radicals' control of courts and their reformist faith in
neutral, racially color-blind legal process became for conservative whites the
very symbol of what they had lost in Reconstruction, the ability to control
local politics and legal culture.[91] Accordingly, for many white Louisianans
lynching became an alternative means of exercising control over the local
social order, and especially a means for policing African American resistance
and criminality.

Lynching had become a normal part of the social landscape by the early
1870s, a seemingly typical response to allegations of African American deviancy. In January 1873, in Claiborne Parish, a large mob executed Henry
Moore, an African American whom they accused of raping and murdering
a white woman, Mrs. Kidd. The mob, reportedly consisting of whites and
blacks, seized Moore from men who were conveying him to legal authorities, tied him to a pine tree, and burned him.[92] In an incident displaying the
racial and political complexity of the postbellum Sugarland, in Iberia Parish,
in June 1873, a mob reported at more than a thousand hanged three African
American men accused of robbing and murdering two men who operated a
store together, Daniel Lanet, a white Creole, and Alexander Snaer, a Creole of
Color who held the office of justice of the peace. Alexander Snaer's brother,
Louis, served as representative for Iberia Parish in the state legislature. Another brother of Snaer's, Seymour, an attorney, conducted an investigation
that found the accused men guilty. Seymour Snaer sought to dissuade the

mob from lynching the three black men, and he left the scene before the mob execution.[93] In Grant Parish in November 1873, whites killed at least four African Americans accused of raping two white women. The incident became heavily enmeshed in Reconstruction politics, as conservative whites asserted that the New Orleans Metropolitan Police, dispatched to Grant Parish to assist the deputy U.S. marshal, were complicit in African American criminality in the parish.[94] In response to the rape allegation but prior to the mob killings, a meeting of whites at Alexandria endorsed resolutions mimicking the Radical emphasis on racial equality but rejecting the validity of the Radical state government of Louisiana and asserting the legitimacy of extralegal violence that defended white interests. " . . . we understand the Government under which we live is for the protection of the white people as well as the black, that the white people have at least as many rights as the black, and all have the same duty of obedience to law to observe, and if those having or claiming authority do not dispense equal justice to both races, we shall take care of ourselves and of those to whom we owe protection."[95]

The 1873 lynchings reveal how the experience of Reconstruction had transformed collective killing into a standard weapon in the social control arsenal of postbellum white Louisianans. Social disorder, the disruption of native white political control and white supremacy, and the thorough reconstitution of political and legal authority helped to legitimize extensive homicidal collective violence. By the mid-1870s, lynching had become a central means by which white Louisianans responded to African American criminality and resistance. For example, in July 1874, near Shreveport, a mob seized an African American man from a posse and killed him. The mob's victim, unnamed in a press report, had allegedly murdered a planter, George Simpson.[96] In another example, in 1875, in East Feliciana Parish, mobs shot John Gair and hanged his sister-in-law for attempting to poison their white employer.[97] Even though the scale of the violence would diminish as conservative whites reclaimed power after the election of 1876, the implication of Reconstruction, which was that collective killing might better serve purposes of racial control than courts or formal politics could, would persist for decades in Louisiana and across the South, providing the ideological and cultural groundwork for the lynching of thousands of African Americans in the late nineteenth and early twentieth centuries.[98]

Epilogue

The conflict between rough justice and due process sentiments persisted for decades after Reconstruction in the American regions beyond the Alleghenies. Vividly remembering Reconstruction as an era in which they had lost control of criminal courts and political offices, many white southerners turned once again to collective murder outside the law amid racial and political conflict shaped by the depressed cotton economy of the 1890s. In a contagion of collective murder that was less overtly political and less systematically organized but even more racial than the collective violence of Reconstruction, lynching became a prime means of punishing black resistance and criminality for white southerners skeptical of the efficacy of law and legal processes in the perpetuation of racial order in the New South. Southern urbanization and industrialization at the turn of the twentieth century catalyzed anxieties over racial mixing and in some cases evoked large-scale spectacle lynchings, but eventually a southern middle class coalesced against mob violence. Embarrassed by the increasing spotlight African American activists and a nationalizing culture shone upon lynching and fearing the loss of investment that might promote economic growth and prosperity in the region, middle class white southerners in the early twentieth century pressed instead for "legal lynchings," expedited trials and executions that merged legal forms with the popular clamor for rough justice. As the frequency of lynchings in the South plummeted in the middle decades of the twentieth century, the practice went underground as lynchers no longer acted in large public mobs but instead in small, secretive groups that murdered in an expression of racial intimidation that by the late twentieth century was more often called a hate crime than a lynching.[1]

The Midwest and the West were not as directly burdened by the legacy of antebellum racial slavery, and the trajectory of rough justice and lynching took different forms in those regions. North and west of Dixie, the practice slowly waned after the Reconstruction period but persisted into the middle decades of the twentieth century, occasionally reviving after allegations of particularly heinous crimes and under the influence of events such as the Mexican Revolution (precipitating the lynching of persons of Mexican descent), World War I (the racial leveling of the war inspired the lynching of African Americans in several northern locales, while nativist and antiradical sentiment informed acts of collective murder in the West and the Midwest), and the social tensions of the Great Depression. In the Midwest and West, as in the South, legislators reshaped the death penalty in the early twentieth century to make capital punishment more efficient and more racial, achieving a compromise between the observation of legal forms long emphasized by due process advocates and the lethal, ritualized retribution long sought by rough justice supporters. Thus, as lynching came from the early modern death penalty, the modern death penalty came from lynching; the contemporary American death penalty carries forth the cultural legacy of the battle over rough justice and due process that marked the United States' distinctive path during the long nineteenth century, with the United States constituting the only major western nation that retains the death penalty today. The United States, however, is not distinctive in its lynching.[2]

In recent decades, group killing across global cultures has, like American lynching in the long nineteenth century, reflected ambivalence about alterations in law and social values and rejection of seemingly ineffectual legal regimes that ostensibly do not offer sufficient protections for the property or security of particular communities. Though most recent group killings across cultures do not stem in any direct way from the extended nineteenth-century American contestation of law and cultural change, contemporary collective killing across global cultures often flows from local dynamics contesting the anxieties and ambiguities of legal change in the context of decentralized, weak, or fragmented states. Reflecting American linguistic influences, such collective murders have sometimes been labeled with the appellation *lynching* in local media and in Anglo-American press coverage.

Group killings invoking concerns about rampant crime have flourished across Latin America in recent decades. Researchers have documented 482 *linchamientos* (acts of vigilantism that include collective killings as well as group violence falling short of group murder) in Guatemala from 1996 to 2002, 103 such acts in Mexico from 1987 through 1998, 164 in Venezuela in 2000 and 2001, and 30 such incidents in Cochabamba, Bolivia, in 2001. In

Guatemala, enormous crowds have burned, stoned, and hanged to death many victims, the majority accused of minor offenses such as theft. Guatemalan lynchers have often staged informal trials of their victims, simultaneously denounced the government and formal justice systems, and sought to publicize their resort to communal violence through the media. A scholar of Guatemalan and Latin American lynching violence argues that the actions of Guatemalan lynchers take meaning as grassroots justice by disenfranchised indigenous populations shaped by cultures of violence waged for decades by a genocidal state, angered by slow, unrepresentative, and ineffectual state courts, deprived by the erosion of traditional nonviolent indigenous forms of dispute mediation, and profoundly affected by the economic and social dislocations wrought by neoliberal, market-oriented development policies and globalization. In this view, the rise of highly ritualized collective murder in Latin America in recent years represents not a throwback to traditional indigenous modes of justice, but rather a perverse response by marginalized rural and urban communities to legal and social conditions caused by radically incomplete and inequitable democratization across Latin America.[3]

Vigilantism and group murder has also flourished across sub-Saharan Africa in recent years. In South Africa, numerous autonomous vigilante organizations, both well-organized and loosely formed, arose in the 1970s and '80s in black neighborhoods in response to the neglect of the townships by the apartheid regime. With the end of apartheid and the transition to a democratic constitutionalist government in 1994, vigilantism has persisted amid concerns about rampant crime. Mixing traditional notions and practices with shifts in social and legal circumstances, groups of South Africa vigilantes have fined and lashed some of their victims, but have also killed many of them by necklacing (execution by placing a tire filled with gasoline over the shoulders and neck and lighting it on fire), shooting, macheteing, stabbing, and stoning. Punishing those accused of theft, murder, rape, and witchcraft, among other offenses, South Africa vigilantes killed 137 persons between January 1999 and March 2000.[4] Supporters of South African vigilantism typically argue that it "upholds the values of compensatory justice, immediate justice, and capital/corporal justice." In contrast, they deride the formal criminal justice system, with its concern for individual and human rights, for its inefficiency and ineffectiveness.[5] Nonstate policing and violence has similarly thrived in recent years in postcolonial West Africa. In Nigeria, vigilante organizations with only a tenuous relationship to the official state have flowered amid fears of rising crime, complaints about a weak and slow criminal justice system, and ubiquitous police corruption. In Anambra State, one such group, the Anambra Vigilante Service, also known as the Bakassi Boys, reportedly extralegally executed 130 robbers after its formation in the late 1990s, decapitating many of them and setting their corpses afire, transposing an older Nigerian tradition of collectively immolating suspected robbers alive.[6] Vigilantism similarly surfaced in the latter decades of the twentieth century in pastoral societies in East Africa. In eastern Uganda, vigilante gangs arose in the 1960s to apprehend, try, and execute thieves and witches after the government transferred law enforcement authority from local chiefs to distant police posts and magistrates' courts. In the early 1980s, in northwest Tanzania, village vigilantes captured, tried, and, in some cases, lethally punished (with poison arrows) cattle thieves and witches in a rejection of what they viewed as inadequate and corrupt police and of alien "state values" regarding criminality, its adjudication, and its punishment. In both Uganda and Tanzania, the state eventually co-opted vigilantes by formalizing them into official agents of state law enforcement.[7]

Group killing has also occurred in the wake of the social and legal disorder engendered by catastrophic natural events, albeit in the context of much longer histories of informal violence and popular distrust of brutal, unreliable, and corrupt police forces. In January 2010, a powerful earthquake leveled Port-au-Prince, Haiti, killing approximately three hundred thousand persons, destroying much of the government and law enforcement apparatus, and emptying the city's prison of inmates. Several days after the earthquake, police turned over a man they said they had arrested for looting to a growing crowd. As the police officers watched, the crowd stripped the alleged looter, beat him severely, improvised a pyre by piling trash, and burned the man to death. A week later, another crowd in the devastated capital stoned an alleged thief to death.[8]

In short, the practice of collective murder is as old and as new as anything in human societies, but the phenomenon of lynching motivated by notions of criminal justice, ethnicity, or race over the last several hundred years can most aptly be interpreted as a response to legal and cultural change in the context of contested, fragile or decentralized states, not least of them the southern, midwestern, and western regions of the United States during the long nineteenth century.

Appendix

Lists of Confirmed Lynchings

Lynchings of African Americans in the South, 1824–1862

Status
U = unknown; S = male slave; F = free black male; FS = female slave

Method
B = burning; H = hanging; S = shooting; U = unknown

State	County / Locale and/or County	Date	Name	Status	Alleged Offense	Method	Source
AL	Near Mobile	5/1835	"Negro"	U	Murdered children	B	James Elbert Cutler, *Lynch-Law and Investigation into the History of Lynching in the United States* (New York: Longman, Green, and Co., 1905), 108; source: *Liberator*, July 4, 1835.
AL	Near Mobile	5/1835	"Negro"	U	Murdered children	B	Cutler, *Lynch-Law*, 108; source: *Liberator*, July 4, 1835.
AL	Mount Meigs, Montgomery Co.	8/1854	"Negro of Dr. McDonald"	S	Murder of master	B	James Benson Sellers, *Slavery in Alabama* (1940; repr., Tuscaloosa: University of Alabama Press, 1994), 262–264.
AL	Sumter Co.	5/1855	"negro man"	U	Murder and rape	B	*New York Times*, June 2, 1855; Sellers, *Slavery in Alabama*, 263.
AL	Clayton, Barbour Co.	8/6/1855	"Bob"	S	Unknown	H	Sellers, *Slavery in Alabama*, 263–264.
AL	Near Tuskegee, Macon Co.	10/9/1860	"boy belonging to Maj. Cocke"	S	Unknown	B	Sellers, *Slavery in Alabama*, 264.
AR	Phillips Co.	1849	Unknown	S	Murder of master	B	Orville W. Taylor, *Negro Slavery in Arkansas* (Durham, N.C.: Duke University Press, 1958), 235.
AR	Phillips Co.	1849	Unknown	S	Murder of master	B	Taylor, *Negro Slavery in Arkansas*, 235.
AR	Hot Spring County	1836	"William"	S	Murder of master, another white man, and 5 slaves	B	Taylor, *Negro Slavery in Arkansas*, 235–236.

Lynchings of African Americans in the South, 1824–1862 (cont.)

State	Locale and/or County	Date	Name	Status	Alleged Offense	Method	Source
AR	Chicot Co.	1857	Unknown	U	Murder and rape	B	Bertram Wyatt-Brown, *Southern Honor: Ethics and Behavior in the Old South* (New York: Oxford University Press, 1982), 389, 564n38; source: *Fuller Diary*, October 16, November 15, 1857. *Boston Liberator*, October 16, December 4, 1857.
AR	Chicot Co.	1857	Unknown	U	Murder and rape	B	Wyatt-Brown, *Southern Honor*, 389, 564n38; source: *Fuller Diary*, October 16, November 15, 1857. *Boston Liberator*, October 16, December 4, 1857.
GA	Columbus	1851	"Jarrett"	S	Rape	H	Ralph Betts Flanders, *Plantation Slavery in Georgia* (Chapel Hill: University of North Carolina Press, 1933), 268–269.
GA	"Georgia's plantation belt"	1861	"George"	S	Rape	B	Martha Hodes, *White Women, Black Men: Illicit Sex in the 19th-Century-South* (New Haven, Conn.: Yale University Press, 1997), 58; source: *Daily Sun* (Columbus, Ga.), February 22, 29, 1861.
LA	East Feliciana Parish	1842	"two runaways"	S	Murder, rape, and kidnapping	B	Wyatt-Brown, *Southern Honor*, 388–389, 564n38; source: Davis, *Barrow Diary*, June 17, 1842, p. 262.
LA	East Feliciana Parish	1842	two runaways	S	Murder, rape, and kidnapping	B	Wyatt-Brown, *Southern Honor*, 388–389, 564n38; source: Davis, *Barrow Diary*, June 17, 1842, p. 262.
LA	Unknown	10/1858	"Free negro"	F	Rape and murder of white child	U	H.E. Sterkx, *The Free Negro in Ante-Bellum Louisiana* (Rutherford, N.J.: Fairleigh Dickinson, N.J., 1972), 189–190; source: *New Orleans Bee*, October 9, 1858.
KY	Louisville	1857	"George"	S	Murder	H	Cutler, *Lynch-Law*, 125; source: *Liberator*, October 16, 1857.
KY	Louisville	1857	"Bill"	S	Murder	H	Cutler, *Lynch-Law*, 125; source: *Liberator*, October 16, 1857.
KY	near Peak's Mill, Franklin Co.	1/1862	Slave of "Miss Pearce"	S	Rape and murderous assault	H	*New York Times*, Jan. 14, 1862.
MD	Denton, Caroline Co.	10/1854	Dave Thomas	F	Murder	H	*Baltimore Republican and Argus*, October 10, 1854.

Lynchings of African Americans in the South, 1824–1862 (cont.)

State	Locale and/or County	Date	Name	Status	Alleged Offense	Method	Source
MS	Near Union Point	1841?	"runaway slave"	S	Murder, rape, and robbery	B	Christopher Waldrep, ed., *Lynching in America: A History in Documents* (New York: New York University Press, 2006), 76–77, source: *Mississippi Free Trader*, March 8, 1854.
MS	Near Union Point	1841?	"runaway slave"	S	Murder, rape, and robbery	B	Waldrep, ed., *Lynching in America*, 76–77, source: *Mississippi Free Trader*, March 8, 1854.
MS	Near Gallatin, Copiah Co.	2/1843	"negro men . . . of Mr. Burdy"	S	Rape, murderous assault, and robbery	H	*Courier de La Louisiane* (*Louisiana Courier*), March 1, 1843.
MS	Near Gallatin,	2/1843	"negro men . . . of Mr. Burdy"	S	Rape, murderous assault, and robbery	H	*Courier de La Louisiane* (*Louisiana Courier*), March 1, 1843.
MO	St. Louis	4/28/1836	Francis L. McʻIntosh	F	Murder of deputy sheriff, stabbed deputy constable	B	Janet S. Hermann, "The McIntosh Affair," *Bulletin of the Missouri Historical Society* 26 (January 1970): 123–143; John F. Darby, *Personal Recollections* (St. Louis: G. I. Jones and Company, 1880): 237–241.
MO	Near Peverly, Jefferson Co.	1842?	"negro"	U	Murder and robbery	H	Goodspeed's History of Franklin, Jefferson, Washington, Crawford, & Gasconade Counties, Missouri (Chicago: The Goodspeed Publishing Co, 1888), 405; http://www.rootsweb.ancestry.com/~nebuffal/jeffcomo/courts.htm.
MO	Franklin Co.	4/1847	"Eli"	S	Murder and attempted rape of white woman, attempt to kill her son	U	Harrison Anthony Trexler, *Slavery in Missouri 1804–1865* (Baltimore: The John Hopkins Press, 1914), 254n61; source: History of Franklin, Jefferson, Washington, Crawford and Gasconade Counties, 283.
MO	Clay Co.	5/1850	"slave woman"	FS	Assaulted mistress w/ an ax	H	R. Douglas Hurt, *Agriculture and Slavery in Missouri's Little Dixie* (Columbia, Mo.: University of Missouri Press, 1992), 248; source: *Missouri Statesman* (Columbia), May 24, 1850; Trexler, *Slavery in Missouri 1804–1865*, 254n61; source: *History of Clay and Platte Counties* (St. Louis, 1885), 158–159.
MO	Boone Co.	8/1853	"a slave"	S	Attempted rape	H	Hurt, *Agriculture and Slavery in Missouri's Little Dixie*, 249; source: *Weekly Tribune* (Liberty, Mo.), September 2, 1853.

Lynchings of African Americans in the South, 1824–1862 (cont.)

State	Locale and/or County	Date	Name	Status	Alleged Offense	Method	Source
MO	Carroll Co.	10/1855	Slave of Judge Thomas Clingman	S	Murder of master	H	*New York Times*, October 16, 1855.
MO	Troy, Lincoln Co.	1/1/1859	"negro" of "Mr. Simeon Thornhill"	S	Murder of master	B	*Maysville Eagle* (Maysville, Ky.), January 8, 1859.
MO	Arrow Rock, Saline Co.	7/18/1859	"slave belonging to Dr. William Price"	S	Assaulted white girl	H	Thomas G. Dyer, "A Most Unexampled Exhibition of Madness and Brutality: Judge Lynch in Saline County, Missouri," in *Under Sentence of Death: Lynching in the South*, ed. W. Fitzhugh Brundage (Chapel Hill: University of North Carolina Press, 1997), 87.
MO	Marshall, Saline Co.	7/20/1859	"John"	S	Murder	B	Hurt, *Agriculture and Slavery in Missouri's Little Dixie*, 250; source: *Glasgow Weekly Times* (Glasgow, Mo.), July 21, 1859; Dyer, "A Most Unexampled Exhibition of Madness and Brutality," 87.
MO	Marshall, Saline Co.	7/20/1859	"Jim"	S	Attempted rape	H	Hurt, *Agriculture and Slavery in Missouri's Little Dixie*, 250; source: *Glasgow Weekly Times*, July 21, 1859; Dyer, "A Most Unexampled Exhibition of Madness and Brutality," 87.
MO	Marshall, Saline Co.	7/20/1859	Holman	S	Had allegedly stabbed white man	H	Hurt, *Agriculture and Slavery in Missouri's Little Dixie*, 250; source: *Glasgow Weekly Times*, July 21, 1859; Dyer, "A Most Unexampled Exhibition of Madness and Brutality," 87.
MO	Callaway County	11/1860	Unknown	FS	Murder of young white woman	H	*St. Louis Bulletin*, November 8, 1860, quoted in *Santa Fe Gazette*, December 15, 1860.
NC	Unknown	Unknown	"slave"	S	Rape of slaveholder's daughter	B	Diane Miller Sommerville, *Race and Rape in the Nineteenth-Century South* (Chapel Hill: University of North Carolina Press, 2004), 29–30; source: p. 270n55 cites Guion Griffis Johnson, *Antebellum North Carolina*, p. 508.
NC	Unknown	1840	"runaway slaves"	S	Cattle theft, murder of member of posse	S	David Grimsted, *American Mobbing, 1828–1861: Toward Civil War* (New York: Oxford University Press, 1998), 111–112; 311n72; sources: *Wilmington Chronicle* in *Fayetteville Observer*, January 13, 1840; *Raleigh Register* in *Liberator*, January 22, 1841.

Lynchings of African Americans in the South, 1824–1862 (cont.)

State	Locale and/or County	Date	Name	Status	Alleged Offense	Method	Source
NC	Unknown	1840	"runaway slaves"	S	Cattle theft, murder of member of posse	S	Grimsted, American Mobbing, 1828-1861, 111–112, 311n72; sources: Wilmington Chronicle in Fayetteville Observer, January 13, 1840; Raleigh Register in Liberator, January 22, 1841.
SC	Charleston	1824	"young slave"	S	Murder	B	Christopher Waldrep, The Many Faces of Judge Lynch: Extralegal Violence and Punishment in America (New York: Palgrave Macmillan, 2002); source: Adam Hodgson, Letters from North America Written During a Tour in the United States and Canada (London, 1824), 188.
SC	Interior of state	1861	"favorite household servants"	S	"Revolt"/murder of master's family	B	New York Times, December 1, 1861.
SC	Interior of state	1861	"favorite household servants"	S	"Revolt"/murder of master's family	B	New York Times, December 1, 1861.
TN	Unknown	1854	Unknown	U	Murder and rape of white woman	B	Hodes, White Women, Black Men, 58; source: New York Daily Tribune, July 4, and 11, 1854.
TN	Near La Grange	1855	"negro boy . . . belonging to Mr. Wm. Turner"	S	Murder of overseer	H	Waldrep, ed., Lynching in America, 74; source: Boston Liberator, October 19, 1855.
TN	Near Sparta	9/1855	"runaway negro"	S	Murder of woman	H	Waldrep, ed., Lynching in America, 74; source: Boston Liberator, October 19, 1855.
TN	Near Rogersville?	1857	"negro"	U	"sundry foul, revolting, and hellish crimes"	B	New York Times, Sept. 17, 1857.
TX	Near Fannin	1854	"negro woman"	FS	Murder of mistress and mistress's 2 children	H	Frederick Law Olmstead, The Cotton Kingdom; A Traveler's Observations on Cotton and Slavery in the American Slave States (New York: Alfred A. Knopf, 1953; repr., New York: Da Capo Press, 1996), 303.
TX	Near Austin	7/1851	"Negro"	S	Murder	H	Enda Junkins, "Slave Plots, Insurrections, and Acts of Violence in the State of Texas, 1828–1865" (MA thesis, Baylor University, 1969), 40; source: San Antonio Ledger, July 31, 1851.

Lynchings of African Americans in the South, 1824–1862 (cont.)

State	Locale and/or County	Date	Name	Status	Alleged Offense	Method	Source
TX	Ft. Bend Co.	5/1853	"young man"	S	Murder of master	H	Junkins, "Slave Plots, Insurrections, and Acts of Violence in the State of Texas, 1828–1865," 44; source: *State Gazette* (Austin, Tx.), May 28, 1853.
TX	Ft. Bend Co.	5/1853	"Negro Preacher"	S	Had influenced young man to murder master	H	Junkins, "Slave Plots, Insurrections, and Acts of Violence in the State of Texas, 1828–1865," 44; source: *State Gazette*, May 28, 1853.
TX	Smith Co.	8/1853	"Negro"	S	Rape and murder	H	Junkins, "Slave Plots, Insurrections, and Acts of Violence in the State of Texas, 1828–1865," 45; Source: *The Standard* (Clarksville, Tx.), August 13, 1853.
TX	Montgomery, Montgomery Co.	5/1857	"negro"	S	Attempted murder of mistress	H	*Galveston Weekly News*, June 2, 1857.
TX	Near Smithfield, Polk Co.	4/30/1859	"Alfred, was the property of a Mr. Roper"	S	Murder and robbery of master	B	*Galveston Weekly News*, May 17, 1859.
TX	Dresden, Navarro Co.	7/1859	"A negro man, belonging to a Mr. Blanton, of Ellis county"	S	Murder and robbery	H	*Galveston Weekly News*, August 6, 1859.
TX	Hopkins Co.	7/1859	Unknown	S	Attempted rape of white woman	H	Randolph B. Campbell, *An Empire for Slavery: The Peculiar Institution in Texas, 1821–1865* (Baton Rouge: Louisiana State University Press, 1989), 105.
TX	Harrison	9/1861	"Green"	S	Rape and murder of 12-year-old white girl	B	*Marshall Republican* (Marshall, Tx.), September 7, 1861, quoted in *New Orleans Picayune*, September 12, 1861.

Lynchings in the Northeast, Midwest, and West, 1840–1877

Race
U = unknown; W = white; N = Native American (Indian); B = black; H = Hispanic
Method
H = hanging; S = shooting; St = stoning; F = flogged to death; U = unknown

State	County	Date	Name	Race	Alleged Offense	Method	Source
IA	Dubuque, Dubuque Co.	9/1840	"Nat"	B	Theft	F	*Chicago American*, September 18, 1840.
IA	Linn Co.	7/1849	John Wilson	W	Horse theft?	U	*Dubuque Weekly Miner's Express*, July 25, 1849.
IA	Council Bluffs, Pottawatamie County	5/17/1853	Baltimore Muir	W	Murder	H	*Pottawatamie County History*, 101–103, in Black, "Lynching Research Notes," box 2, Pottawatamie County Folder, Archives, State Historical Society of Iowa, Iowa City.
IA	Jackson Co.	4/11/1857	Alexander Gifford	W	Murder	H	Paul Walton Black, "Lynchings in Iowa," *The Iowa Journal of History and Politics* 10 (April 1912): 187; *Burlington Daily Hawkeye and Telegraph*, May 30, 1857.
IA	Jackson Co.	5/29/1857	William Barger	W	Murder	H	Black, "Lynchings in Iowa," 190–191; *Daily Iowa State Democrat* (Davenport), June 2, 1857.
IA	Cedar Co.	6/18/1857	Alonzo Page	W	Connected with horse thieves	S	Black, "Lynchings in Iowa," 192; *Tipton Cedar County Advertiser*, June 2, 1857.
IA	Clinton Co.	6/24/1857	Bennett Warren	W	Horse theft?	H	Black, "Lynchings in Iowa," 192–194; *Weekly Eureka* (Anamosa), June 30, 1857.
IA	Clinton Co.	6/27/1857	Peter Conklin	W	Theft	S	Black, "Lynchings in Iowa," 194.
IA	Jones Co.	6/29/1857	Unknown	W	Horse theft	H	Black, "Lynchings in Iowa," 194
IA	Cedar Co.	7/2/1857	Alonzo Gleason	W	Horse theft	H	Black, "Lynchings in Iowa," 195; *Tipton Cedar County Advertiser*, July 4, 1857.
IA	Cedar Co.	7/2/1857	Edwin Soper	W	Horse theft	H	Black, "Lynchings in Iowa," 195; *Tipton Cedar County Advertiser*, July 4, 1857.
IA	Jones Co.	7/10/1857	"Dr. Long's brother"	W	Horse theft	H	Black, "Lynchings in Iowa," 196; *Daily Hawkeye and Telegraph* (Burlington), July 18, 1857.
IA	Jones Co.	7/10/1857	"An accomplice of Dr. Long"	W	Horse theft	H	Black, "Lynchings in Iowa," 196; *Daily Hawkeye and Telegraph*, July 18, 1857.

Lynchings in the Northeast, Midwest, and West, 1840–1877 (cont.)

State	Locale and/or County	Date	Name	Race	Alleged Offense	Method	Source
A	Cascade, Dubuque Co.	7/13/1857	Jack Parrott	W	Horse theft	H	*Dubuque Weekly Express and Herald,* July 15, 1857; *Dubuque Daily Times,* July 13, 1857.
IA	Cedar Co.	7/14/1857	"Kelso"	W	Unknown	H	Black, "Lynchings in Iowa," 197; *Muscatine Daily Journal,* July 20, 1857.
IA	Cedar Co.	7/14/1857	"Associate of Kelso"	W	Unknown	H	Black, "Lynchings in Iowa," 197; *Muscatine Daily Journal,* July 20, 1857
IA	Cedar Co.	7/21/1857	Kieth	W	Horse theft and counterfeiting	H	Black, "Lynchings in Iowa," 198; *Iowa Democratic Enquirer* (Muscatine), July 23, 1857.
IA	Jones Co.	12/4/1857	Hiram Roberts	W	Horse theft and counterfeiting	H	*Tipton Cedar County Advertiser,* December 12, 1857; *Weekly Eureka,* December 8, 1857.
IA	Montezuma, Poweshiek Co.	7/14/1857	William B. Thomas, or "Comequick"	W	Murder	H	*Montezuma Republican,* July 18, August 1, 1857.
IA	Batavia, Jefferson Co.	7/5/1860	John Kephart	W	Murder	H	*Fairfield Ledger,* July 13, 1860.
IA	Pottawattamie Co.	10/16/1860	Philip McGuire	W	Kidnapping and attempting selling a man and woman into slavery; theft	H	Black, "Lynchings in Iowa," 209.
IA	Pottawattamie Co.	7/1863	Miller	W	Horse theft	H	Black, "Lynchings in Iowa," 210.
IA	Appanoose Co.	2/1864	John Seaman	W	Arson, horse theft.	S	Black, "Lynchings in Iowa," 212.
IA	Mills Co.	5/28/1865	James Henderson	W	Horse theft, threat to blow up treasurer's office.	H	Black, "Lynchings in Iowa," 217.
IA	Pottawattamie Co.	6/1865	"Lacey"	W	Theft	H	Black, "Lynchings in Iowa," 217–218.
IA	Clinton Co.	10/18/1865	James Hiner	W	Horse theft	H	Black, "Lynchings in Iowa," 219.
IA	Monroe Co.	6/9/1866	Garrett F. Thompson	W	Horse theft	H	Black, "Lynchings in Iowa," 220.
IA	Mills Co.	6/14/1867	Patrick Lawn	W	Horse theft	U	Black, "Lynchings in Iowa," 222–223.
IA	Mills Co.	6/14/1867	William Lawn	W	Horse theft	U	Black, "Lynchings in Iowa," 222–223.
IA	Bremer Co.	1868	John McRoberts	W	Horse theft	H	Black, "Lynchings in Iowa," 223–224.
IA	Mahaska Co.	9/21/1868	Charles Brandon	W	Horse theft	H	Black, "Lynchings in Iowa," 224.

Lynchings in the Northeast, Midwest, and West, 1840–1877 (cont.)

State	Locale and/or County	Date	Name	Race	Alleged Offense	Method	Source
IA	Fremont Co.	1/18/1869	William Jackson	W	Murder	H	Black, "Lynchings in Iowa," 224–225.
IA	Fremont Co.	1/18/1869	James Orton	W	Murder	H	Black, "Lynchings in Iowa," 224–225.
IA	Fremont Co.	11/16/ 1869	"Murdock"	W	"Ruffian"	H	Black, "Lynchings in Iowa," 225–226.
IA	Lucas Co.	6/1870	Hiram Wilson	W	Killed sheriff, horse theft	H	Black, "Lynchings in Iowa," 227.
IL	Alton, Madison Co.	11/7/1837	Elijah Lovejoy	W	Abolitionist editor	S	*Daily Commercial Bulletin* (St. Louis. Mo.), November 9, 1837.
IL	Carthage, Hancock Co.	6/27/1844	Joseph Smith	W	Destruction of printing press, inciting riot and treason	S	Leonard Arrington and Davis Bitton, *The Mormon Experience: A History of the Latter-Day Saints* (Urbana: University of Illinois Press), 81–82.
IL	Charleston, Coles Co.	2/1856	A. F. Monroe	W	Murder	H	*New York Times*, February 22, 1856.
IL	Mound City, Pulaski Co.	10/1859	James Vaughan	W	Murder	H	*New York Times*, October 17, 1859.
IL	Nashville, Washington Co.	7/1865	"White"	W	Murder and arson	H	*New York Times*, July 16, 1865.
IL	Vienna, Johnson Co.	12/1868	Unknown	W	Murder and horse theft	H	*New York Times*, July 16, 1865.
IL	Pekin, Tazewell Co.	7/1869	"Berry"	W	Murder of deputy sheriff	H	*New York Times*, August 4, 1865.
IL	Salem, Marion Co.	4/1870	Hank Leonard, alias Rogers	W	Robbery	H	*New York Times*, April 22, 1870.
IL	Watseka, Iroquois Co.	7/1871	Martin Mera	W	Murder of 10-year-old son	H	*New York Times*, July 7, 1871.
IL	Olney, Richland Co.	8/1872	Jefferson White	W	Murder	H	*New York Times*, August 22, 1871.
IL	Mt. Carbon, Jackson Co.	2/1874	Alexander White	B	Murder	H	*New York Times*, February 12, 1874.
IL	Near Peoria	10/9/1875	William Pemberton	W	Horse theft	S, H	*New York Times*, October 10, 1875.
IL	Winchester, Scott Co.	9/1877	Andrew Richards	B	Rape	H	*New York Times*, September 12, 1877.
IN	Ligonier, Noble Co.	1/1858	"McClain, McDougal"	W	Counterfeiting	H	*New York Times*, January 30, 1858; February 8, 1858.
IN	Shelburn, Sullivan Co.	8/1865	"Miller"	W	Murderous Assault	H	*New York Times*, August 5, 1865.

Lynchings in the Northeast, Midwest, and West, 1840–1877 (cont.)

State	Locale and/or County	Date	Name	Race	Alleged Offense	Method	Source
IN	Franklin, Johnson Co.	10/1867	John Patterson	W	Murder	H	*New York Times*, November 6, 1867.
IN	Seymour, Jackson Co.	7/1868	Val. Elliot	W	Attempted robbery	H	*New York Times*, July 22, 1868.
IN	Seymour, Jackson Co.	7/1868	Chas. Roseberry	W	Attempted robbery	H	*New York Times*, July 22, 1868.
IN	Seymour, Jackson Co.	7/1868	Phil Clifton	W	Attempted robbery	H	*New York Times*, July 22, 24, 1868.
IN	Seymour, Jackson Co.	7/1868	"Moore"	W	Attempted robbery	H	*New York Times*, July 30, 1868.
IN	Seymour, Jackson Co.	7/1868	"Jerrell"	W	Attempted robbery	H	*New York Times*, July 30, 1868.
IN	Seymour, Jackson Co.	7/1868	"Sparks"	W	Attempted robbery	H	*New York Times*, July 30, 1868.
IN	New Albany, Floyd Co.	12/1868	John Reno	W	Attempted robbery	H	*New York Times*, December 13, and 14, 1868.
IN	New Albany, Floyd Co.	12/1868	Frank Reno	W	Attempted robbery	H	*New York Times*, December 13, and 14, 1868.
IN	New Albany, Floyd Co.	12/1868	Simon Reno	W	Attempted robbery	H	*New York Times*, December 13, and 14, 1868.
IN	New Albany, Floyd Co.	12/1868	Charles Anderson	W	Attempted robbery	H	*New York Times*, December 13, and 14, 1868.
IN	Franklin, Johnson Co.	10/1867	Hatchell	W	Murder	H	*New York Times*, November 6, 1867
IN	Clear Springs Jackson Co.	10/1869	Stephen Clark	W	"Thief and desperado"	H	*New York Times*, October 9, 1869.
IN	Near Orleans, Orange Co.	10/1870	"Tougatt"	W	Members of gang of robbers	H	*New York Times*, October 27, 1870, and July 4, 1873.
IN	Near Orleans, Orange Co.	10/1870	"Pickett"	W	Members of gang of robbers	H	*New York Times*, October 27, 1870, and July 4, 1873.
IN	Clarke Co.	11/1871	Unknown	B	Murder of Park family	U	*New York Times*, November 26, 1871, and July 4, 1873.
IN	Clarke Co.	11/1871	Unknown	B	Murder of Park family	U	*New York Times*, November 26, 1871, and July 4, 1873.
IN	Clarke Co.	11/1871	Unknown	B	Murder of Park family	U	*New York Times*, November 26, 1871, and July 4, 1873.
IN	Salem, Washington Co.	6/28/1873	"Heffren"	W	Murder	H	*New York Times*, July 4, 1873.
IN	Near French Lick Springs, Orange Co.	7/20/1874	Unknown	W	Petty larceny	H	*New York Times*, July 21, 1874.
IN	Greenfield, Hancock Co.	6/1875	"Kurner"	B	Rape	H	*New York Times*, June 27, 1875.
ME	Mapleton, Aroostook Co.	4/30/1873	James Cullen	W	Murder	H	Dena Lynn Winslow York, "'They Lynched Jim Cullen': New England's Only Lynching," (PhD diss., University of Maine, 2001), 86.
MI	Mason, Ingham Co.	8/27/1866	John Taylor	B	Murderous assault	H	*Lansing State Republican*, August 29, 1866; *Detroit Free Press*, August 29, 1866.

Lynchings in the Northeast, Midwest, and West, 1840–1877 (cont.)

State	Locale and/or County	Date	Name	Race	Alleged Offense	Method	Source
MN	St. Croix Valley	1848	"Paunais"	N	Murder of white trader	H	Marilyn Ziebarth, "Judge Lynch in Minnesota," *Minnesota History* 55, no. 2 (Summer 1996): 72.
MN	Gull Lake, Morrison Co.	8/1857	Joe Shambeau	N	Murder	H	Robert D. Pomeroy, "Morrison County's Only Lynching" (1966, unpublished manuscript, Minnesota Historical Society, St. Paul); John D. Bessler, *Legacy of Violence: Lynch Mobs and Executions in Minnesota* (Minneapolis: University of Minnesota Press, 2003), 5; Marilyn Ziebarth, "Judge Lynch in Minnesota," 72.
MN	Gull Lake, Morrison Co.	8/1857	"Jimmy"	N	Murder	H	Pomeroy, "Morrison County's Only Lynching"; Bessler, *Legacy of Violence*, 5; Ziebarth, "Judge Lynch in Minnesota," 72.
MN	Gull Lake, Morrison Co.	8/1857	Charles Gebabish	N	Murder	H	Pomeroy, "Morrison County's Only Lynching"; Bessler, *Legacy of Violence*, 5; Ziebarth, "Judge Lynch in Minnesota," 72.
MN	Lexington, Le Sueur Co.	12/27/1858	Charles Rinehart	W	Murder	H	Bessler, *Legacy of Violence*, 5–6.
MN	Wright Co.	4/25/1859	Oscar F. Jackson	W	Unknown	U	*New York Times*, August 17, 1859; Bessler, *Legacy of Violence*, 6–8.
MN	Mankato	5/3/1865	John Campbell	N	Murder	H	Ziebarth, "Judge Lynch in Minnesota," 72; Bessler, *Legacy of Violence*, 8–10.
MN	New Ulm	12/25/1866	George Liscomb	W	Murder	H	Ziebarth, "Judge Lynch in Minnesota," 72; *New York Times*, January 1, 14, 1867; Bessler, *Legacy of Violence*, 10–11.
MN	New Ulm	12/25/1866	Charles Campbell	W	Murder	H	Ziebarth, "Judge Lynch in Minnesota," 72; Bessler, *Legacy of Violence*, 10–11.
MN	Brainerd	7/23/1872	Gegoonce (Albert Smith)	N	Murder	H	Ziebarth, "Judge Lynch in Minnesota," 72; Bessler, *Legacy of Violence*, 12–13.
MN	Brainerd	7/23/1872	Tebekokechickwabe	N	Murder	H	Ziebarth, "Judge Lynch in Minnesota," 72; Bessler, *Legacy of Violence*, 12–13.
NB	Omaha	1/8/1859	"Bruden"	W	Horse theft	H	*New York Times*, January 19, 1859.
NB	Omaha	1/8/1859	"Daily"	W	Horse theft	H	*New York Times*, January 19, 1859.
NB	Omaha	1861	"Bouve"	W	Member of gang of thieves	H	*New York Times*, March 22, 1861.

Lynchings in the Northeast, Midwest, and West, 1840–1877 (cont.)

State	Locale and/or County	Date	Name	Race	Alleged Offense	Method	Source
NB	Ponca	1870	"Miller"	W	Murder	H	*New York Times*, August 15, 1870.
NB	Sidney	10/29/75	Charles Patterson	W	Murder	H	*New York Times*, October 31, 1875.
NB	Plum Creek	6/1876	"Howell"	W	Murder of deputy sheriff	H	*New York Times*, June 19, 1876.
NY	Newburgh, Orange Co.	6/21/1863	Robert Mulliner	B	Rape	H	*Newburgh Daily Telegraph*, June 22, 1863, p. 3; *Whig Press* (Middletown), July 1, 1863.
NY	Huntington, Suffolk Co.	9/1873	Charles G. Kelsey	W	Affair with younger woman	U	*New York Times*, September 6, 1873.
OH	Manchester, Adams Co.	11/25/1856	"Bill"	B	Rape	H	*New York Times*, December 4, 1856.
OH	Celina, Mercer Co.	7/1872	Absalom Kimmel	W	Murder	H	*New York Times*, July 10, 1872, and March 30, 1874.
OH	Celina, Mercer Co.	7/1872	Alex. McCleod	W	Murder	H	*New York Times*, July 10, 1872, and March 30, 1874.
OH	Urbana, Champaign Co.	1/17/1875	G.W. Ullery	W	Rape of 9-year-old girl	H	*New York Times*, January 18, 1875.
OH	Bellefontaine, Logan Co.	9/1875	James W. Schell	W	Murder of young woman	H	*New York Times*, September 26, 1875.
OH	New Richmond	7/1876	George Williams	W	Rape	H	*New York Times*, July 9, 1876.
OH	Oxford, Butler Co.	9/1877	Simon Garnett	B	Rape	S	*New York Times*, September 4, 1877.
OH	Geauga Co.	11/1877	Luther or Levi Scott	W	Unknown	H	*New York Times*, November 23, 1877.
OR	Northwest Oregon	late 1850s	Unknown	N	Murder	H	David Peterson del Mar, *Beaten Down: A History of Interpersonal Violence in the West* (Seattle: University of Washington Press, 2002), 29.
OR	La Grande	8/1865	"Mexican"	H	Horse theft	H	*Seattle Weekly*, August 26, 1865.
WA	Puget Sound	4/1854	Unknown	N	Murder	H	*Pioneer and Democrat* (Olympia), April 8, 1854.
WA	Seattle	early 1850s	Unknown	N	Murder	H	Alexandra Harmon, *Indians in the Making: Ethnic Relations and Indian Identities around Puget Sound* (Berkeley: University of California Press, 1998), 67.
WA	Seattle	early 1850s	Unknown	N	Murder	H	Harmon, *Indians in the Making*, 67.
WA	Seattle	early 1850s	Unknown	N	Murder of Indians and threats to kill whites	H	Harmon, *Indians in the Making*, 68.

Lynchings in the Northeast, Midwest, and West, 1840–1877 (cont.)

State	Locale and/or County	Date	Name	Race	Alleged Offense	Method	Source
WA	Steilacoom, Pierce Co.	early 1860s	"Indian"	N	Murder	H	Herbert Hunt, *Tacoma: its History and its Builders; a Half Century of Activity, Volume 1* (Chicago: S. J. Clarke, 1916), 90–91.
WA	Steilacoom, Pierce Co.	1/23/1863	J.M. Bates	W	Murder	H	*Tacoma Weekly Ledger*, February 17, 1893; Leland Athow, "A Brief History of the Adam Byrd Branch of the Byrd Family," Tacoma Public Library.
WA	Walla Walla	4/1865	"McKenzie"	W	Cattle and horse theft	H	*Seattle Weekly*, April, 1865.
WA	Walla Walla	4/1865	Doc. Reed	W	Cattle and horse theft	H	*Seattle Weekly*, April 27, 1865.
WA	Walla Walla	4/1865	"Nigger Jim"	B	Cattle and horse theft	H	*Seattle Weekly*, April 27, 1865.
WA	Walla Walla	4/1865	Tom Reeves	W	Cattle and horse theft	H	*Seattle Weekly*, April 27, 1865.
WA	Walla Walla	4/1865	Charles Wilson	W	Cattle and horse theft	H	*Seattle Weekly*, April 27, 1865.
WA	Walla Walla	4/1865	Joseph Petit	W	Cattle and horse theft	H	*Seattle Weekly*, April 27, 1865.
WA	Pierce Co.	1/22/1870	B. Gibson	W	Claims-jumping and threats of violence	S	*Olympia Transcript*, January 29, 1870.
WA	Pierce Co.	1/22/1870	Charles MacDonald	W	Claims-jumping and threats of violence	S	*Olympia Transcript*, January 29, 1870.
WA	Tacoma, Pierce Co.	4/27/1873	Jim Shell	N	Murder	H	Hunt, *Tacoma*, 219.
WI	Chippewa Falls	7/4/1849	Unknown	N	Stabbed lumberjack	H	Western Historical Company, *History of Northern Wisconsin* (Chicago, 1881), 195.
WI	Waushara Co.	2/1854	Frederick Cartwright	W	Murder	H	*Oshkosh Democrat*, March 3, 1854; *Milwaukee Daily Sentinel*, March 6, 1854.
WI	Janesville, Rock Co.	7/12/1855	David F. Mayberry	W	Murder	H	*Democrat Standard* (Janesville), July 12, 1855; *Janesville Gazette*, July 14, 1855.
WI	West Bend, Washington Co.	8/7/1855	George DeBar	W	Murder	H	*Milwaukee Daily Free Democrat*, August 8, 1855; *Milwaukee Daily News*, August 8, 1855.
WI	Milwaukee	9/6/1861	Marshall Clarke	B	Accessory to murder	H	*Milwaukee Sentinel*, September 9, 1861; *Daily Wisconsin* (Milwaukee), September 9, 1861.
WI	Richland Center, Richland Co.	9/26/1868	John Nevel	W	Murder	H, St	*Richland Center Republican*, October 1, 1868; *Milwaukee Sentinel*, September 30, 1868.
WI	New Lisbon, Juneau County	9/1869	"Indian"	N	Murder	H	Richard N. Current, *The History of Wisconsin, Volume II: The Civil War Era, 1848–1873* (Madison: The State Historical Society of Wisconsin, 1976), 523.

Lynchings in the Northeast, Midwest, and West, 1840–1877 (cont.)

State	Locale and/or County	Name	Date	Race	Alleged Offense	Method	Source
WI	Portage, Columbia County	William H. Spain	1869	W	Murder	H	Ray A. Billington, "Young Fred Turner," *Wisconsin Magazine of History* 46 (Autumn 1962): 38–52; Richard D. Durbin, "Two Wisconsin River Stories: Part II, That Bloody September," *Wisconsin Magazine of History* 77 (Spring 1994): 177–195.
WI	Portage, Columbia County	Patrick Wildrick	1869	W	Murder	H	Ray A. Billington, "Young Fred Turner," *Wisconsin Magazine of History* 46 (Autumn 1962): 38–52; Richard D. Durbin, "Two Wisconsin River Stories: Part II, That Bloody September," *Wisconsin Magazine of History* 77 (Spring 1994): 177–195.
WI	Oconto, Oconto Co.	Ludwig Neher	5/1871	W	Murder	H	*New York Times*, June 9, 1871.
WI	Steven's Point, Portage Co.	Ames Courtwright	10/19/1875	W	Murder of sheriff	H	*New York Times*, October 20, 1875.
WI	Steven's Point, Portage Co	Isaac Courtwright	10/19/1875	W	Murder of sheriff	H	*New York Times*, October 20, 1875.
WY	Dale City	Unknown	1/1868	W	Drunkenly shot into dance hall	H	T. A. Larson, *History of Wyoming* (Lincoln: University of Nebraska Press, 1965), 47–48; Carl Stanley Gustafson, "History of Vigilante and Mob Activity in Wyoming," (MA thesis, University of Wyoming, 1961), 41–69.
WY	Dale City	Unknown	1/1868	W	Drunkenly shot into dance hall	H	Larson, *History of Wyoming*, 47–48; Gustafson, "History of Vigilante and Mob Activity in Wyoming," 41–69.
WY	Dale City	Unknown	1/1868	W	Drunkenly shot into dance hall	H	Larson, *History of Wyoming*, 47–48; Gustafson, "History of Vigilante and Mob Activity in Wyoming," 41–69.
WY	Cheyenne	Charles Martin	3/1868	W	Murder	H	Larson, *History of Wyoming*, 47–48; Gustafson, "History of Vigilante and Mob Activity in Wyoming," 41–69.
WY	Cheyenne	Charles Morgan	3/1868	W	Horse theft	H	Larson, *History of Wyoming*, 47–48; Gustafson, "History of Vigilante and Mob Activity in Wyoming," 41–69.
WY	Cheyenne	"Landgraber"	1868	W	Refused to pay debt	H	Larson, *History of Wyoming*, 47–48; Gustafson, "History of Vigilante and Mob Activity in Wyoming," 41–69.
WY	Laramie	"The Kid"	8/1868	W	Robbery	U	Larson, *History of Wyoming*, 59–62; Gustafson, "History of Vigilante and Mob Activity in Wyoming," 70–94.

Lynchings in the Northeast, Midwest, and West, 1840–1877 (cont.)

State	Locale and/or County	Date	Name	Race	Alleged Offense	Method	Source
WY	Laramie	10/1868	Unknown	W	After vigilantes raided drinking, dancing, and gambling establishments	H	Larson, *History of Wyoming*, 59–62; Gustafson, "History of Vigilante and Mob Activity in Wyoming," 70–94.
WY	Laramie	10/1868	Unknown	W	After vigilantes raided drinking, dancing, and gambling establishments	H	Larson, *History of Wyoming*, 59–62; Gustafson, "History of Vigilante and Mob Activity in Wyoming," 70–94.
WY	Laramie	10/1868	Unknown	W	After vigilantes raided drinking, dancing, and gambling establishments	H	Larson, *History of Wyoming*, 59–62; Gustafson, "History of Vigilante and Mob Activity in Wyoming," 70–94.
WY	Laramie	10/1868	Unknown	W	After vigilantes raided drinking, dancing, and gambling establishments	H	Larson, *History of Wyoming*, 59–62; Gustafson, "History of Vigilante and Mob Activity in Wyoming," 70–94.
WY	Laramie	11/1868	H. C. Thomas	W	Theft	H	Larson, *History of Wyoming*, 59–62; Gustafson, "History of Vigilante and Mob Activity in Wyoming," 70–94.
WY	Bear River City	11/1868	Unknown	W	"Desperado"	H	Larson, *History of Wyoming*, 59–62; Gustafson, "History of Vigilante and Mob Activity in Wyoming," 70–94.
WY	Bear River City	11/1868	Unknown	W	"Desperado"	H	Larson, *History of Wyoming*, 59–62; Gustafson, "History of Vigilante and Mob Activity in Wyoming," 70–94.
WY	Bear River City	11/1868	Unknown	W	"Desperado"	H	Larson, *History of Wyoming*, 59–62; Gustafson, "History of Vigilante and Mob Activity in Wyoming," 70–94.
WY	Bear River City	11/1868	Unknown	W	"Desperado"	H	Larson, *History of Wyoming*, 59–62; Gustafson, "History of Vigilante and Mob Activity in Wyoming," 70–94.

Lynchings in the Northeast, Midwest, and West, 1840–1877 (cont.)

State	Locale and/or County	Date	Name	Race	Alleged Offense	Method	Source
WY	Bear River City	11/1868	Unknown	W	"Desperado"	H	Larson, *History of Wyoming*, 59–62; Gustafson, "History of Vigilante and Mob Activity in Wyoming," 70–94.
WY	Bear River City	11/11/1868	Unknown	W	Robbery	H	Larson, *History of Wyoming*, 59–62; Gustafson, "History of Vigilante and Mob Activity in Wyoming," 70–94.
WY	Bear River City	11/11/1868	Unknown	W	Robbery	H	Larson, *History of Wyoming*, 59–62; Gustafson, "History of Vigilante and Mob Activity in Wyoming," 70–94.
WY	Bear River City	11/11/1868	Unknown	W	Robbery	H	Larson, *History of Wyoming*, 59–62; Gustafson, "History of Vigilante and Mob Activity in Wyoming," 70–94.

For lists of lynchings in California, Colorado, and New Mexico, consult Ken Gonzales-Day, *Lynching in the West, 1850–1935* (Durham, N.C.: Duke University Press, 2006), 207–228; Stephen J. Leonard, *Lynching in Colorado 1859–1919* (Boulder: University Press of Colorado, 2002), 163–174; Robert J. Tórrez, *Myth of the Hanging Tree: Stories of Crime and Punishment in New Mexico* (Albuquerque: University of New Mexico Press, 2008), 159–162; West C. Gilbreath, *Death on the Gallows: The Story of Legal Hangings in New Mexico 1847–1923* (Silver City, N.M.: High-Lonesome Books, 2002), 215–219.

Notes

Introduction

1. For southern cases studies, see, for example, James R. McGovern, *Anatomy of a Lynching: The Killing of Claude Neal* (Baton Rouge: Louisiana State University Press, 1982); Dominic Capeci, Jr., *The Lynching of Cleo Wright* (Lexington: University Press of Kentucky, 1998); Bruce E. Baker, "Under the Rope: Lynching and Memory in Laurens County, South Carolina," in *Where These Memories Grow: History, Memory, and Southern Identity,* ed. W. Fitzhugh Brundage (Chapel Hill: University of North Carolina Press, 2000), 319–346; Christine Arnold-Lourie, "'A Madman's Deed—A Maniac's Hand': Gender and Justice in Three Maryland Lynchings," *Journal of Social History* 41, no. 4 (Summer 2008): 1031–1045.

2. George C. Wright, *Racial Violence in Kentucky, 1865–1940* (Baton Rouge: Louisiana State University Press, 1990) was a pioneering state study of lynching. Subsequent state studies include Stephen J. Leonard, *Lynching in Colorado 1859–1919* (Boulder: University Press of Colorado, 2002); William Carrigan, *The Making of a Lynching Culture: Violence and Vigilantism in Central Texas, 1836–1916* (Urbana: University of Illinois Press, 2004). Ken Gonzales-Day, *Lynching in the West, 1850–1935* (Durham, N.C.: Duke University Press, 2006), analyzes lynching in California.

3. Two pathbreaking regional studies were W. Fitzhugh Brundage, *Lynching in the New South: Georgia and Virginia, 1880–1930* (Urbana: University of Illinois Press, 1993), and Stewart E. Tolnay and E. M. Beck, *A Festival of Violence: An Analysis of Southern Lynchings, 1882–1930* (Urbana: University of Illinois Press, 1995). Additional important treatments of racial lynching in the postbellum South include Edward Ayers, *The Promise of the New South: Life After Reconstruction* (New York: Oxford University Press, 1992), 156–157; Leon F. Litwack, *Trouble in Mind: Black Southerners in the Age of Jim Crow* (New York: Vintage, 1999), 280–325; Margaret Vandiver, *Lynchings and Legal Executions in the South* (Piscataway, N.J.: Rutgers University Press, 2006).

4. Michael J. Pfeifer, *Rough Justice: Lynching and American Society, 1874–1947* (Urbana: University of Illinois Press, 2004).

5. Jacquelyn Dowd Hall, *Revolt Against Chivalry: Jesse Daniel Ames and the Women's Campaign Against Lynching* (1979; rev. ed., New York: Columbia University Press, 1993); Crystal N. Feimster, *Southern Horrors: Women and the Power of Rape and Lynching* (Cambridge, Mass.: Harvard University Press, 2009).

6. Examples include Jonathan Markovitz, *Legacies of Lynching: Racial Violence and Memory* (Minneapolis: University of Minnesota Press, 2004); Dora Apel, *Imagery of Lynching: Black Men, White Women, and the Mob* (Piscataway, N.J.: Rutgers University Press, 2004); Jacqueline Goldsby, *A Spectacular Secret: Lynching in American Life and Literature* (Chicago: University of Chicago Press, 2006); Amy Louise Wood, *Lynching and Spectacle: Witnessing Racial Violence in America, 1890–1940* (Chapel Hill: University of North Carolina Press, 2009).

7. In their important work on the lynching of Hispanics, William Carrigan and Clive Webb have argued that the majority of mob killings of Mexican Americans occurred in the mid-nineteenth-century West, several decades before the widespread lynchings of African Americans in the South. Carrigan and Webb have documented at least 571 Mexican American victims of lynching between 1848 and 1928. Carrigan and Webb, "Muerto Por Unos Desconocidos (Killed by Persons Unknown): Mob Violence against African Americans and Mexican Americans," in *Beyond Black and White: Race, Ethnicity, and Gender in the US South and Southwest,* ed. Stephanie Cole and Alison Parker (College Park: Texas A&M University Press, 2004). For an analysis of the lynching of Hispanics in California, see Gonzales-Day, *Lynching in the West.*

8. For a valuable early scholarly analysis of the origins of American lynching, see James Elbert Cutler, *Lynch Law: An Investigation into the History of Lynching in the United States* (1905; repr., New York: Negro Universities Press, 1969), 1–136. Phillip Dray, *At the Hands of Persons Unknown: The Lynching of Black America* (New York: Random House, 2002), 18–32, is a popular treatment that includes a brief but suggestive discussion of lynching violence before the Civil War.

9. Wright, *Racial Violence in Kentucky,* 19–60.

10. Carrigan, *The Making of a Lynching Culture,* 112–131; Gilles Vandal, *Rethinking Southern Violence: Homicides in Post-Civil War Louisiana, 1866–1884* (Columbus: Ohio State University Press, 2000), 90–109; Bruce E. Baker, *This Mob Will Surely Take My Life: Lynching in the Carolinas, 1871–1947* (London: Hambledon and London, 2008); Bruce E. Baker, *What Reconstruction Meant: Historical Memory in the American South* (Charlottesville: University of Virginia Press, 2007), 84–87; Julius E. Thompson, *Lynchings in Mississippi: A History, 1865–1965* (Jefferson, N.C.: McFarland Press, 2007), 4–16.

11. Leonard, *Lynching in Colorado,* 15–53. A useful recent analysis of vigilante violence and capital punishment in the nineteenth-century West can be found in Howard W. Allen, Jerome M. Clubb, and Vincent A. Lacey, *Race, Class, and the Death Penalty* (Albany: State University of New York Press, 2008), 119–145.

12. Eugene Genovese, *Roll, Jordan, Roll: The World the Slaves Made* (New York: Vintage, 1974), 32; Clement Eaton, "Mob Violence in the Old South," *Mississippi Valley Historical Review* 29, no. 3 (December 1942), 351–370.

13. Kenneth M. Stampp, *The Peculiar Institution: Slavery in the Ante-Bellum South* (New York: Knopf, 1956), 190–191; Bertram Wyatt-Brown, *Southern Honor: Ethics and Behavior in the Old South* (New York: Oxford University Press, 1982), 388–389; Philip Schwarz,

Twice Condemned: Slaves and the Criminal Laws of Virginia, 1705–1865 (Baton Rouge: Louisiana State University Press, 1988), 291–292.

14. Christopher Waldrep, *The Many Faces of Judge Lynch: Extralegal Violence and Punishment in America* (New York: Palgrave Macmillan, 2002); Christopher Waldrep, ed., *Lynching in America: A History in Documents* (New York: New York University Press, 2006). For a recent interpretation examining African American responses to lynching, see Christopher Waldrep, *African Americans Confront Lynching: Strategies of Resistance from the Civil War to the Civil Rights Era* (Lanham, Md.: Rowman and Littlefield Publishers, 2008).

15. For a brief effort at writing a history of American lynching in a global context, see Michael J. Pfeifer, "Lynchings," *International Encyclopedia of the Social Sciences,* 2nd ed. (Farmington Hills, Mich.: MacMillan Reference USA, 2008).

16. The ethnic identity of recently arrived European immigrants was also a factor in American lynching in the late nineteenth century. For the Norwegian community's collective murder of a Norwegian farmer accused of mistreating his family in Trempealeau County, Wisconsin, in 1889, see Jane M. Pederson, "Gender, Justice, and a Wisconsin Lynching, 1889–1890," *Agricultural History* 67, no. 2 (Spring 1993): 65–82. For an argument that participation in lynching violence against African Americans was a means for Irish, Czechs, and Italians in Brazos County, Texas, to assert "whiteness," see Cynthia Skove Nevels, *Lynching to Belong: Claiming Whiteness Through Racial Violence* (College Station: Texas A&M University Press, 2007).

17. For the conceptualization of the British Atlantic, see Bernard Bailyn, *Atlantic History: Concept and Contours* (Cambridge, Mass.: Harvard University Press, 2005); David Armitage and Michael J. Braddick, *The British Atlantic World, 1500–1800,* 2nd ed. (New York: Palgrave Macmillan, 2009). For an argument that violence enjoyed considerably greater legal toleration on the western and southern peripheries of the British empire than in the metropole of Britain proper in the eighteenth century, see Eliga H. Gould, "Zones of Law, Zone of Violence: The Legal Geography of the British Atlantic, circa 1772," *The William and Mary Quarterly* 60, no. 3 (July 2003): 474–475.

18. Waldrep, *The Many Faces of Judge Lynch,* 13–47.

19. For discussions of the complexities of defining the term *lynching,* see Waldrep, *African Americans Confront Lynching,* xiii, and Pfeifer, *Rough Justice,* 6–7, 187n15.

20. Sara Forsdyke, "Street Theater and Popular Justice in Ancient Greece: Shaming, Stoning, and Starving Offenders Inside and Outside the Courts," *Past and Present* 201, no. 1 (November 2008): 3–50; P. A. Brunt, "The Roman Mob," *Past and Present* 35, no. 1 (December 1966): 3–27.

21. Roberta Senechal de la Roche, "The Sociogenesis of Lynching," in *Under Sentence of Death: Lynching in the South,* ed. W. Fitzhugh Brundage (Chapel Hill: University of North Carolina Press, 1997), 51, 70n27.

22. Eric Monkkonen, "Homicide: Explaining America's Exceptionalism," *American Historical Review* 111, no. 1 (February 2006): 76–94; Pieter Spierenburg, "Democracy Came Too Early: A Tentative Explanation for the Problem of American Homicide," *American Historical Review* 111, no. 1 (February 2006): 104–114; Pieter Spierenburg, *A History of Murder: Violence in Europe from the Middle Ages to the Present* (Malden, Mass.: Polity, 2008); Norbert Elias, *The Civilizing Process,* trans. Edmund Jephcott (Cambridge, Mass.: Blackwell, 1994); Elizabeth Dale, "Criminal Justice in the United States, 1790–1920: A Gov-

ernment of Laws or Men?" in *The Cambridge History of Law in America, Vol. 2: The Long Nineteenth Century, 1789–1920,* ed. Christopher Tomlins and Michael Grossberg (New York: Cambridge University Press, 2008), 133–167. For an argument that the United States developed elevated rates of homicide, the highest among Western nations, as a product of the disruption of social hierarchies, political instability, and a lack of confidence in government from the mid-to-late nineteenth century, see Randolph Roth, *American Homicide* (Cambridge, Mass: Belknap Press, 2009), 16–26, 297–385. For extensive documentation of governmental surveillance of "popular disturbances" in England in the early nineteenth century that reflects, in significant contrast to the United States, Britain's development by that time of a national, centralized state that claimed a full monopoly on violence, see British Home Office Records on Disturbances, HO 41, National Archives, London.

23. Charles Townshend, *Political Violence in Ireland: Government and Resistance Since 1848* (Oxford, U.K.: Clarendon Press, 1983), 1–19, 47–48; Carolyn A. Conley, *Melancholy Accidents: The Meaning of Violence in Post-Famine Ireland* (Lanham, Md.: Lexington Books, 1999), 1–6.

Chapter 1. Collective Violence in the British Atlantic

1. Roger B. Manning, *Village Revolts: Social Protests and Popular Disturbances in England, 1509–1640* (Oxford, U.K.: Clarendon Press, 1988); John Brewer and John Styles, *An Ungovernable People: The English and Their Law in the Seventeenth and Eighteenth Centuries* (New Brunswick, N.J.: Rutgers University Press, 1980), 14–20; Martin Ingram, "Ridings, Rough Music and the 'Reform of Popular Culture' in Early Modern England," *Past and Present* 105, no. 1 (November 1984): 79–113; Tim Harris, *London Crowds in the Reign of Charles II: Propaganda and Politics From the Restoration Until the Exclusion Crisis* (New York: Cambridge University Press, 1987), 17–24; Norma Landau, *Law, Crime, and English Society, 1660–1830* (New York: Cambridge University Press, 2002), 4; Douglas Greenberg, "Crime, Law Enforcement, and Social Control in Colonial America," *The American Journal of Legal History* 26, no. 4 (October 1982): 293–325; Pauline Maier, "Popular Uprisings and Civil Authority in Eighteenth-Century America," *William and Mary Quarterly* 27, no. 1 (January 1970): 4–21; Paul A. Gilje, *Rioting in America* (Bloomington: Indiana University Press, 1996), 7–33; William Pencak, Matthew Dennis, and Simon P. Newman, eds., *Riot and Revelry in Early America* (University Park: The Pennsylvania State University Press, 2002). For an interesting discussion of Anglo-European antecedents and the role of women and children in American collective violence from the colonial era through the early twentieth century, see Helen McLure, "'I Suppose You Think Strange the Murder of Women and Children': The American Culture of Collective Violence, 1652–1930" (PhD diss., Southern Methodist University, 2009). The discretionary and symbolic qualities of the administration of criminal justice on one periphery of the Anglo-American world can be discerned through reading the comprehensive files of mid-eighteenth-century criminal cases adjudicated by the Scottish high court. Justiciary Court Records, JC 26/141, National Archives of Scotland, Edinburgh.

2. Alastair Bellany, "The Murder of John Lambe: Crowd Violence, Court Scandal and Popular Politics in Early Seventeenth-Century England," *Past and Present* 200, no. 1 (August 2008): 37–76.

3. The events surrounding the crowd execution of Porteous are documented in Sir Walter Scott, *The Heart of Mid-Lothian* (1818; repr., Edinburgh: Edinburgh University Press, 2004), 21–64; T. A. Critchley, *The Conquest of Violence: Order and Liberty in England* (New York: Schocken Books, 1970), 76.

4. James Axtell, "The Vengeful Women of Marblehead: Robert Roules's Deposition of 1677," *William and Mary Quarterly* 31, no. 4 (October 1974), 647–652; Gilje, *Rioting in America*, 19.

5. Axtell, "The Vengeful Women of Marblehead," 652.

6. For a discussion of language describing localistic, small-scale practices of summary justice in medieval and early modern England and Scotland, "Lydford law," "Halifax law," "Cowper justice," and "Jeddart justice," see James Elbert Cutler, *Lynch-Law: An Investigation into the History of Lynching in the United States* (1905; repr., New York: Negro Universities Press, 1969), 7–9. Cutler argues that the usage of these particular terms was not widely dispersed in the British Isles, that they denoted practices that did not completely eschew formal legal proceedings (as later American lynchings would), and that the American term *lynching* originally described flogging, not capital punishment, and thus the word *lynching* could not have evolved from these British terms that referred to summary execution.

7. Gilje, *Rioting in America*, 38–48; Cutler, *Lynch-Law*, 20–76; Maier, "Popular Uprisings and Civil Authority," 28; Ingram, "Ridings, Rough Music." Christopher Waldrep, *The Many Faces of Judge Lynch: Extralegal Violence and Punishment in America* (New York: Palgrave Macmillan, 2002), 13–25, is the definitive treatment of the origins of the terms *lynch-law* and *lynching*. For regulation in the Carolinas, see Gregory H. Nobles, "Breaking into the Backcountry: New Approaches to the Early American Frontier," *William and Mary Quarterly* 46, no. 4 (October 1989), 659–662; Rachel N. Klein, "Ordering the Backcountry: The South Carolina Regulation," *William and Mary Quarterly* 38, no. 4 (October 1981), 661–680.

8. For the evolution of American politics and society from the Revolution through the early Republic, see Gordon S. Wood, *The Radicalism of the American Revolution* (New York: Vintage Books, 1991); Gordon S. Wood, *Empire of Liberty: A History of the Early Republic, 1789–1815* (New York: Oxford University Press, 2009); Sean Wilentz, *Chants Democratic: New York City and the Rise of the American Working Class, 1788–1850* (New York: Oxford University Press, 1984). For the transformation of capital punishment from colonial America through the early Republic, see Stuart Banner, *The Death Penalty: An American History* (Cambridge, Mass.: Harvard University Press, 2002), 53–111. For the ambiguous and contested constitutional legacy of the Revolution with regard to popular violence, see Maier, "Popular Uprisings and Civil Authority," 33–35; Gilje, *Rioting in America*, 38.

Chapter 2. Vigilantes, Criminal Justice, and Antebellum Cultural Conflict

1. Abraham Lincoln, "Address to the Young Men's Lyceum of Springfield, Illinois," January 27, 1838, in *Lincoln: Selected Speeches and Writings,* ed. Don E. Fehrenbacher (New York: Vintage Books, 1992), 13–21. For the context for Lincoln's address to the Young Men's Lyceum, see Carl F. Wieck, *Lincoln's Quest for Equality: the Road to Gettysburg* (Dekalb:

Northern Illinois University, 2002), 29–33. Lincoln's speech responded to the mob assassination of abolitionist editor Elijah P. Lovejoy in Alton, Illinois, on November 7, 1837. Lovejoy had been driven out of St. Louis by a mob infuriated by his denunciation of the legal proceedings that had exonerated the lynchers that had burned to death Francis McIntosh, a "mulatto" boatman from Pittsburgh who had killed a deputy sheriff. *Missouri Republican* (St. Louis), April 30, 1836, reprinted in Janet S. Hermann, "The McIntosh Affair," *Bulletin of the Missouri Historical Society* 26 (January 1970): 123–143; John F. Darby, *Personal Recollections* (St. Louis: G. I. Jones and Company, 1880), 237–241.

2. Lincoln, "Address to the Young Men's Lyceum," 14.

3. Ibid., 16.

4. Ibid., 18, 21.

5. For analyses of the history of popular constitutionalism in the United States, see Larry Kramer, *The People Themselves: Popular Constitutionalism and Judicial Review* (New York: Oxford University Press, 2004); Christian G. Fritz, *American Sovereigns: The People and America's Constitutional Tradition before the Civil War* (New York: Cambridge University Press, 2008). For a treatment of articulations of constitutionalism by whites and blacks in the context of lynching, see Waldrep, *African-Americans Confront Lynching* (Lanham, Md.: Rowman and Littlefield Publishers, 2009), 1–37.

6. Lincoln, "Address to the Young Men's Lyceum," 18.

7. For an overview of the history of American vigilantism that stresses its roots in the era of the American Revolution, see Richard Maxwell Brown, *Strain of Violence: Historical Studies of American Violence and Vigilantism* (New York: Oxford University Press, 1975), esp. 41–66. The ideology and practice of collective violence, particularly rioting, in the Revolutionary era, is considered in Paul A. Gilje, *Rioting in America* (Bloomington: Indiana University Press, 1996), 35–59.

8. For an influential interpretation of the claim clubs, organizations that sought to punish claims-jumping on the midwestern frontier, see Allan G. Bogue, "The Iowa Claim Clubs: Symbol and Substance," *Mississippi Valley Historical Review* 45 (June–March 1958–1959): 231–253.

9. This transformation of criminal justice in the context of the death penalty in the Northeast is charted in Louis P. Masur, *Rites of Execution: Capital Punishment and the Transformation of American Culture, 1776–1865* (New York: Oxford University Press, 1989); Stuart Banner, *The Death Penalty: An American History* (Cambridge, Mass.: Harvard University Press, 2002), 88–137, 141. For overviews of the transformation of criminal justice from the colonial era through the mid–nineteenth century, see Lawrence M. Friedman, *Crime and Punishment in American History* (New York: Basic Books, 1993), 22–82; Samuel Walker, *Popular Justice: A History of American Criminal Justice* (New York: Oxford University Press, 1980), 13–111.

10. John H. Langbein, *The Origins of Adversary Criminal Trial* (New York: Oxford University Press, 2003); Allyson May, *The Bar and the Old Bailey, 1758–1850* (Chapel Hill: University of North Carolina Press, 2006); James D. Rice, "The Criminal Trial Before and After the Lawyers: Authority, Law, and Culture in Maryland Jury Trials, 1681–1837," *American Journal of Legal History* 40, no. 4 (October 1996): 455–475.

11. Elizabeth Dale, "Northerners and Their Laws: Legal Pluralism in Antebellum Era Philadelphia" (unpublished manuscript in possession of author, n.d.); Elizabeth Dale,

"Popular Sovereignty: A Case Study from the Antebellum Era," (University of Florida Levin College of Law Research Paper No. 2009–17, March 16, 2009), accessed June 17, 2009, http://ssrn.com/abstract=1361322.

12. These tendencies in local criminal justice in the South are analyzed perceptively in an introduction and essays by Sally Hadden, Timothy S. Huebner, Judith Kelleher Schafer, and Ariela Gross in Christopher Waldrep and Donald G. Nieman, eds., *Local Matters: Race, Crime, and Justice in the Nineteenth-Century South* (Athens: University of Georgia Press, 2001), ix–124. Banner analyzes the relatively minor reform of capital punishment in the antebellum South in *The Death Penalty*, 137–143, arguing that slavery thwarted the development of the significant culture of reform that emerged in the North. A treatment of antebellum criminal justice in Mississippi can be found in Christopher Waldrep, *Roots of Disorder: Race and Criminal Justice in the American South, 1817–1880* (Urbana: University of Illinois Press, 1998), 7–58. Michael S. Hindus, *Prison and Plantation: Crime, Justice, and Authority in Massachusetts and South Carolina, 1767–1868* (Chapel Hill: University of North Carolina Press, 1980) compares criminal justice in South Carolina and Massachusetts.

13. Gregory H. Nobles, "Breaking into the Backcountry: New Approaches to the Early American Frontier," *William and Mary Quarterly* 46, no. 4 (October 1989): 661.

14. Allan G. Bogue suggested that the cultural competition of southerners and Yankees may have played a role in claim club organization and violence in Iowa, as claim club counties, located in the east central portion of the state and settled during the 1830s and 1840s, tended to have mixed populations of southerners, Yankees, and foreign immigrants. Bogue, "The Iowa Claim Clubs," 235. Tensions between southerners and Yankees also profoundly shaped the political culture and social fabric of antebellum Illinois. James E. Davis, *Frontier Illinois* (Bloomington: Indiana University Press, 1998), 3, 247–251. For cultural tensions in early Michigan, see James Z. Schwartz, *Conflict on the Michigan Frontier: Yankee and Borderland Cultures, 1815–1840* (Dekalb: Northern Illinois University Press, 2009).

15. For a summary of interpretations of regulator violence in the Carolinas in the eighteenth century, see Nobles, "Breaking into the Backcountry," 658–667. For North British folkways and their transposition to the American backcountry, see David Hackett Fischer, *Albion's Seed: Four British Folkways in America* (New York: Oxford University Press, 1989), 605–782, esp. 765–771. For important critiques arguing that Hackett Fischer elides the complexity of cultural transformation over time in the pre-emigration British Isles and in North America, consult Jack P. Greene, "Transplanting Moments: Inheritance in the Formation of Early American Culture," *William and Mary Quarterly* 48, no. 2 (April 1991): 224–230, and Ned C. Landsman, "Border Cultures, the Backcountry, and North British Emigration to America," *William and Mary Quarterly* 48, no. 2 (April 1991): 253–259. For an early treatment of eighteenth- and early-nineteenth-century regulation movements and their relationship to the origins of the collective violence that would come to be known as *lynching*, see James Elbert Cutler, *Lynch-Law: An Investigation Into the History of Lynching in the United States* (New York: Longman, Greens, and Co., 1905), 38–105, esp. 88–89. Reviewing eighteenth- and early-nineteenth-century collective violence, Cutler found that its emphasis tended to be nonlethal and only rarely included capital punishment; as discussed, Cutler identified a lethal turn in vigilante violence in the 1830s.

16. For an insightful treatment of a complex antebellum regulator movement in southern Illinois that descended into prolonged internecine conflict over the legitimacy of the

use of violence to achieve "law and order," see Nicole Etcheson, "Good Men and Notorious Rogues: Vigilantism in Massac County, Illinois, 1846–1850," in *Lethal Imagination: Violence and Brutality in American History,* ed. Michael Bellesiles (New York: New York University Press, 1999), 149–169. Etcheson, p. 151, stresses that lawlessness and violence in Massac occurred not because the county lacked criminal justice institutions but rather "because its legal institutions possessed little if any commonly accepted legitimacy." For regulator violence in east Texas, in 1856, that pitted free black landholders allied with some white officeholders (Regulators) against an opposing faction of white farmers (Moderators), see A. F. Muir, "The Free Negroes of Jefferson and Orange Counties, Texas," *Journal of Negro History* 35 (April 1950): 183–206, esp. 200–203. For an account from the perspective of the white Moderator faction, see *Galveston Weekly News,* July 15, 1856.

17. For analyses of a corresponding lethal turn in rioting in the 1830s, see Gilje, *Rioting in America,* 60–86, and David Grimsted, *American Mobbing, 1828–1861: Toward Civil War* (New York: Oxford University Press, 1998). Gilje connects a pattern of greater loss of life and property in rioting in the early to mid–nineteenth century to the American Revolution's unraveling of traditional notions of hierarchy, a newly ascendant ethos of democratic egalitarianism, and the rise of profound cultural and social divisions involving class, race, and ethnicity. Grimsted, less persuasively, argues that the tensions of the sectional conflict set the contours of antebellum mob violence. For the antebellum evolution of the language of lynching, see Christopher Waldrep, *The Many Faces of Judge Lynch: Extralegal Violence and Punishment in America* (New York: Palgrave Macmillan, 2002), 27–47.

18. For an overview of "rough justice" and "due process" perspectives on criminal justice and lynching in the postbellum United States, see Michael J. Pfeifer, *Rough Justice: Lynching and American Society, 1874–1947* (Urbana: University of Illinois Press, 2004), 2–5. For the broadening of the ideology of republicanism from the American Revolution through the mid–nineteenth century, see Gordon S. Wood, *The Radicalism of the American Revolution* (New York: Vintage Books, 1991) and Sean Wilentz, *Chants Democratic: New York City and the Rise of the American Working Class, 1788–1850* (New York: Oxford University Press, 1984).

19. For recent treatments of the development of the cotton frontier, see Adam Rothman, *Slave Country: American Expansion and the Origins of the Deep South* (Cambridge, Mass.: Harvard University Press, 2005), and Ira Berlin, *Generations of Captivity: A History of African-American Slaves* (Cambridge, Mass.: Harvard University Press, 2003), 160–244.

20. For early modern and colonial Anglo-American traditions of collective violence and morals regulation in north Britain and the American backcountry, see Fischer, *Albion's Seed,* 765–776, 889–895.

21. James W. Bragg, "Captain Slick, Arbiter of Early Alabama Morals," *Alabama Review* 11 (April 1958): 125–126.

22. Ibid., 126.

23. Ibid., 126.

24. Ibid., 126–127.

25. Ibid., 126–127.

26. E. G. Richards, "Reminiscences of the Early Days in Chambers County," *Alabama Historical Quarterly* 4, no. 3 (Fall 1942): 434–435.

27. Bragg, "Captain Slick," 128.

28. Ibid., 125–128; Richards, "Reminiscences," 434–435.

29. *Southern Advocate* (Huntsville, Ala.), quoted in Bragg, "Captain Slick," 128.

30. Ibid., 126.

31. *Vicksburg Register* (Vicksburg, Miss.), July 9, 1835.

32. Ibid.

33. Ibid.

34. Ibid. For the emergence of the northern culture of sentimentalism, particularly among middle class women, see Karen Halttunen, *Confidence Men and Painted Women: A Study of Middle-Class Culture in America* (New Haven: Yale University Press, 1982), 56–152, 191–197.

35. Quoted in *Vicksburg Register*, July 30, 1835.

36. Waldrep, *The Many Faces of Judge Lynch*, 28–31.

37. H. R. Howard, *The History of Virgil A. Stewart* (New York: Harper and Brothers, 1836), 222–261; Henry S. Foote, *Casket of Reminiscences* (Washington, D.C.: Chronicle Publishing Company, 1874), 253. For background on the Murrell Conspiracy, see John L. Penick, Jr., "John Andrews Murrell, 1806–1844," *Tennessee Encyclopedia of History and Culture*, accessed June 11, 2009, http://tennesseeencyclopedia.net/imagegallery.php?EntryID=M133.

38. For analyses of the collective violence with which whites suppressed real and purported slave insurrections, see Berlin, *Generations of Captivity*, 154; Grimsted, *American Mobbing*, 135–136; Rothman, *Slave Country*, 106–117.

39. "Proceedings" [of the Committee at Livingston], Howard, *The History of Virgil A. Stewart*, 235.

40. Ibid., 223, 235.

41. Ibid., 234.

42. Ibid., 235.

43. Ibid., 236.

44. *San Antonio Weekly Herald*, June 13, 1857.

45. Ibid., June 11, 13, 1857; William Corner, *San Antonio de Bexar: A Guide* (San Antonio: Bainbridge and Corner, 1890), 116.

46. Corner, *San Antonio de Bexar*, 30.

47. *San Antonio Weekly Herald*, September 18, 1858.

48. For detailed treatments of the 1857 eastern Iowa vigilante movement, see Paul Walton Black, "Lynchings in Iowa," *Iowa Journal of History and Politics* 10 (April 1912): 187–199; Michael J. Pfeifer, "Law, Society, and Violence in the Antebellum Midwest: The 1857 Eastern Iowa Vigilante Movement," *Annals of Iowa* 64, no. 2 (Spring 2005): 139–166.

49. For an interpretation of the social and legal context of an earlier episode of vigilantism in Iowa, the "Bellevue War" in 1840, see Pfeifer, "Law, Society, and Violence in the Antebellum Midwest," 149–151. In a procedure that displayed the transitional nature of regulator practices in the antebellum era, the vigilantes at Bellevue polled the crowd at a summary trial and narrowly voted to flog rather than to hang their victims.

50. Leland L. Sage, *A History of Iowa* (Ames: Iowa State University Press), 112–115.

51. Iowa's population more than tripled in the 1850s, from 192,000 in 1850 to 674,913 in 1860. William J. Petersen, *The Story of Iowa: The Progress of an American State,* vol. 1 (New York: Lewis Historical Publishing Company, 1952), 356. For a parallel analysis of late frontier Illinois, see Davis, *Frontier Illinois*, 181–182, 319, 333–336, 422–423. Davis

argues that the early years of settlement in Illinois in the 1820s and 1830s saw substantial communalism and republican civic participation in cultural and legal institutions, but that substantial in-migration in the late frontier era from the late 1830s through 1850s fragmented social cohesion and destabilized social institutions; the lethal vigilantism of regulator movements in Winnebago County in northern Illinois and Massac County in the southern portion of the state ensued.

52. *Ninth Census of the United States, 1870: Population* (Washington, D.C.: Government Printing Office, 1872). Cedar County grew from 3,941 in 1850 to 12,949 in 1860 (371 percent), Jackson County from 7,210 to 18,493 (256 percent), Jones County from 3,007 to 13,306 (442 percent), Scott County from 5,986 to 25,959 (434 percent), and Clinton County from 2,822 to 18,938 (671 percent).

53. *Daily Hawkeye and Telegraph* (Burlington, Ia.), quoted in *Dubuque Weekly Express and Herald* (Dubuque, Ia.), June 10, 1857.

54. *Macquoketa Excelsior* (Macquoketa, Ia.), quoted in *Cedar County Advertiser* (Tipton, Ia.), June 20, 1857.

55. *Macquoketa Excelsior,* quoted in *Anamosa Eureka* (Anamosa, Ia.), June 16, 1857.

56. *Dubuque Weekly Express and Herald,* August 5, 1857.

57. Ibid., December 2, 1857.

58. For an editorial linking the problem of "mob law and lynching" in Iowa to the way in which incompetent prosecutors and "badly constructed juries" thwarted the punishment of criminals, see *Dubuque Weekly Express and Herald,* July 22, 1857.

59. *Muscatine Daily Journal* (Muscatine, Ia.), August 1, 1857; Paul Walton Black, "Lynching Research Notes," box 1, folder 4, "Lynchings Anti-Mob Association," Special Collections, State Historical Society of Iowa, Iowa City. Thomas Winn's service as a delegate to the Republican state convention is described in *Cedar County Advertiser,* August 8, 1857.

60. *Daily Iowa State Democrat* (Davenport), July 2, 1857.

61. *Maquoketa Excelsior* quoted in *Daily Hawkeye and Telegraph* (Burlington, Ia.), June 9, 1857, in Black, "Lynching Research Notes," box 1, folder 8, "Lynching Research Materials."

62. The account of Finch's suicide comes from the *Anamosa Eureka,* quoted in *Daily Iowa State Democrat* (Davenport), July 22, 1857.

63. *Maquoketa Excelsior,* quoted in *Tipton Cedar County Advertiser,* July 25, 1857. For information on Samuel A. Bissell, accessed August 2, 2005, http://members.aol.com/BissellGenealogy/BHAMI2–3b.html. For more on Judge Wells Spicer's colorful career, which included exonerating Wyatt Earp after the shootout at the O.K. Corral in Tombstone, Arizona Territory, in 1881, see Robert R. Dykstra, *Bright Radical Star: Black Freedom and White Supremacy on the Hawkeye Frontier* (Cambridge, Mass.: Harvard University Press, 1993), 177.

64. Judge William Tuthill's biographical information is in "Biographies-Center Township," *History of Cedar County, Iowa* (Chicago: Western Historical Company, 1878).

65. *Weekly Eureka* (Anamosa, Ia.), June 30, 1857.

66. *Tipton Cedar County Advertiser,* September 26, 1857.

67. *Daily Hawkeye and Telegraph,* quoted in *Dubuque Weekly Express and Herald,* June 10, 1857.

68. *Dubuque Weekly Express and Herald,* July 7, 1857. For a discussion of Democratic and Whig values and social bases in Iowa, see Robert Cook, "The Political Culture of Antebellum Iowa: An Overview," in *Iowa History Reader,* ed. Marvin Bergman (Ames: Iowa State University Press, 1996), 86–104.

69. *Muscatine Daily Journal,* June 28, 1857, in Black, "Lynching Research Notes," box 1, folder 8, "Lynching Research Materials."

70. *Annals of Jackson County, Iowa,* no. 1 (1905), 29–34, in Black, "Lynching Research Notes," box 1, folder 8, "Lynching Research Materials"; *Daily Hawkeye and Telegraph,* quoted in *Dubuque Weekly Express and Herald,* June 10, 1857. For an analysis of mid-nineteenth-century midwestern vigilante movements and their constitutions, see Patrick Bates Nolan, "Vigilantes on the Middle Border: A Study of Self-Appointed Law Enforcement in the States of the Upper Mississippi from 1840 to 1880" (PhD diss., University of Minnesota, 1971).

71. See the accounts of the lynch trial of Jacob (a.k.a. Benjamin) Warner in Cedar County in *Davenport Gazette,* June 27, 1857, quoted in *Daily Hawkeye,* July 1, 1857, in Black, "Lynching Research Notes," box 2, Cedar County folder; and the lynch trial and execution of Bennett Warren in Clinton County, *Cedar Valley Times* (Cedar Rapids, Ia.), July 9, 1857, in Black, "Lynching Research Notes," box 2, Clinton County folder. In the latter case, a constable from Big Rock, Mr. Gates, observed the proceeding and told the regulators that Warren had been "convicted on the most slimy evidence I ever heard."

72. "John Chappell's Diary," *Cedar County Historical Review,* July 1984, 97–98.

73. "Arrivals in 1837," "Biographies-Red Oak Township," and "Hi. Roberts," in *History of Cedar County, Iowa*; Hale and Rome Townships, Jones County, 1856 Iowa State Census (transcribed by Richard Harrison), accessed August 4, 2005, http://www.rootsweb.com/~iajones/census/56hale.htm, http://www.rootsweb.com/~iajones/census/56rome.htm.

74. Natalie Zemon Davis, "The Reasons of Misrule," in *Society and Culture in Early Modern France: Eight Essays by Natalie Zemon Davis* (Stanford: Stanford University Press, 1975), 97–123; E. P. Thompson, "'Rough Music': Le Charivari Anglais," *Annales: Economics, Societies, Civilization* 27 (March–April 1972): 286–287.

75. Michael J. Pfeifer, "Lynching and Criminal Justice in Regional Context: Iowa, Wyoming, and Louisiana, 1878–1946," (PhD diss., University of Iowa, 1998), 58; *New York Times,* November 26, 1871.

76. On the early territorial period and vigilantism in Wyoming, see T. A. Larson, *History of Wyoming* (Lincoln: University of Nebraska Press, 1965), 36–63, in which Baker and the *Cheyenne Leader* are quoted extensively; Carl Stanley Gustafson, "History of Vigilante and Mob Activity in Wyoming," (MA thesis, University of Wyoming, 1961), 41–94.

77. Larson, *History of Wyoming,* 45–68, 59–60; Gustafson, "History of Vigilante and Mob Activity," 41–90. Larson argues that levels of personal violence and crime were high in the recently settled railroad towns.

78. Larson, 47–48; Gustafson, 41–69.

79. Larson, 59–62; Gustafson, 70–94.

80. Larson, 46–48, 59–62; Gustafson, 41–94. Although admitting the vigilante committees' excesses, Gustafson charitably argues that they were an understandable response to the chaotic conditions in "end-of-the-track" towns and that they had a deterrent effect on criminal activity in Cheyenne and Laramie.

81. The formative, classic account of western vigilantism, highly sympathetic to the vigilantes, is Hubert Bancroft, *Popular Tribunals* (San Francisco: The History Company, 1887). For the San Francisco vigilante movements in the 1850s, see Robert M. Senkewicz, *Vigilantes in Gold Rush San Francisco* (Stanford: Stanford University Press, 1985); David Johnson, "Vigilance and the Law: The Moral Authority of Popular Justice in the Far West," *American Quarterly* 33 (1981): 558–586; Philip Ethington, *The Public City: The Political Construction of Urban Life in San Francisco, 1850–1900* (Berkeley: University of California Press, 2001), 86–169; Waldrep, *The Many Faces of Judge Lynch,* 50–56. For vigilantism in Montana, see Thomas J. Dimsdale, *The Vigilantes of Montana* (1866; repr., Norman: University of Oklahoma Press, 1953); Frederick Allen, *A Decent Orderly Lynching: The Montana Vigilantes* (Norman: University of Oklahoma Press, 2004); Waldrep, *The Many Faces of Judge Lynch,* 63–66. For vigilante committees in Colorado in the early 1860s, see Stephen J. Leonard, *Lynching in Colorado 1859–1919* (Boulder: University Press of Colorado, 2002), 22–23.

82. In a well-known example of an antebellum collective killing that grew out of a conflict over social values, a mob of approximately two hundred attacked the jail in Carthage, Illinois, on June 27, 1844, killing the leader of the Latter-Day Saints, Joseph Smith. Authorities had arrested and jailed Smith after he had ordered the destruction of the press of the *Nauvoo Expositor.* Leonard Arrington and Davis Bitton, *The Mormon Experience: A History of the Latter-Day Saints* (Urbana: University of Illinois Press), 81–82. For an argument that both the early Mormons and their opponents acted from perspectives shaped by republican ideology, see Kenneth Winn, *Exiles in a Land of Liberty: Mormons in America* (Chapel Hill: University of North Carolina Press, 1989), 2–6.

Chapter 3. Racial and Class Frontiers: Lynching and Social Identity in Antebellum America

1. *Galveston Weekly News,* August 6, 1859.

2. Eugene D. Genovese, *Roll, Jordan, Roll: The World the Slaves Made* (New York: Pantheon, 1974), 32–33. For additional interpretations stressing the infrequency of the lynching of slaves, see Clement Eaton, "Mob Violence in the Old South," *Mississippi Valley Historical Review* 29 (December 1942): 351–370; Gilles Vandal, *Rethinking Southern Violence: Homicides in Post-Civil War Louisiana, 1866–1884* (Columbus: Ohio State University Press, 2000), 94, 244–245n20; Vandal found five instances of lynching that claimed eight black victims in Louisiana in the 1850s. In parallel with Genovese's estimates, David Grimsted enumerated approximately forty-nine African American victims of "anticriminal mobs" in the antebellum South. Grimsted, *American Mobbing, 1828–1861: Toward Civil War* (New York: Oxford University Press, 1998), 101, 103.

3. Kenneth M. Stampp, *The Peculiar Institution: Slavery in the Ante-Bellum South* (New York: Knopf, 1956), 190–191. Additional interpretations arguing that the lynching of slaves was fairly common can be found in Ulrich B. Phillips, *American Negro Slavery* (1918; repr., Gloucester, Mass.: Peter Smith, 1959), 511–512; Bertram Wyatt-Brown, *Southern Honor: Ethics and Behavior in the Old South* (New York: Oxford University Press, 1982), 388–389; and Philip Schwarz, *Twice Condemned: Slaves and the Criminal Laws of Virginia, 1705–1865* (Baton Rouge: Louisiana State University Press, 1988), 291–292.

4. See Thomas G. Dyer, "'A Most Unexampled Exhibition of Madness and Brutality:

Judge Lynch in Saline County, Missouri," in *Under Sentence of Death: Lynching in the South,* ed. W. Fitzhugh Brundage (Chapel Hill: University of North Carolina Press, 1997), 98–99.

5. Orville W. Taylor, *Negro Slavery in Arkansas* (Durham, N.C.: Duke University Press, 1958), 235–236; James Benson Sellers, *Slavery in Alabama* (1940; repr., Tuscaloosa: University of Alabama Press, 1994), 262–264; Randolph B. Campbell, *An Empire for Slavery: The Peculiar Institution in Texas, 1821–1865* (Baton Rouge: Louisiana State University Press, 1989), 105; Ralph Betts Flanders, *Plantation Slavery in Georgia* (Chapel Hill: University of North Carolina Press, 1933), 268–269; R. Douglas Hurt, *Agriculture and Slavery in Missouri's Little Dixie* (Columbia, Mo.: University of Missouri Press, 1992), 248–250.

6. Christopher Waldrep, ed., *Lynching in America: A History in Documents* (New York: New York University Press, 2006), 61. For an important discussion that emphasizes growing northern criticism of southern collective violence after the mid-1830s, violence that was increasingly labeled *lynching* and that included mob executions of slaves, see Christopher Waldrep, *The Many Faces of Judge Lynch: Extralegal Violence and Punishment in America* (New York: Palgrave Macmillan, 2002), 27–47, esp. 41–45.

7. See Dyer, "A Most Unexampled Exhibition," 81–108; Martha Hodes, *White Women, Black Men: Illicit Sex in the 19th-Century-South* (New Haven, Conn.: Yale University Press, 1997), 58–59, 60, 235–236n56; Diane Miller Sommerville, *Race and Rape in the Nineteenth-Century South* (Chapel Hill: University of North Carolina Press, 2004), 29–30, 52–53.

8. For vital analyses of the history of popular constitutionalism in the United States, see Larry Kramer, *The People Themselves: Popular Constitutionalism and Judicial Review* (New York: Oxford University Press, 2004); Christian G. Fritz, *American Sovereigns: The People and America's Constitutional Tradition Before the Civil War* (New York: Cambridge University Press, 2008). For a cogent interpretation that analyzes the history of the federal response to lynching in the context of popular constitutionalism, see Christopher Waldrep, "National Policing, Lynching, and Constitutionalism," *Journal of Southern History* 74, no. 3 (August 2008): 589–626.

9. Missouri and Texas tallied, respectively, twelve and nine documented African American victims of mobs. The proximity of Kansas, the locus of a fierce national debate over the territorial expansion of slavery and the site of intense conflict between proslavery and abolitionist settlers, may have heightened white fears about the effects of abolitionism upon an "insufficiently obsequious slave population" in Missouri. Dyer, "A Most Unexampled Exhibition," 82–83. The nearness of Mexico, a haven for escaping slaves, and the presence of large numbers of culturally distinct Tejanos, whom Anglo-American slaveholders suspected might aid slave insurrection, lent a distinctive character to slaveholding culture in Texas. William Carrigan, *The Making of a Lynching Culture: Violence and Vigilantism in Central Texas, 1836–1916* (Urbana: University of Illinois Press, 2004); Campbell, *An Empire for Slavery*, 218–219; Enda Junkins, "Slave Plots, Insurrections, and Acts of Violence in the State of Texas, 1828–1865" (MA thesis, Baylor University, 1969), 9, 17–24. Comparatively low rates of legal execution on slavery's western periphery may also have played a role in the relative prevalence of the lynching of slaves there. Although his evidence is incomplete, Watt Espy documents merely 11 executions of blacks in Missouri and ten of African Americans in Texas from 1835 to 1862, compared with 185 executions of African Americans in Alabama and 174 executions of blacks in Virginia. For Watt Espy's

historical execution database, see http://www.deathpenaltyinfo.org/executions-us-1608-
-2002-espy-file, accessed September 1, 2009.

10. Evidence suggests that the collective killings of slaves began before the nineteenth
century. For instance, in Accomack County, Virginia, in 1791, a group of "disguised men,
numbering from six to fifteen," hanged Ralph Singo and James Richards, for reasons
not specified in the historical record. (Wm. P. Palmer, and Sherwin McRae, *Calendar
of Virginia State Papers* [Richmond, Va.: 1885], 328). This incident is cited in Phillips,
American Negro Slavery, 311. Race is not specified in the source, and Phillips's discussion
of the episode is ambiguous on the question of the race of the offenders. Less ambigu-
ously, Waldrep, *Lynching in America*, 62, includes documentation of a 1797 Georgia case
in which a posse decided to burn to death a slave accused of murder.

11. Thirty-nine of the fifty-six documented lynchings of slaves and free blacks occurred
between 1850 and 1862. While northern abolitionist newspapers relished reporting such
events during this period of sectional crisis, southern newspapers reported them as well,
albeit with concern over how Northerners might interpret such incidents.

12. Insurrection panics precipitated extensive episodes of lethal violence against African Americans, sometimes legally constituted, sometimes extralegally. David Grimsted
tabulated that 35 incidents of collective violence by southern whites against real and
purported slave insurrections claimed 448 lives in the antebellum era, with most of the
victims slaves. Grimsted, *American Mobbing*, 135–136. For the dozens of slaves killed by
militia or executed in highly public punishments following judicial proceedings in the
suppression of a large-scale slave rebellion in the Louisiana sugar parishes of St. John the
Baptist and St. Charles in 1811, see Adam Rothman, *Slave Country: American Expansion
and the Origins of the Deep South* (Cambridge, Mass.: Harvard University Press, 2005),
106–117. For the summary executions of blacks and whites amid an insurrection panic in
Texas in 1860, see Donald E. Reynolds, *Texas Terror: The Slave Insurrection Panic of 1860
and the Secession of the Lower South* (Baton Rouge: Louisiana State University Press, 2007).
For the hangings and lethal floggings with which whites sought to suppress an alleged
slave conspiracy in Mississippi in 1861, see Winthrop D. Jordan, *Tumult and Silence at
Second Creek: An Inquiry into a Civil War Slave Conspiracy*, rev. ed. (Baton Rouge: Louisiana State University Press, 1996). The classic interpretation of African American slave
resistance and the white response is Herbert Aptheker, *American Negro Revolts* (New
York: International Publishers, 1963).

13. Campbell, *An Empire for Slavery*, 101.

14. Ibid.

15. *Boston Liberator*, October 16, 1857; James Elbert Cutler, *Lynch-Law and Investigation
into the History of Lynching in the United States* (New York: Longman, Green, and Co.,
1905), 125.

16. For analyses of the treatment of slaves in the formal criminal justice system and in
extralegal "plantation justice," see Michael Stephen Hindus, *Crime, Justice, and Authority
in Massachusetts and South Carolina, 1767–1878* (Chapel Hill: University of North Carolina
Press, 1980), 130–161; Edward L. Ayers, *Vengeance and Justice, Crime and Punishment in
the 19th-Century American South* (New York: Oxford University Press, 1984), 132–137.

17. Howell M. Henry, *The Police Control of the Slave in South Carolina* (New York: Negro
Universities Press, 1968), 4–6; Walter Hening, *The Statutes at Large: Being a Collection*

of All the Laws of Virginia, from the First Session of the Legislature in the Year 1619, vol. 1 (New York: R & W & G. Bartow, 1823).

18. Judith Kelleher Schafer, "Slaves and Crime: New Orleans, 1846–1862," in Christopher Waldrep and Donald G. Nieman, eds., *Local Matters: Race, Crime, and Justice in the Nineteenth-Century South* (Athens: University of Georgia Press, 2001), esp. 56, 74, 84–85n5.

19. Ibid., 62.

20. Ibid., 58.

21. Ibid., 56, 84–85n5.

22. For a case study with these dynamics, see Timothy Huebner, "The Roots of Fairness, *State v. Caesar* and Slave Justice in Antebellum North Carolina," in Waldrep and Nieman, eds., *Local Matters*, 29–52. For evidence of concern for slaves' legal rights, proper legal procedure, and a variety of legal outcomes in cases involving slaves in Texas, see Campbell, *An Empire for Slavery*, 106–108. For the legal culture of southern slavery, see Daniel J. Flanigan, *The Criminal Law of Slavery and Freedom 1800–1868* (New York: Garland Publishing, 1987); Mark V. Tushnet, *The American Law of Slavery 1810–1860* (Princeton: Princeton University Press, 1981); Thomas D. Morris, *Southern Slavery and the Law, 1619–1860* (Chapel Hill: University of North Carolina Press, 1996); Ariela J. Gross, *Double Character: Slavery and Mastery in the Antebellum Southern Courtroom* (Princeton: Princeton University Press, 2000).

23. Schwarz, *Twice Condemned*, 27–29; Stuart Banner, "Traces of Slavery: Race and the Death Penalty in Historical Perspective," in *From Lynch Mobs to the Killing State: Race and the Death Penalty in America*, ed. Charles Ogletree, Jr., and Austin Sarat (New York: New York University Press, 2006), 100.

24. Works Progress Administration (WPA) Slave Narratives, Oklahoma Narratives, vol. 13, Octavia George, 113.

25. Moses Roper to Thomas Price, London, June 27, 1836, *Slavery in America*, no. 2 (August 1836): 45–46, quoted in *Slave Testimony: Two Centuries of Letters, Speeches, Interviews, and Autobiographies*, ed. John W. Blassingame (Baton Rouge: Louisiana State University Press, 1977), 24–25.

26. For analyses of the slave patrol, see Sally E. Hadden, "Colonial and Revolutionary Era Slave Patrols of Virginia," in *Lethal Imagination: Violence and Brutality in American History*, ed. Michael Bellesiles (New York: New York University Press, 1999), 69–85, and Hadden, *Slave Patrols: Law and Violence in Virginia and the Carolinas* (Cambridge, Mass.: Harvard University Press, 2001).

27. For the commentary of ex-slaves on the slave patrol see, for instance, WPA Slave Narratives, Ohio Narratives, vol. 12, Perry Sid Jemison, 52; WPA Slave Narratives, Georgia Narratives, vol. 4, pt. 2, Easter Huff, 24. For analysis of the clash between masters and the slave patrol, and how this was informed by a tension between slaveholders and nonslaveholders regarding the regulation of African American behavior, see Henry, *The Police Control of the Slave in South Carolina*, 39–41.

28. For the profound social effects of the expansion of slavery in the early to mid–nineteenth century, an event that Ira Berlin terms "the Second Middle Passage," see Berlin, *Generations of Captivity: A History of African-American Slaves* (Cambridge, Mass.: Harvard University Press, 2003), 161–243.

29. *Galveston Weekly News,* May 17, 1859.

30. Taylor, *Negro Slavery in Arkansas,* 235–236.

31. Sellers, *Slavery in Alabama,* 262–264.

32. *Huntsville Democrat,* September 7, 1854, quoted in Sellers, *Slavery in Alabama,* 263.

33. *Maysville Eagle* (Maysville, Ky.), January 8, 1859. *New York Times,* January 28, 1859, erroneously reports that this incident occurred in Kentucky.

34. *Maysville Eagle,* January 8, 1859. For the ritual of the condemned person's "dying declaration" in eighteenth- and early-nineteenth-century England and America, see Stuart Banner, *The Death Penalty: An American History* (Cambridge, Mass.: Harvard University Press, 2002), 48–52.

35. Frederick Law Olmstead, *The Cotton Kingdom; A Traveler's Observations on Cotton and Slavery in the American Slave States* (New York: Alfred A. Knopf, 1953; repr., New York: Da Capo Press, 1996), 303.

36. R. Douglas Hurt, *Agriculture and Slavery in Missouri's Little Dixie* (Columbia: University of Missouri Press, 1992), 248; Harrison Anthony Trexler, *Slavery in Missouri 1804–1865* (Baltimore: The John Hopkins Press, 1914), 254n61; *St. Louis Bulletin,* November 8, 1860, quoted in *Santa Fe Gazette,* December 15, 1860.

37. *Mississippi Free Trader* (Natchez, Miss.), March 8, 1854, reprinted in Waldrep, ed., *Lynching in America,* 76–77.

38. Hodes, *White Women, Black Men,* 39–122; Sommerville, *Race and Rape in the Nineteenth-Century South,* 19–101. Hodes, 59–60, cites the 1861 Georgia case.

39. Campbell, *An Empire for Slavery,* 105.

40. Sommerville, *Race and Rape in the Nineteenth-Century South,* 29–30.

41. Dyer, "A Most Unexampled Exhibition," 87; Hurt, *Agriculture and Slavery in Missouri's Little Dixie,* 249–250.

42. Banner, *The Death Penalty,* 70–72.

43. Ibid., 72–76, 88–111, 151.

44. I am grateful to Peter Charles Hoffer for information on this point. "Execution by Burning in the 19th century U.S.?" thread, H-Law, July 18, 2008. I am also indebted to Michael Radelet for information on this matter, e-mail correspondence with the author, July 15, 16, 2008. For a description of a legal execution by burning in South Carolina in the 1830s, see Moses Roper to Thomas Price, London, June 27, 1836, from *Slavery in America,* no. 2 (August 1836): 45–46, in Blassingame, *Slave Testimony,* 24–25. Special freeholder courts tried slaves and free blacks in South Carolina from the colonial era through the antebellum period; blacks gained the right to appeal the decisions of the "negro courts" in 1833. Henry, "The Police Control of the Slave in South Carolina," 58–65.

45. *Boston Liberator,* July 4, 1835, quoted in Cutler, *Lynch-Law,* 108.

46. Junkins, "Slave Plots, Insurrections, and Acts of Violence," 40. The quotation is from Junkins's source, *San Antonio Ledger,* July 31, 1851.

47. *Gallatin Signal* (Gallatin, Miss.), quoted in *Courier de La Louisiane (Louisiana Courier)* (New Orleans), March 1, 1843.

48. Hurt, *Agriculture and Slavery in Missouri's Little Dixie,* 249. Hurt quotes *Weekly Tribune* (Liberty, Mo.), September 2, 1853.

49. Wyatt-Brown, *Southern Honor,* 389; *Boston Liberator,* October 16, and December 4, 1857.

50. *New York Times*, September, 17, 1857. For another northern editor's condemnation of a "negro-burning" in Tennessee as the inevitable product of "the inhuman relations of slave and owner," see *New York Tribune*, July 11, 1854.

51. Sellers, *Slavery in Alabama*, 263.

52. Ibid., 263–264.

53. *Boston Liberator*, October 19, 1855, reprinted in Waldrep, ed., *Lynching in America*, 74–75.

54. *Galveston Weekly News*, June 2, 1857.

55. Flanders, *Plantation Slavery in Georgia*, 268–269.

56. Trexler, *Slavery in Missouri 1804–1865*, 254n61; Hurt, *Agriculture and Slavery in Missouri's Little Dixie*, 248.

57. *Baltimore Republican and Argus*, October 10, 1854.

58. For the declining social and legal status of free blacks in the antebellum South, see Berlin, *Generations of Captivity*, 182–184, 224–225; Campbell, *An Empire for Slavery*, 112–114; John Hope Franklin, *The Free Negro in North Carolina 1790–1860* (Chapel Hill: University of North Carolina Press, 1943), 67–81.

59. H. E. Sterkx, *The Free Negro in Ante-Bellum Louisiana* (Rutherford, N.J.: Fairleigh Dickinson, N.J., 1972), 189–190.

60. *Missouri Republican* (St. Louis, Mo.), April 30, 1836, reprinted in Janet S. Hermann, "The McIntosh Affair," *Bulletin of the Missouri Historical Society* 26 (January 1970): 123–143; John F. Darby, *Personal Recollections* (St. Louis: G. I. Jones and Company, 1880), 237–241.

61. For an interpretation that argues that the unevenness and flexibility of local criminal justice in the antebellum South stemmed from the need for courts to mediate class differences among whites, see Bertram Wyatt-Brown, "Community, Class, and Snopesian Crime: Local Justice in the Old South," in *Class, Conflict, and Consensus: Antebellum Southern Community Studies,* ed. Orville Vernon Burton and Robert C. McMath Jr. (Westport, Conn.: Greenwood Press, 1982), 173–206.

62. Genovese argues that Kentucky's slave code was comparatively mild, but that Kentucky apparently saw more "personal violence and lynching" than many other southern states, "although much more often directed against allegedly negrophile whites than against blacks." *Roll, Jordan, Roll*, 32.

63. Dyer, "A Most Unexampled Exhibition," 89–91.

64. Ibid., 86, 92.

65. Ibid., 93.

66. Ibid., 93–94.

67. "Charge of Hon. Judge Watts to the Grand Jury of Taos County, in Relation to the Mora Execution," *Santa Fe Gazette*, December 18, 1852; Robert J. Tórrez, *Myth of the Hanging Tree: Stories of Crime and Punishment in New Mexico* (Albuquerque: University of New Mexico Press, 2008), 5–9, 159–162. Tórrez identifies the summary hangings of Vigil and Luhan as "New Mexico's first documented lynchings." Tórrez documents an additional 123 lynching victims in New Mexico between 1852 and 1928, 42 percent with Mexico/Hispano (Spanish) surnames, and 53 percent with American/Anglo surnames.

68. For the transformation of the ideology of republicanism from the American Revolution through the mid–nineteenth century, see Gordon S. Wood, *The Radicalism of the American Revolution* (New York: Vintage Books, 1991); Wood, *Empire of Liberty: A His-*

tory of the American Republic, 1789–1815 (New York: Oxford University Press, 2009); and Sean Wilentz, *Chants Democratic: New York City and the Rise of the American Working Class, 1788–1850* (New York: Oxford University Press, 1984). The racial dimensions of nineteenth-century republicanism, with the West as an important crucible for the forging of racial ideologies, are traced in Alexander Saxton and David Roediger, *The Rise and Fall of the White Republic: Class Politics and Mass Culture in Nineteenth-Century America, New Edition* (New York: Verso Books, 2003).

69. For treatments of violence and society on the mining frontiers of California and Colorado, see Robert M. Senkewicz, *Vigilantes in Gold Rush California* (Stanford: Stanford University Press, 1985); Susan Lee Johnson, *Roaring Camp: The Social World of the California Gold Rush* (New York: W. W. Norton, 2001), 218, 321; Ken Gonzales-Day, *Lynching in the West: 1850–1935* (Durham, N.C.: Duke University Press, 2006); Stephen J. Leonard, *Lynching in Colorado 1859–1919* (Denver: University Press of Colorado, 2002), 1–29. For a recent interpretation arguing that the nineteenth-century West was not particularly violent, see Robert R. Dykstra, "Quantifying the Wild West: The Problematic Statistics of Frontier Violence," *Western Historical Quarterly* 40, no. 3 (Autumn, 2009): 321–347. The carefully controlled collective violence of lynching can be read in multiple, contradictory ways in terms of the long-standing debate over whether the nineteenth-century West was or was not violent, not least because lynching violence substantially declined (and then persisted at a lesser level) after the first years of white American in-migration and settlement at midcentury.

70. For overviews of the development of white racial ideologies regarding Mexican Americans, shaped by centuries of Anglo-American interactions with peoples of the Iberian Peninsula, indigenous peoples of the Americas, and Mexicans, see David J. Weber, "'Scarce More than Apes': Historical Roots of Anglo American Stereotypes of Mexicans in the Border Region," in *New Spain's Far Northern Frontier: Essays on Spain the American West, 1540–1821*, ed. David J. Weber (Albuquerque: University of New Mexico Press, 1979), 295–307; David G. Gutiérrez, "Significant to Whom?: Mexican Americans and the History of the American West," *Western Historical Quarterly* 24 (November 1993): esp. 520–523. For white Americans' perception of and interaction with Natives in the nineteenth century, see Glenda Riley, *Women and Indians on the Frontier, 1825–1915* (Albuquerque: University of New Mexico Press, 1984). For an interpretation stressing the centrality of violence in the encounter of Natives and Euro-American settlers in the West, see Ned Blackhawk, *Violence Over the Land: Indians and Empires in the Early American West* (Cambridge, Mass.: Harvard University Press, 2008).

71. Gonzales-Day, *Lynching in the West*, appendix 1, 206–219. William Carrigan and Clive Webb similarly enumerate 163 Mexican victims of lynching in California from 1848 through 1860 in their pathbreaking interpretation of the lynching of Mexican Americans in U.S. history. William Carrigan and Clive Webb, "Muerto Por Unos Desconocidos (Killed by Persons Unknown): Mob Violence against African Americans and Mexican Americans," in *Beyond Black and White: Race, Ethnicity, and Gender in the U.S. South and Southwest*, ed. Stephanie Cole and Alison Parker (College Park: Texas A & M University Press, 2004), 49.

72. Johnson, *Roaring Camp*; Sucheng Chan, "A People of Exceptional Character: Ethnic Diversity, Nativism, and Racism in the California Gold Rush," and James A. Sandos, "'Be-

cause he is a liar and a thief': Conquering the Residents of 'Old' California, 1850–1880," in *Rooted in Barbarous Soil: People, Culture, and Community in Gold Rush California,* ed. Kevin Starr and Richard J. Orsi (Berkeley: University of California Press, 2000), 44–112; Malcolm J. Rohrbough, *Days of Gold: The California Gold Rush and the American Nation* (Berkeley: University of California Press, 1997), 216–229.

73. David Peterson del Mar, *Beaten Down: A History of Interpersonal Violence in the West* (Seattle: University of Washington Press, 2002), 28–29.

74. Leonard Pitt, *The Decline of the Californios: A Social History of the Spanish-Speaking Californians* (Berkeley: University of California Press, 1966), 104–276; Albert Camarillo, *Chicanos in a Changing Society: From Mexican Pueblos to American Barrios in Santa Barbara and Southern California, 1848–1930* (Cambridge, Mass.: Harvard University Press, 1979), 6–52; Richard Griswold del Castillo, *The Los Angeles Barrio* (Berkeley: University of California Press, 1979), 30–61; Douglas Monroy, *Thrown Among Strangers: The Making of Mexican Culture in Frontier California* (Berkeley: University of California Press, 1990), 163–232; Erlinda Gonzales-Berry and David R. Maciel, *The Contested Homeland: A Chicano History of New Mexico* (Albuquerque: University of New Mexico Press, 2000), 12–22; Armando C. Alonzo, *Tejano Legacy: Rancheros and Settlers in South Texas, 1734–1900* (Albuquerque: University of New Mexico Press, 1998). For an argument suggesting that American officials championed capital punishment in territorial New Mexico and that this was resisted by Hispanic New Mexican jurors who were reluctant to convict in capital cases, see Tórrez, *Myth of the Hanging Tree,* 52–53.

75. Western Historical Company, *History of Northern Wisconsin* (Chicago: Western Historical Company, 1881), 195; Richard N. Current, *The History of Wisconsin, Volume II: The Civil War Era, 1848–1873* (Madison: The State Historical Society of Wisconsin, 1976), 154. For the Ojibwas (Chippewas) in northern Wisconsin in the antebellum era, see Mark Wyman, *The Wisconsin Frontier* (Bloomington: Indiana University Press, 1998), 223–226.

76. Robert D. Pomeroy, "Morrison County's Only Lynching," (unpublished manuscript, 1966, Minnesota Historical Society, St. Paul); John D. Bessler, *Legacy of Violence: Lynch Mobs and Executions in Minnesota* (Minneapolis: University of Minnesota Press, 2003), 5; Marilyn Ziebarth, "Judge Lynch in Minnesota," *Minnesota History* 55 (Summer 1996): 72. Ziebarth documents three additional lynchings of persons of Native ancestry by whites in Minnesota, in 1848, 1865, and 1872.

77. Robert Bunting, *The Pacific Raincoast: Environment and Culture in an American Eden* (Lawrence: University Press of Kansas, 1997), 51–54.

78. Peterson del Mar, *Beaten Down: A History of Interpersonal Violence in the West* (Seattle: University of Washington Press, 2002), 29; *Pioneer and Democrat* (Olympia, Wash.), April 8, 1854, p. 2; Alexandra Harmon, *Indians in the Making: Ethnic Relations and Indian Identities Around Puget Sound* (Berkeley: University of California Press, 1998), 67–68; Brad Asher, *Beyond the Reservation: Indians, Settlers, and the Law in Washington Territory, 1853–1889* (Norman: University of Oklahoma Press, 1999), 19–40.

79. *Pioneer and Democrat,* April 8, 1854.

80. M.T. Simmons, "To the Inhabitants of the Puget Sound Indian Agency District," reprinted in *Pioneer and Democrat,* April 8, 1854.

81. Ibid.

82. Harmon, *Indians in the Making*, 67.

83. Gonzales-Day, *Lynching in the West*, appendix 1, 206–219. For Native people in Gold Rush–era California, see Johnson, *Roaring Camp*, 219–234, 307–311.

84. David Johnson, "Vigilance and the Law: The Moral Authority of Popular Justice in the Far West," *American Quarterly* 33 (1981): 558–586.

85. *Alta California* (San Francisco), March 31, 1851.

86. Paul R. Spitzzeri, "On a Case-by-Case Basis: Ethnicity and Los Angeles Courts, 1850–1875," *California History* 83, no. 2 (Fall 2005): 26–30.

87. *Los Angeles Star*, April 3, 1852.

88. Ibid., December 3, 1853.

89. *Alta California*, November 15, 1850.

90. *Santa Fe Gazette*, July 24, 1858.

91. Ibid., December 18, 1852.

92. Ibid.

93. *Alta California*, August 1, 1850.

94. Rohrbough, *Days of Gold*, 228–229; Gonzales-Day, *Lynching in the West*, appendix 1, 206–219; Carrigan and Webb, "Muerto Por Unos Desconocidos (Killed by Persons Unknown)," 49; Pitt, *The Decline of the Californios*, 53–64, 69–82; Rodolfo Acuña, *Occupied America: A History of Chicanos* (New York: Pearson Education, 1988), 118–121. For social banditry in Gold Rush–era California, see Johnson, *Roaring Camp*, 28–53, 218. For analyses of perhaps the best-known lynching of a Hispanic person in Gold Rush–era California, the informal execution of Josefa (sometimes given as Juanita), a Mexican woman summarily tried and hanged for the murder of an English miner in Downieville, in 1851, see Gonzales-Day, *Lynching in the West*, 185–186; Carrigan and Webb, "Muerto Por Unos Desconocidos (Killed by Persons Unknown)," 42–43; Acuña, *Occupied America*, 118–119; Pitt, *The Decline of the Californios*, 73–74; Coya Paz Brownrigg, "Linchocracia: Performing 'America' in El Clamor Publico," *California History* 84, no. 2 (Winter 2006): 41–42.

95. *Alta California*, December 4, 1851; Walter T. Durham, *Volunteer Forty-Niners: Tenneseeans and the California Gold Rush* (Nashville: Vanderbilt University Press, 1997), 145.

96. *Alta California*, August 1, 1853. Gonzales-Day identifies seven Chilean lynching victims in California, 1850–1860, and another four victims of lynching identified as "Chilean or Mexican." Gonzales-Day, *Lynching in the West*, appendix 1, 206–219.

97. For the lynching of Mexicans for property crime, see Carrigan and Webb, "Muerto Por Unos Desconocidos (Killed by Persons Unknown)," 41–42.

98. *Alta California*, August 1, 1853.

99. Ibid., August 1, 1853. For a cultural shift against lynching in California in the mid-to-late 1850s, with vigilante activity moving to the rural periphery as support declined in urban areas, see Johnson, "Vigilance and the Law," 578, 583.

100. *Los Angeles Star*, October 8, 1853.

101. Ibid., October 22, 1853.

102. Ibid., October 8, 1853; December 10, 1853.

103. Examining vigilante violence in Los Angeles in the 1850s, Leonard Pitt, *The Decline of the Californios*, 154–166, argues that "the better element" of Californios cooperated

with the vigilantes, but that lower class Hispanics bridled at the discriminatory nature of the collective punishments. Pitt emphasizes the important role of white Texan migrants who had served in the Texas Rangers in the orchestration of anti-Mexican vigilantism in Southern California. For a parallel analysis, see Monroy, *Thrown Among Strangers*, 208–211.

104. *Los Angeles Star*, December 4, 1858. For analysis of the events surrounding the Pancho Daniel case, see Gonzales-Day, *Lynching in the West*, 189–197.

105. *Nueces Valley Weekly* (Corpus Christi, Tx.), January 23, 1858; *New York Times*, January 27, 1858.

106. Michael J. Pfeifer, *Rough Justice: Lynching and American Society, 1874–1947* (Urbana: University of Illinois Press, 2004), 85–87.

Chapter 4. Lynchers versus Due Process: The Forging of Rough Justice

1. Account from *Maysville Eagle* (Maysville, Ky.) reprinted in *New York Times*, December 4, 1856.

2. *New York Times*, November 26, 1871; George C. Wright, *Racial Violence in Kentucky, 1865–1940* (Baton Rouge: Louisiana State University Press, 1990), 19–60; David Thelen, *Paths of Resistance: Tradition and Dignity in Industrializing Missouri* (New York: Oxford University Press, 1986), 59–62, 88–90.

3. Abraham Lincoln, "Address to the Young Men's Lyceum of Springfield, Illinois," January 27, 1838, in *Lincoln: Selected Speeches and Writings*, ed. Don E. Fehrenbacher (New York: Vintage Books, 1992), 13–21. For the context for Lincoln's Address to the Young Men's Lyceum, see Carl F. Wieck, *Lincoln's Quest for Equality: The Road to Gettysburg* (Dekalb: Northern Illinois University, 2002), 29–33.

4. *Missouri Republican* (St. Louis), April 30, 1836, reprinted in Janet S. Hermann, "The McIntosh Affair," *Bulletin of the Missouri Historical Society* 26 (January 1970): 123–143; John F. Darby, *Personal Recollections* (St. Louis: G. I. Jones and Company, 1880), 237–241.

5. For the origins of backcountry folkways and culture in the eighteenth-century migration of North British borderers to the Appalachians, see David Hackett Fischer, *Albion's Seed: Four British Folkways in America* (New York: Oxford University Press, 1989), 605–782. For a discussion of the essential role of communal opinion in criminal justice in Appalachia in the mid-to-late nineteenth century, see Altina L. Waller, *Feud: Hatfields, McCoys, and Social Change in Appalachia, 1860–1900* (Chapel Hill: University of North Carolina Press, 1988), 85–93.

6. For tensions between southerners and Yankees in the political culture and social fabric of antebellum Illinois, see James E. Davis, *Frontier Illinois* (Bloomington: Indiana University Press, 1998), 3, 247–251. For these dynamics, more broadly in the early Midwest, see Nicole Etcheson, *The Emerging Midwest: Upland Southerners and the Political Culture of the Old Northwest, 1789–1861* (Bloomington: Indiana University Press, 1996).

7. Larry Kramer, *The People Themselves: Popular Constitutionalism and Judicial Review* (New York: Oxford University Press, 2004); Christian G. Fritz, *American Sovereigns: The People and America's Constitutional Tradition Before the Civil War* (New York: Cambridge University Press, 2008); Christopher Waldrep, "National Policing, Lynching, and Constitutionalism," *Journal of Southern History* 74, no. 3 (August 2008), 589–626. Bertram

Wyatt-Brown, *Southern Honor: Ethics and Behavior in the Old South* (New York: Oxford University Press, 1982), esp. 362–401, remains the indispensable analysis of the conjunction of kin, neighborhood, honor, shame, and informal and formal violence in southern legal systems. For the origins of free labor ideology, see Eric Foner, *Free Soil, Free Labor, Free Men: The Ideology of the Republican Party Before the Civil War*, rev. ed. (New York: Oxford University Press, 1995).

8. *Goodspeed's History of Franklin, Jefferson, Washington, Crawford, and Gasconade Counties, Missouri* (Chicago: Goodspeed Publishing Company, 1888), 280–281.

9. *Montezuma Republican* (Montezuma, Ia.), July 18, and August 1, 1857.

10. *Cincinnati Commercial*, quoted in *New York Times*, February 22, 1856.

11. *Boonsville Observer* (Boonsville, Mo.), quoted in *New York Times*, July 29, 1856.

12. *Louisville Democrat*, quoted in *New York Times*, July 17, 1858.

13. *Fairfield Ledger* (Fairfield, Ia.), July 13, 1860.

14. *Mt. Pleasant News* (Mt. Pleasant, Ia.), quoted in *Fairfield Ledger*, July 20, 1860.

15. *Ibid.*

16. For the abolition of Wisconsin's death penalty, see Richard N. Current, *The History of Wisconsin, Volume II: The Civil War Era, 1848–1873* (Madison: State Historical Society of Wisconsin, 1976), 190–191. Four legal executions in the state and territory, 1836–1851, had preceded abolition, two of American Indians. The abolition movement's origin in the Northeast is described in Louis P. Masur, *Rites of Execution: Capital Punishment and the Transformation of American Culture, 1776–1865* (New York: Oxford University Press, 1989). Antebellum American debates over the death penalty, and their regional dimensions, are analyzed in Stuart Banner, *The Death Penalty: An American History* (Cambridge, Mass.: Harvard University Press, 2002),112–168.

17. Ira C. Jenks, *Trial of David F. Mayberry for the Murder of Andrew Alger* (Janesville, Wis.: Baker, Burnett, and Hall, 1855), 1–4; *Janesville Democrat Standard* (Janesville, Wis.), June 20, 27, July 12, 1855.

18. Jenks, *Trial of David F. Mayberry*, 19.

19. Ibid., 29.

20. *Janesville Democrat Standard*, July 25, 1855.

21. *Janesville Gazette* (Janesville, Wis.), July 21, 1855.

22. *Milwaukee Free Democrat*, August 2, 3, 4, 7, 8, and 9, 1855; *Milwaukee Daily News*, August 3, 4, 8, and 10, 1855; *Milwaukee Sentinel*, August 3, 4, 6, 8, 9, 10, 11, 13, and 14, 1855.

23. Booth was tried and convicted for his participation in the "rescue" of Joshua Glover in March 1854, but was released in February 1855 after the Wisconsin Supreme Court ruled that the Fugitive Slave Act was unconstitutional. *The Rescue of Joshua Glover: A Fugitive Slave, The Constitution, and the Coming of the Civil War* (Athens: Ohio University Press, 2006).

24. *Milwaukee Free Democrat*, August 8, 1855.

25. Ibid., August 10, 1855.

26. *Milwaukee Sentinel*, August 14, 1855.

27. Ibid., August 16, 1855.

28. Michael J. Pfeifer, "Wisconsin's Last Decade of Lynching, 1881–1891: Law and Violence in the Postbellum Midwest," *American Nineteenth Century History* 6, no. 3 (September 2005): 227–239.

29. For Minnesota's death penalty history, see John D. Bessler, *Legacy of Violence: Lynch Mobs and Executions in Minnesota* (Minneapolis: University of Minnesota Press, 2003), 67–182.

30. Michael J. Pfeifer, *Rough Justice: Lynching and American Society, 1874–1947* (Urbana: University of Illinois Press, 2004), 113.

31. For an overview of the cultural context of lynching violence in Gold Rush–era California, see David Johnson, "Vigilance and the Law: The Moral Authority of Popular Justice in the Far West," *American Quarterly* 33 (1981): 558–586. For a statement of the legal critique that was used to justify lynching in the Gold Rush–era, see *Alta California* (San Francisco, Calif.), March 5, 1851.

32. Ibid., February 15, 1851.

33. Ibid.

34. Ibid.

35. Ibid., June 14, 1851.

36. *Alta California*, April 14, and May 31, 1851; Todd L. Shulman, *Napa County Police* (Mt. Pleasant, S.C.: Arcadia Publishing, 2007), 10.

37. *Alta California*, September 1, 1851.

38. Ibid.

39. Ibid.

40. Robert M. Senkewicz, *Vigilantes in Gold Rush San Francisco* (Stanford: Stanford University Press, 1985), 86.

41. Johnson, "Vigilance and the Law," 573–586; Christopher Waldrep, *The Many Faces of Judge Lynch: Extralegal Violence and Punishment in America* (New York: Palgrave Macmillan, 2002), 49–66; Pfeifer, *Rough Justice*, 94–121, 137–139.

Chapter 5. The Civil War and Reconstruction and the Remaking of American Lynching

1. For a comprehensive treatment of the Civil War in its political and social context, see James McPherson, *Battle Cry of Freedom: The Civil War Era* (New York: Ballantine Books, 1989). The definitive treatment of the social and political dimensions of Reconstruction on the regional and national levels remains Eric Foner, *Reconstruction: America's Unfinished Revolution* (New York: Harper and Row, 1988). For a recent interpretation stressing the centrality of the image of the American West in the reconciliation of the North and South in the postbellum era, see Heather Cox Richardson, *West From Appomattox: The Reconstruction of America After the Civil War* (New Haven: Yale University Press, 2007).

2. Allen W. Trelease, *White Terror: The Ku Klux Klan Conspiracy and Southern Reconstruction* (Baton Rouge: Louisiana State University Press, 1971); George C. Rable, *But There Was No Peace: The Role of Violence in the Politics of Reconstruction* (Athens: University of Georgia Press, 1984). Elaine Frantz Parsons, "Midnight Rangers: Costume and Performance in the Reconstruction-Era Ku Klux Klan," *Journal of American History* 92, no. 3 (December 2005): 811–836, is an important recent interpretation of southern Klan violence in Reconstruction.

3. See, for example, David R. Roediger, *The Wages of Whiteness: The Making of the American Working Class*, 2nd ed. (New York: Verso, 1997), esp. 133–163; Noel Ignatiev, *How the Irish Became White* (New York: Routledge, 1995); Alexander Saxton and David

Roediger, *The Rise and Fall of the White Republic: Class Politics and Mass Culture in Nineteenth-Century America,* new ed. (New York: Verso, 2003); Iver Bernstein, *The New York City Draft Riots: Their Significance for American Society and Politics in the Age of the Civil War* (New York: Oxford University Press, 1990); Michael A. Gordon, *The Orange Riots: Irish Political Violence in New York City, 1870 and 1871* (Ithaca, N.Y.: Cornell University Press, 1993). At least 120 persons died in the New York City Draft Riots; Irish rioters burned the corpse of an African American that they had hanged and sexually mutilated some black male victims. Paul Gilje, *Rioting in America* (Bloomington: Indiana University Press, 1996), 92–93; Leslie M. Harris, *In the Shadow of Slavery: African-Americans in New York City, 1626–1863* (Chicago: University of Chicago Press, 2003), 279–288.

4. In this chapter, I use the term *lynching* in the way that Americans did in the 1860s, to connote an unlawful killing by a group of people motivated by an intent to impose harsher and more rapid punishment than that available through legal processes. This meaning of *lynching* coexisted into the twentieth century with a meaning referring to summary group violence that was not lethal. Historian Christopher Waldrep has charted the origins of the term *lynching* to describe summary floggings and hangings in the American Revolution, as well as the term's widespread adoption to connote vigilante killings in the 1830s with the rise of the popular press. Waldrep traces the word's history in the nineteenth and twentieth centuries in the context of politicized debates concerning race, region, and the legitimacy of particular varieties of collective violence. Yet Waldrep understates how prevalent the term had become by the mid–nineteenth century, by which time the word had already come to encompass meanings that would be readily familiar to late-nineteenth- and twentieth-century Americans. Waldrep asserts that "racial violence in the Reconstruction era was not called lynching" and that the usage of the term *lynching* in the mid-to-late nineteenth century was constrained by the fact that it implied the uniform backing of the local community. Waldrep, *The Many Faces of Judge Lynch,* 67–84, esp. 68, 84; Waldrep, "Word and Deed: The Language of Lynching, 1820–1953," in *Lethal Imagination: Violence and Brutality in American History,* ed. Michael Bellesiles (New York: New York University Press, 1999), 232, 245. Waldrep's argument about Reconstruction would be more persuasive if he limited it to Ku Klux Klan violence, as opposed to the broad sweep of racial violence in southern Reconstruction, much of which was called *lynching* by contemporary sources, some of which Waldrep cites. All of the northern racial violence in the early-to-mid-1860s chronicled in this chapter was called *lynching* by participants and observers and by those who chronicled these deeply divisive events, none of which enjoyed the uniform backing of the communities in which they occurred. For example, in describing the events leading to the collective murder of African American Marshall Clarke by Irishmen in Milwaukee, which it deplored, the *Milwaukee Sentinel* wrote of "the preparation for the lynching" (*Milwaukee Sentinel,* September 10, 1861). Local newspapers that described and debated the collective murder of an African American, Robert Mulliner, by Irishmen in Newburgh, New York, also used the word *lynching:* "The Tribune on the Lynching Case" (*Newburgh Daily Telegraph,* June 24, 1863); "Knots and groups about the streets on the river and in the drinking houses, discussed the circumstances with bitter feeling and with threats of lynching" *(Whig Press* [Middletown, New York], July 1, 1863). Finally, Michigan newspapers were unanimous in labeling the illegal collective murder of John Taylor a *lynching.* The *Lansing State Journal,* which excoriated the collective murderers of Taylor, reported that Taylor had been *lynched* and that the event

was a *lynching* (August 29, 1866: "Ingham county has been disgraced by the lynching of the prisoner, Taylor," "Taylor has been lynched by an infuriated mob"; September 19, 1866: "the lynching of the negro"), as did the *Saginaw Enterprise* and the *Grand Rapids Eagle* (quoted in the *Lansing State Journal*, September 29, 1866: "the men who outraged law and humanity by resorting to lynch law" and "the lynching and hanging by a mob"). The *Chicago Tribune* similarly characterized the event as a *lynching* (quoted in *Lansing State Journal*, October 10, 1866: "the lynching is heartily condemned.") The *Detroit Free Press*, a Democratic paper, did not editorialize on the event, but did characterize it as a *lynching* ("The Lynching of the Delhi Murderer," *Detroit Free Press*, August 31, 1866).

5. Roediger, *The Wages of Whiteness*, and Ignatiev, *How the Irish Became White*, emphasize Irish American racial formation in the antebellum United States in the context of labor markets in which Irish Americans competed with free blacks. For Roediger's response to his critics, who have asserted that his interpretation reified whiteness, oversimplified working class identity, and overemphasized race to the detriment of class or ethnicity, see *The Wages of Whiteness*, 2nd ed., 185–189.

6. I am indebted to Carolyn Conley for helping me to think about this point, e-mail exchange with the author, February 8, 2009. Carolyn A. Conley, *Melancholy Accidents: The Meaning of Violence in Post-Famine Ireland* (Lanham, Md.: Lexington Books, 1999), 1–6. For treatments of the mid-nineteenth-century emigration from Ireland and Irish community formation in North America, see Kerby A. Miller, *Emigrants and Exiles: Ireland and the Irish Exodus to North America* (New York: Oxford University Press, 1985); Lawrence J. McCaffrey, *The Irish Catholic Diaspora in America* (1976; repr., Washington, D.C.: Catholic University Press of America, 1997); McCaffrey, *Textures of Irish America* (Syracuse: Syracuse University Press, 1992); Hasia R. Diner, *Erin's Daughters in America: Irish Immigrant Women in the Nineteenth Century* (Baltimore: Johns Hopkins University Press, 1983); Kevin Kenny, *The American Irish* (New York: Longman, 2000); Kenny, ed., *New Directions in Irish-American History* (Madison: University of Wisconsin Press, 2003); David T. Gleeson, *The Irish in the South, 1815–1877* (Chapel Hill: University of North Carolina Press, 2001). Miller's influential interpretation stresses the difficulty of Irish Catholic adjustment to American circumstances, a view disputed by McCaffrey and Gleeson, among others.

7. For another mid-nineteenth-century lynching by Irish Americans, the collective stoning (by women) and hanging (by men) of a white youth, John Nevel, for the alleged murder of an Irish woman, Anna Wallace, in Richland Center, Wisconsin, in 1868, see Michael J. Pfeifer, "Wisconsin's Last Decade of Lynching, 1881–1891: Law and Violence in the Postbellum Midwest," *American Nineteenth Century History* 6, no. 3 (September 2005): 231.

8. Irish Catholic ethnicity may have played a role in the lynching of John Taylor, in 1866, as Irish-Americans composed almost 10 percent of Ingham County's population. But contemporaneous sources did not highlight the role of Irish ethnicity in the lynching. *Eighth Census of the United States* (Washington, D.C.: Government Printing Office, 1864); *Ninth Census of the United States* (Washington, D.C.: Government Printing Office, 1872).

9. For the widespread adoption and dispersal of the term *lynching* in the antebellum era, see Waldrep, *The Many Faces of Judge Lynch*, 27–48.

10. See, for example, *New York Tribune*, July 11, 1854, quoted in Waldrep, ed., *Lynching in America*, 75–76; *New York Times*, September, 17, 1857.

11. For an overview of race riots in the urban North in the early-to-mid-nineteenth century, see Gilje, *Rioting in America*, 88–90. For the racially motivated riot of 1834, in New York City, see Paul Gilje, *The Road to Mobocracy: Popular Disorder in New York City, 1763–1834* (Chapel Hill: University of North Carolina Press, 1987), 162–169. For Irish participation in rioting that targeted blacks in Philadelphia in the 1830s and '40s, see Ignatiev, *How the Irish Became White*, 124–144.

12. Gilje, *Rioting in America*, 88–90.

13. For a comparative analysis of ethnic and civic nationalism among Irish Americans, African Americans, and southern whites during Reconstruction, see Mitchell Snay, *Fenians, Freedmen, and Southern Whites: Race and Nationality in the Era of Reconstruction* (Baton Rouge: Louisiana State University Press, 2007), esp. 1–17. Snay argues that, despite significant differences, Irish Americans, southern blacks, and southern whites each sought "ethnic autonomy and political self-governance" in Reconstruction.

14. For the transformation of American law in the era of the Civil War and Reconstruction, see Herman Belz, *Abraham Lincoln, Constitutionalism, and Equal Rights in the Civil War Era* (New York: Fordham University Press, 1998); Alexander Tsesis, *The Thirteenth Amendment and American Freedom: A Legal History* (New York: New York University Press, 2004).

15. For case studies of racial lynchings in the North in the early twentieth century, see Dennis B. Downey and Raymond M. Hyser, *No Crooked Death: Coatesville, Pennsylvania, and the Lynching of Zachariah Walker* (Urbana: University of Illinois Press, 1991); Michael Fedo, *The Lynchings in Duluth* (1979; repr., St. Paul: Minnesota Historical Society Press, 2000); James H. Madison, *A Lynching in the Heartland: Race and Memory in America* (New York: Palgrave, 2001).

16. William M. Tuttle, *Race Riot: Chicago in the Red Summer of 1919* (1970; repr., Urbana: University of Illinois Press, 1996); Domenic J. Capeci, *Race Relations in Wartime Detroit: The Sojourner Truth Housing Controversy of 1942* (Philadelphia: Temple University Press, 1984); Domenic J. Capeci and Martha Wilkerson, *Layered Violence: The Detroit Rioters of 1943* (Jackson: University Press of Mississippi, 1991).

17. Thomas J. Sugrue, *The Origins of the Urban Crisis: Race and Inequality in Postwar Detroit*, rev. ed. (Princeton: Princeton University Press, 2005); Ronald Formisano, *Boston Against Busing: Race, Class, Ethnicity in the 1960s and 1970s*, 2nd ed. (Chapel Hill: University of North Carolina Press, 2003).

18. Joanne Pope Melish, *Disowning Slavery: Gradual Emancipation and "Race" in New England, 1780–1860* (Ithaca, N.Y.: Cornell University Press, 1998), xii–xiii.

19. Charles Townshend, *Political Violence in Ireland: Government and Resistance Since 1848* (Oxford, U.K.: Clarendon Press, 1983), 2–3, 47–48.

20. Conley, *Melancholy Accidents*, 1–6, 113–114, 150–159, 215–219.

21. *Milwaukee Sentinel*, September 10, 1861.

22. For accounts of the altercation and the lynching, see *Milwaukee Sentinel*, September 7, 9, and 10, 1861; *Daily Wisconsin* (Milwaukee, Wis.), September 7, 9, and 10, 1861; *Milwaukee News*, September 8, and 10, 1861; Richard N. Current, *The History of Wisconsin, Volume II: The Civil War Era, 1848–1873* (Madison: State Historical Society of Wisconsin, 1976), 390; John G. Gregory, *History of Milwaukee, Wisconsin, Volume II* (Chicago: Clarke Publishing Co., 1931), 784–785.

23. *Eighth Census of the United States.* For postfamine urban settlement patterns of Irish Americans, see McCaffrey, *The Irish Catholic Diaspora in America*, 71–73. For an overview of ethnicity and community institutions in antebellum Milwaukee, see Kathleen Neils Conzen, *Immigrant Milwaukee 1836–1860: Accommodation and Community in a Frontier City* (Cambridge, Mass.: Harvard University Press, 1976). For an analysis of population trends in antebellum Milwaukee and the Third Ward, see Conzen, *Immigrant Milwaukee*, 8–9, 14–20, 142–143. For the *Lady Elgin* incident, see Conzen, 171–172, and *Milwaukee News*, September 13, 1861. Perhaps ironically, the Third Ward has been redeveloped since 1995 into a destination neighborhood of luxury condominiums and high end shops located in refurbished nineteenth-century warehouses, simultaneously evocative of Milwaukee's picturesque working class ethnic past and current attempts to revive and gentrify its struggling urban core. For contemporary commercial representations of the Third Ward, see http://www.historicthirdward.org/.

24. *Milwaukee Sentinel*, September 7, 9, and 10, 1861; *Daily Wisconsin*, September 7, 9, and 10, 1861; *Milwaukee News*, September 8, and 10, 1861. The lynching of Marshall Clarke in Milwaukee, in September 1861, anticipated the pattern of violence in the New York City Draft Riots in July 1863 in many ways. For parallel tensions between Irish and Germans in the Draft Riots, see Bernstein, *The New York City Draft Riots*, 34.

25. *Daily Wisconsin*, September 9, 1861.

26. For the "rescue" of Joshua Glover, a case that would reverberate in Wisconsin law and politics into the 1860s, see H. Robert Baker, *The Rescue of Joshua Glover: A Fugitive Slave, The Constitution, and the Coming of the Civil War* (Athens: Ohio University Press, 2006); Ruby West Jackson and Walter T. McDonald, *Finding Freedom: The Untold Story of Joshua Glover, Runaway Slave* (Madison: Wisconsin Historical Society Press, 2007). The Glover case was an important context for the *Lady Elgin* excursion in 1860. For similar political dynamics in the New York City Draft Riots, see Bernstein, *The New York City Draft Riots*, 35–36. Bernstein finds that Irish industrial workers directed their riot activities against the Republican elite, whereas the violence of Irish laborers involved "sexually charged purges of black men."

27. *Chicago Post*, quoted in *Milwaukee News*, September 13, 1861.

28. *Daily Wisconsin*, September 7, 1861. For African Americans in early Milwaukee and antebellum Wisconsin, see Conzen, *Immigrant Milwaukee*, 8; Baker, *The Rescue of Joshua Glover*, 59–64; John O. Holzhueter, "Ezekiel Gillespie, Lost and Found," *Wisconsin Magazine of History* 60, no. 3 (Spring 1977): 178–184.

29. *Daily Wisconsin*, September 9, 1861. For the important role of Irish American phobias regarding sexual liaisons between black men and white women in the New York City Draft Riots, see Bernstein, *The New York City Draft Riots*, 35–36.

30. *Milwaukee News*, September 8, 1861.

31. *Daily Wisconsin*, September 9, 1861.

32. For the context for Butler's "contraband of war" designation, see Louis S. Gerteis, *From Contraband to Freedom* (Westport, Conn.: Greenwood Press, 1973), 11–15. For references to Clarke, Shelton, and other Milwaukee blacks as "contraband," see *Milwaukee Press and News*, September 8, and 11, 1861; and *Daily Wisconsin*, September 7, 1861.

33. For analyses of lynching and constitutionalism, see Christopher Waldrep, "National Policing, Lynching, and Constitutionalism," *Journal of Southern History* 74, no. 3 (August

2008): 589–626; Waldrep, *African Americans Confront Lynching: Strategies of Resistance from the Civil War to the Civil Rights Era* (Lanham, Md.: Rowman and Littlefield Publishers, 2008).

34. *Milwaukee News*, September 10, 11, 12, 13, and 14, 1861.

35. *Daily Wisconsin*, September 11, 1861; *Milwaukee Sentinel*, September 10, and 11, 1861. The *Sentinel* scored the "ignorance, led by fanaticism, or clannish hatred" expressed by the Irish community in the lynching and asserted that "ignorance cannot be transmuted into the highest order of citizenship." For the broader context of anti-Irish Catholic nativism in the mid–nineteenth century, see McCaffrey, *The Irish Catholic Diaspora in America*, 97–103.

36. Current, *The History of Wisconsin, Volume II,* 390; *Milwaukee Sentinel*, October 9, 1861.

37. Current, *The History of Wisconsin, Volume II,* 390; *Milwaukee Sentinel*, November 16, 18, 19, 20, and 21, 1861; *Milwaukee News*, November 15, 16, 18, 19, 21, and 25, 1861.

38. *Daily Wisconsin*, November 25, 1861.

39. *Milwaukee News*, November 26, 1861.

40. *Newburgh Daily Telegraph*, June 22, and 23, 1863; *Whig Press*, July 1, 1863.

41. *Newburgh Daily Telegraph*, June 23, 24, and 26, July 17, 1863.

42. *Eighth Census of the United States.* In 1860, the U.S. Census enumerated 536 of Newburgh's population of 15,196 as "free colored." The Census reported 3.4 percent of the population of Orange County, seated at Newburgh, as "free colored" (2,112 of 61,700). For the history of African Americans in the downstate region, see Edythe Ann Quynne, "'The Hills' in the Mid-Nineteenth Century: The History of a Rural Afro-American Community in Westchester County, New York, *"Afro-Americans in New York Life and History (AANYLH)* 14, no. 2 (July 1990): 35–50; Ralph Watkins, "A Survey of the African American Presence in the History of the Downstate New York Area," *AANYLH* 15, no. 1 (January 1991): 53–79. For the larger context of African Americans and race in New York State, see David N. Gellman and David Quigley, *Jim Crow New York: A Documentary History of Race and Citizenship, 1777–1877* (New York: New York University Press, 2003).

43. *Newburgh Daily Telegraph*, June 26, 1863; *Whig Press*, July 1, 1863.

44. *Ninth Census of the United States.* The 1870 U.S. Census counted as foreign-born 4,346 of Newburgh's population of 17,014.

45. *Newburgh Daily Telegraph*, June 22, 23, 1863; *Whig Press*, July 1, 1863.

46. Ibid., July 1, 1863.

47. Ibid.

48. *Newburgh Daily Telegraph*, June 29, 1863.

49. Ibid., July 13, 1863.

50. Ibid., June 22, and 23, 1863.

51. Ibid., June 22, 1863.

52. Ibid., June 23, 1863.

53. *Whig Press*, July 1, 1863.

54. *Lansing State Republican*, August 29, September 19, and 29, October 10, 1866; *Detroit Free Press*, August 28, 29, and 31, 1866.

55. *Lansing State Republican*, August 29, 1866.

56. For racial tensions in wartime Michigan, including a riot in Detroit, in March 1863,

precipitated by the trial of William Faulkner, an African American, for the alleged rape of two white girls, see Willis F. Dunbar, *Michigan: A History of the Wolverine State*, rev. ed. (Grand Rapids, Mich.: Eerdmans, 1980), 391–392. The riot, in which whites targeted the African American community, began when a guard thwarted a white mob from taking Faulkner from jail by shooting into the crowd, killing one.

57. *Eighth Census of the United States.* The total population enumerated by the census for Ingham County in 1860 was 17,435.

58. *Ninth Census of the United States.* The census tallied an aggregate population of 25,268 for Ingham County in 1870.

59. Ibid. The U.S. Census did not enumerate any blacks in Delhi Township in 1860 or 1870. *Lansing State Republican*, September 19, 1866.

60. Ibid.

61. Ibid., September 5, and 19, October 10, and 17, November 7, 1866. For the national election of 1866, a referendum on the Fourteenth Amendment in which Republicans won an overwhelming majority in Congress at the expense of Johnsonian conservatives and Democrats, see Foner, *Reconstruction*, 264–271.

62. Ibid., August 29, 1866. For an analysis of the 1866 riots in Memphis and New Orleans and their political contexts, see Rable, *But There Was No Peace*, 33–58.

63. *Lansing State Republican*, August 29, 1866.

64. Ibid., September 5, 1866.

65. Quoted in *Detroit Free Press*, August 31, 1866.

66. *Lansing State Republican*, September 29, 1866.

67. For the lynching of Alexander White in Mt. Carbon, Illinois, see *New York Times*, February 12, 1874; for the collective murder of Andrew Richards in Winchester, Illinois, *New York Times*, September 12, 1877; for the mob executions of three African Americans in Clarke County, Indiana, *New York Times*, November 26, 1871, and July 4, 1873; for the lynching of a black man identified as "Kurner" in Greenfield, Indiana, *New York Times*, June 27, 1875; and for the collective killing of Simon Garnett in Oxford, Ohio, *New York Times*, September 4, 1877. Richards, "Kurner," and Garnett were accused of raping white women. For an insightful analysis of the lynching of African Americans in Reconstruction-era Kansas, see Brent M. S. Campney, "'Light is bursting upon the world': White Supremacy and Racist Violence Against Blacks in Reconstruction Kansas," *Western Historical Quarterly* 41, no. 2 (Summer 2010): 171–194.

68. Key analyses of the rise of organized terrorist violence in the Reconstruction South are Trelease, *White Terror*, 92–98, 127–136, and Rable, *But There Was No Peace*, 74–78, 122–143. The term *counterrevolution* is Rable's. Trelease, p. xlvi, emphasizes the "decentralized" nature of the Klan's organization across state lines and particular localities. For the performative qualities of the Klan, see Parsons, "Midnight Rangers."

69. George C. Wright, *Racial Violence in Kentucky, 1865–1940* (Baton Rouge: Louisiana State University Press, 1990), 19–60; William D. Carrigan, *The Making of a Lynching Culture: Violence and Vigilantism in Central Texas, 1836–1916* (Urbana: University of Illinois Press, 2004), 112–131; Bruce Baker, *What Reconstruction Meant: Historical Memory in the American South* (Charlottesville: University of Virginia Press, 2007), 84–87; Julius E. Thompson, *Lynchings in Mississippi: A History, 1865–1965* (Jefferson, N.C.: McFarland Press, 2007), 4–16. For a brief but useful treatment of lynching in North Carolina during

Reconstruction, see Vann R. Newkirk, *Lynching in North Carolina: A History, 1865–1941* (Jefferson, N.C.: McFarland Press, 2009), 7–9.

70. Gilles Vandal, *Rethinking Southern Violence: Homicides in Post-Civil War Louisiana, 1866–1884* (Columbus: Ohio State University Press, 2000), 67–93. For an interpretation of the evolution of politics and violence in the Florida Parishes of Louisiana that stresses the formative role of Reconstruction, including the Radicals' abuses of power, in precipitating a profound contempt for authority and pattern of lawless violence in eastern Louisiana, see Samuel C. Hyde Jr., *Pistols and Politics: The Dilemma of Democracy in Louisiana's Florida Parishes, 1810–1899* (Baton Rouge: Louisiana State University Press, 1996), esp. 139–188. Essential treatments of society and politics in Reconstruction Louisiana, which include considerations of the role of violence, can be found in Joe Gray Taylor, *Louisiana Reconstructed 1863–1877* (Baton Rouge: Louisiana State University Press, 1974); Ted Tunnell, *War, Radicalism, and Race in Louisiana, 1862–1877* (Baton Rouge: Louisiana State University Press, 1984); and John C. Rodrigue, *Reconstruction in the Cane Fields: From Slavery to Free Labor in Louisiana's Sugar Parishes, 1862–1880* (Baton Rouge: Louisiana State University Press, 2001).

71. Vandal, *Rethinking Southern Violence*, 92, defines *lynching* as "the killing of one or more persons who/is are seized and illegally executed for an alleged crime." Although organized terrorist violence and politically motivated collective killings would become less significant after Reconstruction, lynchings for alleged criminal offenses would persist and take on new prominence in the decades that followed.

72. The activities of lynchers would also be concentrated in the Red River Delta and, to a lesser extent, the Sugarland, in the late nineteenth and early twentieth centuries. For a discussion of lynching in Jim Crow era Louisiana, see Michael J. Pfeifer, *Rough Justice: Lynching and American Society* (Urbana: University of Illinois Press, 2003), chapter 3.

73. Ibid., 90–105.

74. Ibid., 104.

75. Vandal, *Rethinking Southern Violence*, 244–245n20, cites five lynchings in which whites killed eight African Americans in Louisiana in the 1850s.

76. *New York Times*, November 4, 1859.

77. For the 1859 Attakapas vigilante movements and ensuing collective violence in southwestern Louisiana, consult Carl A. Brasseaux, *Acadian to Cajun: Transformation of a People, 1803–1877* (Jackson: University Press of Mississippi, 1992), 112–149; Carl A. Brasseaux, Keith P. Fontenot, and Claude F. Oubre, *Creoles of Color in the Bayou Country* (Jackson: University Press of Mississippi, 1994), 85. For guerilla warfare against Union forces in the Florida Parishes, see Samuel C. Hyde Jr., *A Fierce and Fractious Frontier: The Curious Development of Louisiana's Florida Parishes, 1699–2000* (Baton Rouge: Louisiana State University Press, 2004), 109–124.

78. Col. S. M. Quincey to Bvt. Maj. J. S. Crosby, AAG, New Orleans, October 22, 1866, Department of the Gulf and Louisiana, 1756 LR box 16, Q 8 (1866), RG [record group] 393, United States Army Continental Commands, National Archives, Washington, D.C. This 1866 Union Army source uses the terms *lynch trial* and *lynching* to describe vigilante violence against African Americans in Franklin Parish. This usage would seem to call into question lynching historian Christopher Waldrep's assertion that "racial violence in the Reconstruction era was not called lynching" and that southern racial violence only

acquired this appellation in the late nineteenth century. Waldrep, *The Many Faces of Judge Lynch*, 84. Additional examples of the use of the term *lynching* and its variants to describe racial violence in Reconstruction can be found in the *New Orleans Daily Picayune* in the late 1860s. On April 4, 1868, the *Picayune* reported "lynch law violence in the back portion of Rapides parish" in which former "Union men" hanged "Dorinda Huffman, and her son, Moses, and Henry Cornies, all colored." In another example, on February 23, 1866, the *Picayune* headlined a report on the mob hanging in Knoxville, Tennessee, of a black soldier who had murdered a white lieutenant colonel of the First Tennessee Calvary, with the phrase, "A Murderer Lynched."

79. Col. S. M. Quincey to Bvt. Maj. J. S. Crosby, AAG, New Orleans, October 22, 1866, Department of the Gulf and Louisiana, 1756 LR box 16, Q 8 (1866), RG 393, United States Army Continental Commands, National Archives, Washington, D.C.

80. Ibid. Similarly the same month, October 1866, in Avoyelles Parish, a Freedmen's Bureau agent complained of a skewed administration of the local courts, with twelve freedmen but no whites convicted and sent to the penitentiary. October 31, 1866, Marksville, La., Agent and Assistant Subassistant Commissioner 1691 Letters Sent (July 1866–Oct. 1867 and May–Dec. 1868), A-8729, La. Marksville 1691 vol. 319, p. 20–22, pp. 40–43, RG 105 Freedmen's Bureau Records, National Archives, Washington, D.C.

81. Capt. N. B. Blanton to Capt. A. F. Hayden, Sparta, La., August 31, 1866, Department of the Gulf and Louisiana, 1756 LR box 15, B 58 (1866), RG 393, United States Army Continental Commands, National Archives, Washington, D.C.

82. *Opelousas Courier* (Opelousas, La.), August 30, 1873, reprinted in *New Orleans Daily Picayune*, September 3, 1873.

83. *New Orleans Daily Picayune*, April 28, 1866.

84. *New Orleans Daily Picayune*, September 14, 1873, and Vandal, *Rethinking Southern Violence*, 51, 95, 98–99, 108. While the vigilante hangings in Vermilion provoked substantial opposition in southern Louisiana, vigilance committees were reconstituted in the parish in 1875, 1876, and 1879. Vandal, *Rethinking Southern Violence*, 51.

85. For several cases of African American and racially mixed mobs in Reconstruction-era Louisiana, see Vandal, *Rethinking Southern Violence*, 95. For black and racially mixed mobs in Louisiana in the late nineteenth and early twentieth centuries, see Pfeifer, *Rough Justice*, 119–120.

86. Tunnell, *War, Radicalism, and Race in Louisiana* (Baton Rouge: Louisiana State University Press, 1984), 111–154. Samuel C. Hyde distinguishes between the Knights of the White Camelia and the Ku Klux Klan in the Florida Parishes, arguing that the former group acted publicly through economic intimidation to achieve racial and political goals, whereas the latter group deployed terrorist violence to assert a far-reaching white supremacy while retaining Klansmen's secrecy. Hyde, *Pistols and Politics*, 164–165.

87. For treatments of the 1868 violence, see Tunnell, *War, Radicalism, and Race in Louisiana*, 154–157; Vandal, *Rethinking Southern Violence*, 178–180.

88. Warmoth's letter, quoted in *New Orleans Daily Picayune*, August 6, 1868.

89. *New Orleans Daily Picayune*, August 11, 1868.

90. Tunnell, *War, Radicalism, and Race in Louisiana*, 189–209.

91. For a parallel discussion of the ramifications of Reconstruction for legal culture and extralegal violence in Warren County, Mississippi, see Christopher Waldrep, *Roots of*

Disorder: Race and Criminal Justice in the American South, 1817–80 (Urbana: University of Illinois Press, 1998), esp. 171–174. Legal culture and lynching in late-nineteenth- and early-twentieth-century Louisiana are analyzed in Pfeifer, *Rough Justice*, 116–121.

92. *New Orleans Daily Picayune*, January 25, 1873. The *Picayune*'s account, a reprint from the *Claiborne Advocate* (Homer, La.), asserts that African Americans also assisted in apprehending Moore.

93. *New Orleans Daily Picayune*, June 15, 18, 1873. Louis A. Snaer, a Republican, represented Iberia Parish in the state legislature from 1872 through 1878. "Membership in the Louisiana House of Representatives, 1874–2008," David R. Poynter Legislative Research Library, Louisiana House of Representatives, accessed February 28, 2007, http://www.legis.state.la.us/members/h1874–2008.pdf.

94. *New Orleans Daily Picayune*, November 2, 12, 16, and 19, 1873.

95. *New Orleans Daily Picayune*, November 2, 1873.

96. *New York Times*, July 21, 1874.

97. *New York Times*, October 18, 1875.

98. The most accurate count available, that of Stewart E. Tolnay and E. M. Beck, is that nearly 2,500 African Americans were murdered by lynch mobs from 1882 through 1930 in the ten southern states of Mississippi, Georgia, Louisiana, Alabama, South Carolina, Florida, Tennessee, Arkansas, Kentucky, and North Carolina. Stewart E. Tolnay and E. M. Beck, *A Festival of Violence: An Analysis of Southern Lynchings, 1882–1930* (Urbana: University of Illinois Press, 1995), ix.

Epilogue

1. Michael J. Pfeifer, *Rough Justice: Lynching and American Society, 1874–1947* (Urbana: University of Illinois Press, 2004), 15, 22–24, 68–86, 139–147. For discussions of the evolution of the legal and rhetorical context for the racially motivated extralegal violence that came to be known as "hate crime" in the 1980s, see Christopher Waldrep, *The Many Faces of Judge Lynch: Extralegal Violence and Punishment in America* (New York: Palgrave Macmillan, 2002), 185–191; Christopher Waldrep, *African Americans Confront Lynching: Strategies of Resistance from the Civil War to the Civil Rights Era* (Lanham, Md.: Rowman and Littlefield Publishers, 2008), 113–127.

2. Pfeifer, *Rough Justice*, 25–33, 94–116, 122–123, 129–139, 149–153.

3. Angelina Snodgrass Godoy, "When 'Justice' is Criminal: Lynchings in Contemporary Latin America," *Theory and Society* 33, no. 6 (December 2004): 621–651. For further analysis of the context for lynching violence in Guatemala, see Angelina Snodgrass Godoy, "Lynchings and the Democratization of Terror in Postwar Guatemala: Implications for Human Rights," *Human Rights Quarterly* 24, no. 3 (August 2002): 640–661.

4. Bruce Baker, *Taking the Law into Their Own Hands: Lawless Law Enforcers in Africa* (Aldershot, U.K.: Ashgate Publishing, 2002), 155–175.

5. Ibid., 160.

6. Ibid., 129–148.

7. Ibid., 190–192.

8. *New York Times*, January 17, 2010; *Montreal Gazette*, January 23, 2010.

Index

MICHAEL J. PFEIFER is an associate professor of history
at John Jay College of Criminal Justice, CUNY, and the author
of *Rough Justice: Lynching and American Society, 1874–1947*.

The University of Illinois Press
is a founding member of the
Association of American University Presses.

University of Illinois Press
1325 South Oak Street
Champaign, IL 61820-6903
www.press.uillinois.edu